ALSO BY THE EDITORS AT AMERICA'S TEST KITCHEN

The America's Test Kitchen Cooking School Cookbook

The Cook's Illustrated Baking Book

The Cook's Illustrated Cookbook

The Science of Good Cooking

The America's Test Kitchen Menu Cookbook

The America's Test Kitchen Quick Family Cookbook

The America's Test Kitchen Healthy Family Cookbook

The America's Test Kitchen Family Baking Book

The America's Test Kitchen Family Cookbook

THE AMERICA'S TEST KITCHEN LIBRARY SERIES AND THE TEST KITCHEN HANDBOOK SERIES:

The Six-Ingredient Solution

Comfort Food Makeovers

The America's Test Kitchen D.I.Y. Cookbook

Pasta Revolution

Simple Weeknight Favorites

Slow Cooker Revolution

The Best Simple Recipes

Pressure Cooker Perfection

THE COOK'S COUNTRY SERIES:

From Our Grandmothers' Kitchens

Cook's Country Blue Ribbon Desserts

Cook's Country Best Potluck Recipes

Cook's Country Best Lost Suppers

Cook's Country Best Grilling Recipes

The Cook's Country Cookbook

America's Best Lost Recipes

THE TV COMPANION SERIES:

The Complete Cook's Country TV Show Cookbook

The Complete America's Test Kitchen TV Show Cookbook 2001–2014

America's Test Kitchen: The TV Companion Cookbook (2002–2009 and 2011–2014 Editions)

AMERICA'S TEST KITCHEN ANNUALS:

The Best of America's Test Kitchen (2007–2014 Editions)

Cooking for Two (2010–2013 Editions)

Light & Healthy (2010–2012 Editions)

THE BEST RECIPE SERIES:

The New Best Recipe

More Best Recipes

The Best One-Dish Suppers

Soups, Stews & Chilis

The Best Skillet Recipes

The Best Slow & Easy Recipes

The Best Chicken Recipes

The Best International Recipe

The Best Make-Ahead Recipe

The Best 30-Minute Recipe

The Best Light Recipe

The Cook's Illustrated Guide to Grilling and Barbecue

Best American Side Dishes

Cover & Bake

Steaks, Chops, Roasts & Ribs

Baking Illustrated

Italian Classics

American Classics

FOR A FULL LISTING OF ALL OUR BOOKS OR TO ORDER TITLES:

CooksIllustrated.com

AmericasTestKitchen.com

or call 800-611-0759

PRAISE FOR OTHER AMERICA'S TEST KITCHEN TITLES

"Ideal as a reference for the bookshelf and as a book to curl up and get lost in, this volume will be turned to time and again for definitive instruction on just about any food-related matter."
PUBLISHERS WEEKLY ON *THE SCIENCE OF GOOD COOKING*

"The perfect kitchen home companion. The practical side of things is very much on display. . . . cook-friendly and kitchen-oriented, illuminating the process of preparing food instead of mystifying it."
THE WALL STREET JOURNAL ON *THE COOK'S ILLUSTRATED COOKBOOK*

"A wonderfully comprehensive guide for budding chefs. . . . Throughout are the helpful tips and exacting illustrations that make ATK a peerless source for culinary wisdom."
PUBLISHERS WEEKLY ON *THE COOK'S ILLUSTRATED COOKBOOK*

"This book upgrades slow cooking for discriminating, 21st-century palates—that is indeed revolutionary."
THE DALLAS MORNING NEWS ON *SLOW COOKER REVOLUTION*

"There are pasta books . . . and then there's this pasta book. Flip your carbohydrate dreams upside down and strain them through this sieve of revolutionary, creative, and also traditional recipes."
SAN FRANCISCO BOOK REVIEW ON *PASTA REVOLUTION*

"If this were the only cookbook you owned, you would cook well, be everyone's favorite host, have a well-run kitchen, and eat happily every day."
THECITYCOOK.COM ON *THE AMERICA'S TEST KITCHEN MENU COOKBOOK*

"The strength of the Best Recipe series lies in the sheer thoughtfulness and details of the recipes."
PUBLISHERS WEEKLY ON THE BEST RECIPE SERIES

"Expert bakers and novices scared of baking's requisite exactitude can all learn something from this hefty, all-purpose home baking volume."
PUBLISHERS WEEKLY ON *THE AMERICA'S TEST KITCHEN FAMILY BAKING BOOK*

"If you're hankering for old-fashioned pleasures, look no further."
PEOPLE MAGAZINE ON *AMERICA'S BEST LOST RECIPES*

"This tome definitely raises the bar for all-in-one, basic, must-have cookbooks. . . . Kimball and his company have scored another hit."
PORTLAND OREGONIAN ON *THE AMERICA'S TEST KITCHEN FAMILY COOKBOOK*

"A foolproof, go-to resource for everyday cooking."
PUBLISHERS WEEKLY ON *THE AMERICA'S TEST KITCHEN FAMILY COOKBOOK*

"These dishes taste as luxurious as their full-fat siblings. Even desserts are terrific."
PUBLISHERS WEEKLY ON *THE BEST LIGHT RECIPE*

"The best instructional book on baking this reviewer has seen."
THE LIBRARY JOURNAL (STARRED REVIEW) ON *BAKING ILLUSTRATED*

"Further proof that practice makes perfect, if not transcendent. . . . If an intermediate cook follows the directions exactly, the results will be better than takeout or mom's."
THE NEW YORK TIMES ON *THE NEW BEST RECIPE*

Slow Cooker
REVOLUTION

VOLUME 2: THE EASY-PREP EDITION

BY THE EDITORS AT
America's Test Kitchen

Slow Cooker Revolution
Volume 2: The Easy-Prep Edition

1st Edition
Paperback: $26.95 US

ISBN-13: 978-1-936493-57-9
ISBN-10: 1-936493-57-8
Library of Congress control number:
2011279393

Manufactured in the United States

10 9 8 7 6 5 4 3 2 1

DISTRIBUTED BY
America's Test Kitchen
17 Station Street, Brookline, MA 02445

EDITORIAL DIRECTOR: Jack Bishop
EDITORIAL DIRECTOR, BOOKS: Elizabeth Carduff
EXECUTIVE FOOD EDITOR: Julia Collin Davison
EXECUTIVE EDITOR: Lori Galvin
SENIOR EDITOR: Dan Zuccarello
ASSOCIATE EDITORS: Kate Hartke, Alyssa King
TEST COOKS: Sara Mayer, Ashley Moore, Stephanie Pixley
ASSISTANT TEST COOK: Lainey Seyler
DESIGN DIRECTOR: Amy Klee
ART DIRECTOR: Greg Galvan
ASSOCIATE ART DIRECTOR: Beverly Hsu
DESIGNER: Allison Pfiffner
PHOTOGRAPHY BY: Keller + Keller
STAFF PHOTOGRAPHER: Daniel J. van Ackere
ADDITIONAL PHOTOGRAPHY: Stephen Klise, Carl Tremblay
PHOTO EDITOR: Stephen Klise
FOOD STYLING: Catrine Kelty, Marie Piraino
PHOTOSHOOT KITCHEN TEAM:
    ASSOCIATE EDITOR: Chris O'Connor
    TEST COOK: Daniel Cellucci
    ASSISTANT TEST COOK: Cecilia Jenkins
PRODUCTION DIRECTOR: Guy Rochford
SENIOR PRODUCTION MANAGER: Jessica Quirk
SENIOR PROJECT MANAGER: Alice Carpenter
PRODUCTION AND TRAFFIC COORDINATOR: Brittany Allen
WORKFLOW AND DIGITAL ASSET MANAGER: Andrew Mannone
SENIOR COLOR AND IMAGING SPECIALIST: Lauren Pettapiece
PRODUCTION AND IMAGING SPECIALISTS: Heather Dube, Lauren Robbins
COPYEDITOR: Barbara Wood
PROOFREADER: Ann-Marie Imbornoni
INDEXER: Elizabeth Parson

PICTURED ON FRONT COVER: Chocolate Cheesecake (page 297)
PICTURED ON BACK COVER: Easy Roast Beef with Mushroom Gravy
(page 163), Poached Salmon (page 261), Penne with Chicken, Sun-Dried
Tomatoes, and Spinach (page 179), Garlicky Shrimp (page 25), Whole
"Roast" Spice-Rubbed Chicken (page 167), Crème Brûlée (page 299)

Contents

Welcome to America's Test Kitchen

This book has been tested, written, and edited by the folks at America's Test Kitchen, a very real 2,500-square-foot kitchen located just outside of Boston. It is the home of *Cook's Illustrated* magazine and *Cook's Country* magazine and is the Monday-through-Friday destination for more than three dozen test cooks, editors, food scientists, tasters, and cookware specialists. Our mission is to test recipes over and over again until we understand how and why they work and until we arrive at the "best" version.

We start the process of testing a recipe with a complete lack of conviction, which means that we accept no claim, no theory, no technique, and no recipe at face value. We simply assemble as many variations as possible, test a half-dozen of the most promising, and taste the results blind. We then construct our own hybrid recipe and continue to test it, varying ingredients, techniques, and cooking times until we reach a consensus. The result, we hope, is the best version of a particular recipe, but we realize that only you can be the final judge of our success (or failure). As we like to say in the test kitchen, "We make the mistakes, so you don't have to."

All of this would not be possible without a belief that good cooking, much like good music, is indeed based on a foundation of objective technique. Some people like spicy foods and others don't, but there is a right way to sauté, there is a best way to cook a pot roast, and there are measurable scientific principles involved in producing perfectly beaten, stable egg whites. This is our ultimate goal: to investigate the fundamental principles of cooking so that you become a better cook. It is as simple as that.

You can watch us work (in our actual test kitchen) by tuning in to *America's Test Kitchen* (AmericasTestKitchenTV.com) or *Cook's Country from America's Test Kitchen* (CooksCountryTV.com) on public television, or by subscribing to *Cook's Illustrated* magazine (CooksIllustrated.com) or *Cook's Country* magazine (CooksCountry.com). We welcome you into our kitchen, where you can stand by our side as we test our way to the "best" recipes in America.

Curious to see what goes on behind the scenes at America's Test Kitchen? The Feed features kitchen snapshots, exclusive recipes, video tips, and much more. **AmericasTestKitchenFeed.com**

f **facebook.com/AmericasTestKitchen**
t **twitter.com/TestKitchen**
You Tube **youtube.com/AmericasTestKitchen**

Preface

I grew up, at least in part, on a Vermont farm and was used to a kitchen that had no appliances to speak of, just a wood-burning Kalamazoo cast-iron stove, a hand pump for water in the sink, and a lot of elbow grease.

Since that time, however, many time-saving appliances have appeared, including the food processor, stand mixer, microwave, pressure cooker, toaster oven, and slow cooker. Of those devices, it is only the slow and pressure cookers that offer a whole new way of preparing finished dishes—the others are there to help prep food, not cook it through.

At first, the slow cooker was nothing more than plug-in convenience; dinner cooks while you are at work or out in the fields. When we published *Slow Cooker Revolution* three years ago, we decided to take a fresh look at this appliance, to use slow cooking as an advantage, not a restriction. To date, we have sold over 300,000 copies.

To do a second book (like *Spider-Man 2*) is risky business. One is apt to produce something half as good and twice as long! But we had a very clear goal in mind with this second volume—we wanted easier preparation (many of the recipes in the first book required front-end sautéing, browning, and flavor development), and we also wanted to explore new territory, including complete pasta dinners, creamy dips, usually quick-cooking seafood recipes, and desserts such as cheesecake, brownies, and even crème brûlée.

Let's start at the beginning. This book includes 200 all-new recipes; there are no repeats from our first volume. All of the recipes in this second volume require no more than 15 minutes of active prep time before everything goes into the slow cooker. We also redefined the slow-cooker timeline. Some recipes are done in an hour or two, and others in 3 to 4 hours. You don't have to wait all day for dinner anymore.

Every year, around April, my neighbors Tom and Nancy and I have a game dinner, usually based on rabbits that ended up in the freezer during the hunting season. One year, we had a dozen or so rabbits that ended up in an all-day slow cooker along with a tomato-based spaghetti sauce. The results were quite good but not ideal since the meat turned out a bit dry. The point is simple—the slow cooker can be an instrument of good cooking or bad; one simply has to pay attention to its strengths and weaknesses.

That, of course, is what we do in our test kitchen—find the good ideas and eliminate the bad ones. Through this process we find that, sometimes, cutting corners works out just fine and other times it doesn't. That reminds me of the story of the Vermont sexton who had held onto his job as the town gravedigger, although he was not known as a model of industry. One day, the head of the cemetery association decided to have a talk with the man and said, "Jeb, I don't like to mention this but it seems that every new grave you dig is a bit shallower than the one before." Jeb replied, "Well, you haven't seen anyone climb out of one yet, have you?"

Our job is to try new things, fix old things, and come up with a reliable repertoire to make you confident each and every time in the kitchen. I hope that you enjoy this book and our hard work—we had a great time testing and tasting.

CHRISTOPHER KIMBALL
Founder and Editor,
Cook's Illustrated and *Cook's Country*
Host, *America's Test Kitchen* and
Cook's Country from America's Test Kitchen

Slow Cooker 101

Introduction

In our very first slow-cooker cookbook (*Slow Cooker Revolution*), the test kitchen tackled the slow cooker head-on, determined to discover new techniques for making classic slow-cooker dishes (soups, stews, chilis, and braises) taste better. In this, our second volume of slow-cooker recipes, we set out with two goals in mind: to deliver a new collection of flavorful family favorites (while making them faster to get into the slow cooker) and to explore new uses for the slow cooker.

In the process, we've learned a lot about the versatility of slow cookers while pressing them into service to make appetizers, cook leaner cuts of meat, poach fish, cook pasta, and even make creamy desserts. Developing these recipes required new strategies (and new mindsets) for using this handy appliance. In short, this book is about using your slow cooker in many different ways, not just to make a meal that is ready when you arrive home from work (though there are plenty of recipes like that in the book). We learned that a slow cooker can sometimes outperform the oven or stovetop, or at least make the cooking process easier or more foolproof when it comes to tasks like gently poaching shrimp, making a hands-free risotto, or turning out a no-fuss creamy cheesecake. Not to mention the fact that it can free up your oven for the main course while you use it to "bake" potatoes or "roast" beets or Brussels sprouts.

One constant throughout this book, however, is that in the spirit of keeping things easy, we made sure that no recipe took more than 15 minutes of prep time before you could press start and walk away. And the recipes require absolutely no stovetop cooking. So whether you are making a dip that takes just an hour, poaching fish that takes about 2 hours, or assembling a hearty braise that can cook all day, getting started will be easy.

Getting Started

While all ovens set to 350 degrees will perform the same (assuming all the ovens are properly cali-brated), heating varies tremendously among slow cookers. We tested more than a dozen models and prepared every recipe in this book in at least three different models. Here's what you need to know.

GET TO KNOW YOUR SLOW COOKER

Some models run hot and fast, while others heat more slowly and gently. Most models perform best on low, but again it's hard to make blanket statements that will apply to all slow cookers. In our testing, we have found that some slow cookers run hot or cool on just one of the settings (either low or high). This is where the cook's experience comes into play. If you have been using a slow cooker for some time, ask yourself if recipes are generally done at the low or high end of the cooking times provided in recipes. The answer should tell you whether you have a "fast" slow cooker or a "slow" model. If you are just getting started with your slow cooker, check all recipes at the beginning of the time range but allow some extra time to cook food longer if necessary.

HOW TO USE TIME RANGES

Through extensive testing using multiple brands of slow cookers, the test kitchen found that we could narrow the window of doneness, which is normally 2 hours or more in slow-cooker recipes, to just an hour, giving you a better expectation of when your food will be done or when you should be home to start checking. We found that this 1-hour time frame worked for all the models we tested. It is especially helpful to have a narrower range when cooking fish or lean meats, which are less forgiving than stews and braises.

MATCHING RECIPES TO SLOW-COOKER SIZES

Slow cookers come in a variety of sizes, from the ridiculously small (1 quart) to the very big (7 quarts or more). In general, we like 6-quart models. That said, we tested our recipes in slow cookers of different sizes. Each recipe in this book lists the size range that will work for that particular recipe. Note that some recipes must be made in a large slow cooker (at least 5½ quarts) or you run the risk of overfilling the insert. In some cases, we found that the cook-ing times and methods varied depending on whether we used a small or large slow cooker, so we included these variations in the recipes. If you don't know the size of your slow cooker, check the underside of the insert (which is usu-ally stamped with the size), or simply measure how much water it takes to fill the insert to just above the lip.

KEEPING FOOD SAFE

For safety reasons, the internal temperature of meat and poultry should reach 140 degrees (the temperature at which bacteria cannot grow) by the 2-hour mark in the cooking time. When you first start using your slow cooker, we suggest that you check the temperature of meat or chicken at this stage to be sure this is happening. If your food doesn't reach this safety zone when cooking on low, you might be able to solve the problem by using the high setting. Note that putting frozen meat or other frozen food into any slow cooker is dangerous as it will dramatically increase the amount of time it takes your food to reach this safe zone.

Take the Fast Lane to Great Slow Food

Here are some of the strategies we used to guarantee flavor-packed dishes with less fuss and effort.

USE NO-PREP AROMATICS

Our recipes call for fresh onions, garlic, and ginger, and our promise to limit prep for every recipe to 15 minutes or less includes time to chop onions, mince garlic, or grate ginger. That said, in our testing we found that frozen chopped onions, granulated garlic, and dried, ground ginger were all good alternatives for cutting down on knife work and reducing prep time even further.

An equal amount of frozen chopped onions can be used in place of fresh chopped onions in any recipe. Granulated garlic (preferred over garlic powder and other substitutes) and ground ginger require some math. Here are the equivalencies of fresh garlic and ginger to their dried counterparts for easy reference.

1 teaspoon minced fresh garlic	=	¾ teaspoon granulated garlic
1 tablespoon minced fresh garlic	=	2 teaspoons granulated garlic
1 teaspoon grated fresh ginger	=	½ teaspoon ground ginger
1 tablespoon grated fresh ginger	=	1 teaspoon ground ginger

CHOOSE WISELY AT THE MEAT COUNTER

To keep things simple, we started with cuts of meat that were easy-prep in nature. Blade steaks went straight from the package to the slow cooker for braises, and steak tips were easier to cut into pieces for stew than a large chuck roast. Boneless country-style pork ribs were easy enough to pull apart into bite-size pieces when tender, and they made stews and our meaty ragù quick to assemble.

USE CONVENIENCE PRODUCTS TO YOUR ADVANTAGE

We turned to convenience products when other ingredients either did not work in the slow cooker or simply took too much time (or advance cooking). For instance, we learned that neither instant rice nor raw rice worked in our casseroles—they just never delivered properly cooked rice. But packaged, precooked rice worked perfectly. When it came to making a creamy sauce for some pasta dishes (like macaroni and cheese and penne with chicken), we found that condensed cheese soup or jarred Alfredo sauce was the only route to a sauce that would not break in the slow cooker.

And for glazed meat and chicken (impossible to achieve in a slow-cooker environment), we turned to easy-to-whip-together glazes made with preserves or jellies—and we brushed on the glaze at the end of the cooking time, sometimes using the broiler for a caramelized finish.

USE YOUR MICROWAVE

Rather than cook aromatics and spices on the stovetop to bloom their flavors, we simply microwaved them for a few minutes. We also used the microwave to parcook hearty vegetables like potatoes, so they'd be cooked through perfectly at the same time as the main ingredient (like chicken, which needs only a short stint in the slow cooker). Microwaving delicate vegetables and adding them to the slow cooker at the end of the cooking time ensured that they remained colorful and crisp-tender. And using the microwave to toast pasta guaranteed that it came out of the slow cooker perfectly tender (for more about cooking pasta in a slow cooker, see page 180).

Ensuring Slow-Cooker Success

After hours of slow cooking, flavors can become muted or one-dimensional, and meat and vegetables can dry out. Here are some tips for turning out satisfying, full-flavored dishes.

DON'T SKIMP ON THE AROMATICS

You'll see hefty amounts of onions, garlic, herbs, and other flavorful ingredients in our recipes. This is because the moist heat environment and long cooking times that come with the slow cooker tend to mute flavors. Also, many recipes need a flavor boost at the end of the cooking time, which is why we often finish with fresh herbs, lemon juice, or other flavorful ingredients.

ADD TOMATO PASTE AND SOY SAUCE FOR MEATY FLAVOR

To replicate the meaty flavor usually achieved by browning meat and vegetables, we turned to *umami*-rich ingredients instead, which offered savory depth and rich flavor. Tomato paste, which we often microwave with aromatics or other ingredients to deepen its flavor, ramps up the meaty richness of everything from soups and stews to pasta sauces. And soy sauce adds flavor to a number of non-Asian dishes, like our meaty ragù and vegetarian chili, without calling attention to itself.

GET OUT YOUR ALUMINUM FOIL

Most slow cookers have a hotter side (typically the back side that's opposite the controls) that can cause pastas, casseroles, and other dense dishes to burn. We found an easy work-around for this problem: We simply lined this side of the slow-cooker insert with an aluminum foil collar. That way, the food on the hot side of the slow cooker is insulated from the heat and doesn't overcook. See page 180 for more details. Also, it is hard to get some foods like meatloaf, salmon, and swordfish out of the slow cooker intact. The solution? Make a simple sling using aluminum foil. See page 144 for more details.

USE AN INSTANT-READ THERMOMETER WHEN PRECISION MATTERS

A few degrees won't make much difference when preparing stews, chilis, and braises in a slow cooker, and it's pretty hard to overcook a pot roast. However, some dishes do require heating food to a precise internal temperature. This list includes roast beef (cooked to medium-rare), fish, pork loin, pork tenderloins, whole chicken, and some desserts (such as cheesecake). We found that with careful monitoring and the help of an instant-read thermometer you can achieve excellent results with all of these dishes. Our time ranges will guide you, but we've also provided doneness temperatures; the first time you make one of these recipes, start checking for doneness at the low end of the range. Once you know how one of these recipes performs in your slow cooker, you'll be able to walk away with confidence knowing just how long it will take.

ADD DELICATE VEGETABLES AT THE END

Certain ingredients need just a short stint in the slow cooker to warm through and meld into the dish, so we saved them until the end of cooking. Delicate vegetables, like frozen peas, baby spinach, and chopped tomatoes, turned mushy when added at the beginning, so we stirred them in at the end; in just a few minutes, they were perfectly tender.

SKIM AWAY EXCESS FAT

During the long cooking time, meat will release fat into a stew or braise, but it is easy to remove it at the end of the cooking time. Simply turn off the slow cooker and let the food sit for a few minutes so the fat can rise to the top. Use a large spoon to skim the excess fat off the surface.

The Test Kitchen's Guide to Buying a Slow Cooker

Today's slow cookers come in a wide array of sizes with lots of different features. In our recipe testing for this book, we found 5½- to 7-quart slow cookers to be the most versatile because they could accommodate a whole chicken or pork loin, the small springform pan and ramekins we used to make many desserts, as well as the soufflé dish we used for some dips and other recipes. That said, it can be handy to use a smaller slow cooker for recipes scaled for two (note that the larger slow cookers do work for smaller-batch recipes) and for many dips.

To find out which models performed best and which features really mattered, we tested seven large (6-quart capacity or more) and eight small (4-quart capacity) slow cookers, using the large models to prepare pot roast, meaty tomato sauce, and French onion soup and the small models to prepare chicken thighs in hearty tomato sauce, smothered steaks, and sweet-and-sour sticky ribs. In short, the features we liked included programmable timers, warming modes, and clear glass lids (which allow the cook to assess the food as it cooks). Inserts that have handles, which make it easy to remove the insert from the slow cooker, and that can be washed in the dishwasher earned extra points.

We rated each slow cooker on cooking ability and design. We also devised a test to measure the maximum temperatures of the models on high and low settings; we found that some models didn't get hot enough, whereas others hovered around or hit the boiling point. The best models quickly brought food into the safe zone (above 140 degrees) then climbed slowly to the boiling point or just below it over a period of hours rather than reaching the boiling point right away and overcooking food. Our top four slow cookers are listed below in order of preference within each category.

LARGE SLOW COOKERS

KEY: GOOD ★★★   FAIR ★★   POOR ★

HIGHLY RECOMMENDED

	CRITERIA		TESTERS' COMMENTS
CROCK-POT Touchscreen 6½-Quart Slow Cooker MODEL: SCVT650-PS PRICE: $129.99 CONTROLS: Digital programmable	COOKING DESIGN	★★★ ★★★	The control panel is extremely easy to use, and the timer counted up to 20 hours, even on high. Sunday gravy thickened to the correct consistency, pot roast was tender and sliceable, and onions caramelized perfectly.

RECOMMENDED

	CRITERIA		TESTERS' COMMENTS
ALL-CLAD 6½-Quart Slow Cooker with Ceramic Insert MODEL: 99009 PRICE: $199.95 CONTROLS: Digital programmable	COOKING DESIGN	★★★ ★★	Pot roast and gravy cooked to the correct consistency, and this model runs at the ideal temperature range. But we got equally good results from our top-ranked model at a much lower price. The button controls are easy to use, but the timer could not be set for more than 6 hours on high.

RECOMMENDED WITH RESERVATIONS

	CRITERIA		TESTERS' COMMENTS
BREVILLE 7-Quart Slow Cooker with EasySear MODEL: BSC 560XL PRICE: $179.95 CONTROLS: Manual	COOKING DESIGN	★★ ★★	Although this large cooker ran a bit hot, the tight seal of its metal lid yielded fall-apart meat in Sunday gravy. Pot roast overcooked, though, and onions for the soup burned. We couldn't see the food through the steel lid. For this price, we expected a timer and "keep warm" cycle.

RECOMMENDED WITH RESERVATIONS	CRITERIA		TESTERS' COMMENTS

KITCHENAID 7-Quart Slow Cooker
MODEL: KSC 700SS
PRICE: $129.99
CONTROLS: Manual, with digital timer

COOKING ★★
DESIGN ★★

The meat in Sunday gravy was tender, but the pot roast was dry. The onions didn't cook evenly. The heavy insert's square shape made pouring easy. The control panel has five cooking settings, but the timer stops after 8 hours on high.

SMALL SLOW COOKERS

RECOMMENDED

CUISINART 4-Quart Programmable Slow Cooker
MODEL: PSC-400
PRICE: $79.95
CONTROLS: Digital programmable

COOKING ★★★
DESIGN ★★½

This model produced perfect chicken, steaks, and ribs. Its programmable timer can be set to cook for up to 24 hours and then automatically switches over to "keep warm" for another 8 hours. We also liked its dishwasher-safe insert, large handles, and retractable cord for easy storage. Our only gripe: Its big, square casing is bulky, taking up almost as much counter space as our 6-quart slow cooker does.

HAMILTON BEACH Stay or Go 4-Quart Slow Cooker
MODEL: 33246T
PRICE: $26.99
CONTROLS: Manual

BEST BUY

COOKING ★★★
DESIGN ★★

This cooker performed well, producing perfect ribs, steak, and chicken. A gasket and clips on the lid let you take your cooker to a potluck without risking spills. It's comparatively low-tech: The "off," "low," "high," and "warm" settings are on a manual dial—which is its drawback. You can't set it to turn off or switch to "keep warm" on its own.

RECOMMENDED WITH RESERVATIONS

WEST BEND 4-Quart Oval Crockery Cooker
MODEL: 84384
PRICE: $29.99
CONTROLS: Manual

COOKING ★★
DESIGN ★½

This model performed fine with chicken Provençal, bringing the thighs north of 140 degrees in about an hour. It cooked steak to tenderness (although the sauce scorched slightly). But ribs developed a tough, leathery crust wherever they touched the hot bottom of the insert. The model is manually controlled, which means you must switch off the cooker to stop cooking.

BREVILLE the Risotto Plus
MODEL: BRC600XL
PRICE: $129.99
CONTROLS: Digital programmable

COOKING ★★
DESIGN ★½

This model has some cool features (it's a combo slow cooker, rice cooker, and risotto maker), and it works OK, as long as you don't cook low-moisture recipes, such as our ribs. The instruction manual calls for a greater minimum amount of liquid than we call for in some of our recipes. Also, the insert lacks handles and isn't dishwasher-safe. On the plus side, the sauté function worked perfectly—no need to brown foods in a separate pan before placing them in the slow cooker.

Easy Appetizers

Spinach and Artichoke Dip

Makes about 5 cups   **Serves** 6 to 8   **Cooking Time** 1 to 2 hours on Low
Slow Cooker Size 1½ to 7 quarts

✔ WHY THIS RECIPE WORKS: Spinach and artichoke dip is a bona fide crowd-pleaser, but it often ends up watery, bland, and left behind on the buffet table. We wanted a reliable dip that was rich, creamy, and packed with flavorful chunks of artichokes and earthy spinach. We discarded versions with flour-thickened cream mixtures in favor of an easy-prep combination of softened cream cheese and mayonnaise that gave our dip both the creaminess we were after and a subtle tanginess that tasters enjoyed. Frozen artichoke hearts and spinach were easier options than their fresh counterparts; we just patted them dry to rid them of excess moisture. With a sprinkle of fresh chives, our dip was ready for the party. Serve with crackers and/or Garlic Toasts (page 16).

6	**ounces cream cheese, softened**
½	**cup mayonnaise**
2	**tablespoons lemon juice**
2	**tablespoons water**
1	**tablespoon minced garlic**
	Salt and pepper
18	**ounces frozen artichoke hearts, thawed, patted dry, and chopped**
10	**ounces frozen spinach, thawed and squeezed dry**
2	**tablespoons minced fresh chives**

1. Mix cream cheese, mayonnaise, lemon juice, water, garlic, 1 teaspoon salt, and ½ teaspoon pepper together in large bowl. Fold in artichokes and spinach until well combined.

2A. FOR A 1½- TO 5-QUART SLOW COOKER: Transfer mixture to slow cooker, cover, and cook until heated through, 1 to 2 hours on high.

2B. FOR A 5½- TO 7-QUART SLOW COOKER: Transfer mixture to 1½-quart soufflé dish. Set dish in slow cooker and pour water into slow cooker until it reaches about one-third up sides of dish (about 2 cups water). Cover and cook until heated through, 1 to 2 hours on high. Remove dish from slow cooker.

3. Stir dip to recombine, sprinkle with chives, and serve. (Dip can be held on warm or low setting for up to 2 hours.)

QUICK PREP TIP USING A SOUFFLÉ DISH IN THE SLOW COOKER

While a large slow cooker is great for cooking up big batches of soups, stews, and braises for a crowd, the large amount of space is problematic for smaller dishes like dips, which end up spreading out too thin and burning or cooking unevenly. To solve this problem, we assemble the recipe in a 1½-quart soufflé dish, then place the dish in the slow cooker. To encourage even heat transfer, we pour about 2 cups of water into the slow cooker to make a simple water bath. Once the dip is cooked, the soufflé dish can be removed from the slow cooker for serving.

Creamy Crab Dip

Makes about 5 cups   **Serves** 6 to 8   **Cooking Time** 1 to 2 hours on Low
Slow Cooker Size 1½ to 7 quarts

✔ **WHY THIS RECIPE WORKS:** For an elegant crab dip that tasted first and foremost of crab, we included a full pound of crabmeat and limited the amount of filler. Patting the crabmeat dry was key to ensuring that the dip was creamy but not watery, and adding some traditional Old Bay seasoning balanced the sweet richness of the crabmeat. We tried adding raw onions to the slow cooker, but they never turned tender, so we softened them in the microwave with butter first to give them a head start. We liked a combination of cream cheese and mayonnaise for the mild tanginess and rich texture it lent to our dip. Finishing with a sprinkle of chives instead of the traditional cheese layer gave our creamy dip a lighter, fresher flavor. Do not substitute imitation crabmeat here. Serve with crackers and/or Garlic Toasts (page 16).

¾	**cup chopped onion**
2	**tablespoons unsalted butter**
2	**teaspoons Old Bay seasoning**
8	**ounces cream cheese, softened**
¼	**cup mayonnaise**
	Salt and pepper
1	**pound lump crabmeat**
2	**tablespoons minced fresh chives**

1. Microwave onion, butter, and Old Bay in large bowl, stirring occasionally, until onion is softened, about 5 minutes. Stir in cream cheese, mayonnaise, ¼ teaspoon salt, and ¼ teaspoon pepper. Spread crab onto paper towel–lined plate, pick over for shells, and pat dry; gently fold crab into mixture.

2A. FOR A 1½- TO 5-QUART SLOW COOKER: Transfer mixture to slow cooker, cover, and cook until heated through, 1 to 2 hours on high.

2B. FOR A 5½- TO 7-QUART SLOW COOKER: Transfer mixture to 1½-quart soufflé dish. Set dish in slow cooker and pour water into slow cooker until it reaches about one-third up sides of dish (about 2 cups water). Cover and cook until heated through, 1 to 2 hours on high. Remove dish from slow cooker.

3. Gently stir dip to recombine. Sprinkle with chives and serve. (Dip can be held on warm or low setting for up to 2 hours.)

SMART SHOPPING GRADES OF CRABMEAT
Differences in grade correspond to the part of the crab the meat comes from and to the size of the pieces. Jumbo lump is from the two large muscles connected to the swimming legs. The most expensive, it boasts large pieces with a bright white color and delicate flavor. Lump is composed of smaller or broken pieces of jumbo lump. It is also white and has a delicate flavor. Backfin is a mix of smaller "flake" pieces of body meat. It is finer textured than lump, but its flavor is similar. Claw meat comes from the swimming fins and claws. Because these are very active muscles, the meat is pink or brown and high in fat, and it has a stronger flavor.

Pepperoni Pizza Dip

Makes about 5 cups   **Serves** 6 to 8   **Cooking Time** 1 to 2 hours on Low
Slow Cooker Size 1½ to 7 quarts

✔ **WHY THIS RECIPE WORKS:** Too often pizza dips try to incorporate the flavors of pizza but end up as dense, greasy cheese bombs. We wanted a pizza-inspired dip that we could actually dip into—without losing half our chip along the way. To start, we combined rich, meltable cream cheese and flavorful pizza sauce for a creamy, tangy base. Then we gradually added mozzarella until we found the perfect balance between a creamy dip and stringy, chewy pizza cheese. Next we added our favorite pizza toppings—spicy pepperoni and earthy mushrooms. To remove the mushrooms' excess moisture and the pepperoni's grease, we briefly microwaved them before stirring them into the slow cooker. Though we liked the idea of further imitating pizza by sprinkling an extra layer of cheese over the top, in practice the extra cheese made our dip over-the-top greasy. Instead we reserved a quarter of the mushrooms and pepperoni for the top and garnished it with a little fresh basil. Margherita Italian Style Pepperoni is the test kitchen's winning brand. Serve with crackers, tortilla chips, and/or Melba toast.

1 **pound white mushrooms, trimmed and sliced thin**

4 **ounces sliced pepperoni, quartered**

1 **pound cream cheese**

1 **cup canned pizza sauce**

2 **cups shredded mozzarella cheese**

2 **tablespoons chopped fresh basil**

1. Line plate with double layer of coffee filters. Spread mushrooms and pepperoni in even layer over filters and microwave until mushrooms have released their liquid and fat begins to render from pepperoni, about 3 minutes. Reserve one-quarter of mixture for topping.

2. Microwave cream cheese and pizza sauce in large bowl, whisking occasionally, until smooth, about 1 minute. Stir in three-quarters of mushroom-pepperoni mixture and mozzarella until well combined.

3A. FOR A 1½- TO 5-QUART SLOW COOKER: Transfer mixture to slow cooker and top with reserved mushroom-pepperoni mixture. Cover and cook until heated through, 1 to 2 hours on high.

3B. FOR A 5½- TO 7-QUART SLOW COOKER: Transfer mixture to 1½-quart soufflé dish and top with reserved mushroom-pepperoni mixture. Set dish in slow cooker and pour water into slow cooker until it reaches about one-third up sides of dish (about 2 cups water). Cover and cook until heated through, 1 to 2 hours on high. Remove dish from slow cooker.

4. Sprinkle dip with basil and serve. (Dip can be held on warm or low setting for up to 2 hours.)

Beef and Black Bean Taco Dip

Makes about 5 cups **Serves** 6 to 8 **Cooking Time** 1 to 2 hours on Low
Slow Cooker Size 1½ to 7 quarts

WHY THIS RECIPE WORKS: Taco dip rarely delivers on its promise of big Tex-Mex flavor. We set out to develop a hearty, meaty taco dip worthy of eating while watching the big game. We wanted our dip to include plenty of flavorful ground beef, but when we simply stirred raw ground beef into the slow cooker, the dip was a watery, greasy mess. So we partially cooked the ground beef in the microwave to remove moisture and render excess fat. A packet of taco seasoning and a little garlic made quick work of seasoning the beef and helped us to shorten our ingredient list. To bulk up the meat, we added lots of hearty black beans. Mashing half of the beans and stirring in some shredded Monterey Jack cheese helped to bind everything together into a cohesive dip. Ro-tel tomatoes added bright acidity and a spicy kick. To finish, we topped the dip with more gooey Monterey Jack and a sprinkling of scallions. Serve with tortilla chips and/or Pita Chips (page 18).

1 pound 85 percent lean ground beef

1 (1-ounce) packet taco seasoning

2 teaspoons minced garlic

2 (10-ounce) cans Ro-tel Diced Tomatoes & Green Chilies

2 (15-ounce) cans black beans, rinsed

2 cups shredded Monterey Jack cheese

2 scallions, sliced thin

1. Microwave ground beef, taco seasoning, and garlic in bowl, stirring occasionally, until beef is no longer pink, about 5 minutes. Break up any large pieces of beef with spoon, then drain off fat.

2. Drain tomatoes, reserving ¼ cup juice. Using potato masher, mash half of beans with reserved tomato juice in large bowl until mostly smooth. Stir in beef mixture, remaining beans, tomatoes, and 1½ cups Monterey Jack until well combined.

3A. FOR A 1½- TO 5-QUART SLOW COOKER: Transfer mixture to slow cooker, cover, and cook until heated through, 1 to 2 hours on high. Stir dip to recombine and sprinkle with remaining ½ cup Monterey Jack. Cover and continue to cook on high until cheese is melted, about 5 minutes.

3B. FOR A 5½- TO 7-QUART SLOW COOKER: Transfer mixture to 1½-quart soufflé dish. Set dish in slow cooker and pour water into slow cooker until it reaches about one-third up sides of dish (about 2 cups water). Cover and cook until heated through, 1 to 2 hours on high. Stir dip to recombine and sprinkle with remaining ½ cup Monterey Jack. Cover and continue to cook on high until cheese is melted, about 5 minutes. Remove dish from slow cooker.

4. Sprinkle dip with scallions and serve. (Dip can be held on warm or low setting for up to 2 hours.)

Rosemary and Garlic White Bean Dip

Makes about 5 cups   **Serves** 6 to 8   **Cooking Time** 1 to 2 hours on Low
Slow Cooker Size 1½ to 7 quarts

✔ **WHY THIS RECIPE WORKS:** For a simple white bean dip to really stand out, it needs to have both a little texture and a lot of flavor. To transform humble legumes into a rich, warm dip worthy of a dinner party, we started with delicately flavored cannellini beans. We processed most of the beans into a smooth puree along with a good dose of extra-virgin olive oil, but we reserved a third of the beans to pulse in at the end for an appealing chunky texture. For bold, aromatic flavor, we stirred in a little garlic, rosemary, lemon zest, and lemon juice. Serve with crackers, Garlic Toasts, and/or Pita Chips (page 18).

3	(15-ounce) cans cannellini beans, rinsed
¼	cup extra-virgin olive oil
1	teaspoon minced garlic
1	teaspoon minced fresh rosemary
¼	teaspoon grated lemon zest plus 1 tablespoon juice
¼	teaspoon salt

1. Process two-thirds of beans, oil, garlic, rosemary, lemon zest and juice, and salt in food processor until smooth, about 10 seconds; scrape down sides of bowl. Add remaining beans and pulse to incorporate (do not puree smooth), about 2 pulses.

2A. FOR A 1½- TO 5-QUART SLOW COOKER: Transfer mixture to slow cooker, cover, and cook until heated through, 1 to 2 hours on high.

2B. FOR A 5½- TO 7-QUART SLOW COOKER: Transfer mixture to 1½-quart soufflé dish. Set dish in slow cooker and pour water into slow cooker until it reaches about one-third up sides of dish (about 2 cups water). Cover and cook until heated through, 1 to 2 hours on high. Remove dish from slow cooker.

3. Drizzle dip with extra olive oil and serve. (Dip can be held on warm or low setting for up to 2 hours.)

ON THE SIDE GARLIC TOASTS
Adjust oven racks to upper-middle and lower-middle positions and heat oven to 400 degrees. Spread two 12-inch baguettes, sliced ½ inch thick on bias, on 2 rimmed baking sheets and bake until dry and crisp, about 10 minutes, rotating sheets and flipping toasts halfway through baking. While warm, rub one side of each toast briefly with peeled garlic clove. Drizzle toasts lightly with extra-virgin olive oil and season with salt and pepper to taste. (Makes 40 toasts.)

Refried Bean Dip

Makes about 5 cups   **Serves** 6 to 8   **Cooking Time** 1 to 2 hours on Low
Slow Cooker Size 1½ to 7 quarts

WHY THIS RECIPE WORKS: Refried bean dip is a staple at any game-day gathering, but while it's easy to throw together, it's often lacking in the flavor department. We were determined to bring this dish back to life. First we ditched the dull-tasting canned refried beans. Instead, we started with canned pinto beans, processed most of them until smooth, then pulsed in some more whole beans to give the dip a chunky texture. Next, we packed in bold flavor with chili powder, garlic, and cumin, as well as a can of spicy Ro-tel tomatoes. Finishing it with some Monterey Jack cheese and fresh, bright cilantro balanced the hearty beans and flavorful spices. Now our dip was quick and easy—and anything but boring. Serve with tortilla chips and/or Pita Chips.

3 **(15-ounce) cans pinto beans, rinsed**

½ **cup chicken broth**

2 **teaspoons chili powder**

1 **teaspoon minced garlic**

1 **teaspoon salt**

½ **teaspoon ground cumin**

1 **(10-ounce) can Ro-tel Diced Tomatoes & Green Chilies, drained**

½ **cup shredded Monterey Jack cheese**

2 **tablespoons minced fresh cilantro**

1. Process two-thirds of beans, broth, chili powder, garlic, salt, and cumin in food processor until smooth, about 10 seconds; scrape down sides of bowl. Add tomatoes and remaining beans and pulse to incorporate (do not puree smooth), about 2 pulses.

2A. FOR A 1½- TO 5-QUART SLOW COOKER: Transfer mixture to slow cooker, cover, and cook until heated through, 1 to 2 hours on high. Sprinkle with Monterey Jack, cover, and cook on high until cheese is melted, about 5 minutes.

2B. FOR A 5½- TO 7-QUART SLOW COOKER: Transfer mixture to 1½-quart soufflé dish. Set dish in slow cooker and pour water into slow cooker until it reaches about one-third up sides of dish (about 2 cups water). Cover and cook until heated through, 1 to 2 hours on high. Sprinkle with Monterey Jack, cover, and cook on high until cheese is melted, about 5 minutes. Remove dish from slow cooker.

3. Sprinkle dip with cilantro and serve. (Dip can be held on warm or low setting for up to 2 hours.)

ON THE SIDE PITA CHIPS
Adjust oven racks to upper-middle and lower-middle positions and heat oven to 350 degrees. Using kitchen shears, cut around perimeter of four 8-inch pita breads to yield 8 rounds; cut each round into 6 wedges. Spread pita wedges, smooth side down, on 2 rimmed baking sheets. Brush tops of wedges lightly with ¼ cup extra-virgin olive oil and sprinkle with 2 teaspoons salt. Bake until wedges are crisp, about 12 minutes, rotating sheets and flipping wedges halfway through baking. Let pita chips cool before serving. (Makes 48 chips.)

Beer and Cheddar Fondue

Makes about 5 cups   **Serves** 8 to 10   **Cooking Time** 1 to 2 hours on Low
Slow Cooker Size 1½ to 7 quarts

✅ **WHY THIS RECIPE WORKS:** Fondue can be tricky because it tends to be fussy; to prevent the cheese from separating, it needs to be melted slowly and gently. Once melted, it must be kept at just the right temperature and frequently stirred to keep the fondue from breaking. We wanted to take advantage of the gentle, steady heat of the slow cooker to make a beer and cheddar fondue that would stay creamy for hours unattended. Sharp cheddar had great flavor, but its texture was consistently grainy when melted. We switched to mild cheddar and added highly meltable American cheese to make it even creamier, but our fondue still turned grainy as it sat. To further stabilize it, we added a mixture of cornstarch and cream cheese. Now we had a fondue that stayed creamy without constant stirring. To bring out the flavor of the cheddar, we added some garlic and dry mustard. Finally, for the characteristic malty flavor, we added American lager—tasters preferred its milder, less bitter flavor over other styles of beer. The fondue tasted best when made with block cheese that we shredded ourselves; buy a block of American cheese from the deli counter. Preshredded cheese will work, but the fondue will be much thicker. For dipping we like to use bread, apple slices, steamed broccoli and cauliflower florets, and cured meats. Be sure to have long skewers on hand for easy dipping.

1   **cup beer**

4   **ounces cream cheese**

1   **tablespoon cornstarch**

1   **teaspoon minced garlic**

1   **teaspoon dry mustard**

¼   **teaspoon pepper**

2   **cups shredded mild cheddar cheese**

2   **cups shredded American cheese**

1. Microwave beer, cream cheese, cornstarch, garlic, mustard, and pepper in large bowl, whisking occasionally, until smooth and thickened, about 5 minutes. Stir in cheddar and American cheeses until combined.

2A. FOR A 1½- TO 5-QUART SLOW COOKER: Transfer mixture to slow cooker, cover, and cook until cheese is melted, 1 to 2 hours on low.

2B. FOR A 5½- TO 7-QUART SLOW COOKER: Transfer mixture to 1½-quart soufflé dish. Set dish in slow cooker and pour water into slow cooker until it reaches about one-third up sides of dish (about 2 cups water). Cover and cook until cheese is melted, 1 to 2 hours on low. Remove dish from slow cooker.

3. Whisk fondue together until smooth and serve. (Adjust consistency with hot water 2 tablespoons at a time as needed. Fondue can be held on warm or low setting for up to 2 hours.)

Chile con Queso

Makes about 5 cups   **Serves** 8 to 10   **Cooking Time** 1 to 2 hours on Low
Slow Cooker Size 1½ to 7 quarts

WHY THIS RECIPE WORKS: Chile con queso has fallen on hard times; often it's just Ro-tel diced tomatoes and chiles mixed with Velveeta, microwaved, and stirred. We wanted to keep the simplicity but ditch the plasticky flavor and waxy texture. We started with a base of chicken broth, cream cheese, and cornstarch to help stabilize the cheese and prevent it from breaking. For the cheeses, we chose Monterey Jack for its great flavor and American cheese for its superior meltability. We kept the classic Ro-tel tomatoes but bumped up their flavor even more with garlic and canned chipotle chile. If you prefer a mild chili con queso, omit the chipotle. The dip tasted best when made with block cheese that we shredded ourselves; buy a block of American cheese from the deli counter. Preshredded cheese will work, but the dip will be much thicker.

1   **cup chicken broth**

4   **ounces cream cheese**

1   **tablespoon cornstarch**

1   **tablespoon minced chipotle chile**

1   **teaspoon minced garlic**

¼   **teaspoon pepper**

2   **cups shredded Monterey Jack cheese**

1   **cup shredded American cheese**

1   **(10-ounce) can Ro-tel Diced Tomatoes & Green Chilies, drained**

1. Microwave broth, cream cheese, cornstarch, chipotle, garlic, and pepper in large bowl, whisking occasionally, until smooth and thickened, about 5 minutes. Stir in Monterey Jack and American cheeses until combined.

2A. FOR A 1½- TO 5-QUART SLOW COOKER: Transfer mixture to slow cooker, cover, and cook until cheese is melted, 1 to 2 hours on low.

2B. FOR A 5½- TO 7-QUART SLOW COOKER: Transfer mixture to 1½-quart soufflé dish. Set dish in slow cooker and pour water into slow cooker until it reaches about one-third up sides of dish (about 2 cups water). Cover and cook until cheese is melted, 1 to 2 hours on low. Remove dish from slow cooker.

3. Whisk cheese mixture until smooth, then stir in tomatoes. (Adjust consistency with hot water 2 tablespoons at a time as needed. Dip can be held on warm or low setting for up to 2 hours.)

SMART SHOPPING RO-TEL TOMATOES
This blend of tomatoes, green chiles, and spices was created by Carl Roettele in Elsa, Texas, in the early 1940s. By the 1950s, Ro-tel tomatoes had become popular in the Lone Star State and beyond. The spicy, tangy tomatoes add just the right flavor to countless regional recipes, such as King Ranch Casserole and Chile con Queso. We call on Ro-tel tomatoes when we need an extra flavor boost in Southwest- and Texas-inspired recipes. If you can't find them, you can substitute 1¼ cups diced tomatoes plus one minced jalapeño for one 10-ounce can.

Warm Marinated Artichoke Hearts with Feta and Olives

Serves 8 to 10   **Cooking Time** 1 to 2 hours on Low   **Slow Cooker Size** 1½ to 7 quarts

WHY THIS RECIPE WORKS: Marinated artichoke hearts are a classic antipasto, but when flavored with little more than oil and garlic, they can be boring and one-dimensional. We wanted to revive this dish by using the gentle heat of the slow cooker to infuse the artichokes with deep, complex flavor. Fresh artichokes are not always readily available and can be a hassle to prepare for cooking, so we started with frozen artichoke hearts. Available year-round, they come fully prepped right out of the package; we simply needed to thaw them and pat them dry to remove excess moisture before tossing them in the slow cooker. To flavor the basic marinade, we added some bright lemon zest and juice, red pepper flakes, and a few sprigs of fresh thyme along with the requisite olive oil and garlic. Briny kalamata olives and rich, tangy feta cheese fit in nicely with the Mediterranean theme; we simply stirred the cheese in at the end of cooking to ensure that the cubes wouldn't lose their shape. Serve with crusty bread for dipping in the infused oil.

18	ounces frozen artichoke hearts, thawed, patted dry, and halved
1	cup extra-virgin olive oil
½	cup pitted kalamata olives, halved
¾	teaspoon grated lemon zest plus 2 tablespoons juice
3	peeled garlic cloves, crushed
2	sprigs fresh thyme
1	teaspoon salt
¼	teaspoon red pepper flakes
1	(4-ounce) block feta cheese

1. Combine artichoke hearts, oil, olives, lemon zest and juice, garlic, thyme, salt, and pepper flakes in slow cooker. Cover and cook until heated through and flavors meld, 1 to 2 hours on low.

2. Discard thyme. Cut feta into ½-inch pieces, gently stir into slow cooker, and let sit until heated through, about 5 minutes. Serve. (This dish can be held on warm or low setting for up to 2 hours.)

SMART SHOPPING FROZEN ARTICHOKES
Artichokes boast a sweet, earthy, nutty flavor that works well in a variety of dishes, but fresh artichokes can be a hassle to prep and cook. Luckily, frozen artichoke hearts are widely available and simply need to be thawed and patted dry to remove excess moisture prior to cooking.

Garlicky Shrimp

Serves 8 to 10   **Cooking Time** about 1 hour on High   **Slow Cooker Size** 3½ to 7 quarts

✔ **WHY THIS RECIPE WORKS:** Delicate, fast-cooking shrimp and the slow cooker may seem like an impossible pairing, but the slow, gentle heat of the slow cooker is actually terrific for producing tender shrimp without the fear of overcooking. With that in mind, we set out to create a classic garlic shrimp recipe that would infuse the shrimp with plenty of rich garlicky flavor. We started by cooking sliced garlic and spices in oil for 30 minutes to soften the raw flavor of the garlic and allow the spices' flavors to bloom. Once the oil was sufficiently flavored, we stirred in the shrimp. A mere 20-minute poach in the garlicky oil was enough to cook and season the shrimp. While we prefer the flavor of smoked paprika in this recipe, you can substitute sweet paprika. Serve with crusty bread for dipping in the infused oil.

¾	cup extra-virgin olive oil
6	garlic cloves, sliced thin
1	teaspoon smoked paprika
	Salt and pepper
¼	teaspoon red pepper flakes
2	pounds large shrimp (26 to 30 per pound), peeled and deveined
1	tablespoon minced fresh parsley

1A. FOR A 3½- TO 5-QUART SLOW COOKER: Combine oil, garlic, paprika, 1 teaspoon salt, ¼ teaspoon pepper, and pepper flakes in slow cooker, cover, and cook until flavors meld, about 30 minutes on high. Stir in shrimp, cover, and cook on high until opaque throughout, about 40 minutes, stirring halfway through cooking.

1B. FOR A 5½- TO 7-QUART SLOW COOKER: Combine oil, garlic, paprika, 1 teaspoon salt, ¼ teaspoon pepper, and pepper flakes in slow cooker, cover, and cook until flavors meld, about 30 minutes on high. Stir in shrimp, cover, and cook on high until opaque throughout, about 20 minutes, stirring halfway through cooking.

2. Transfer shrimp and oil mixture to serving dish. Sprinkle with parsley and serve.

QUICK PREP TIP
PEELING AND DEVEINING SHRIMP
To devein shrimp, hold shrimp firmly in 1 hand, then use paring knife to cut down back side of shrimp, about ⅛ to ¼ inch deep, to expose vein. Using tip of knife, gently remove vein. Wipe knife against paper towel to remove vein and discard.

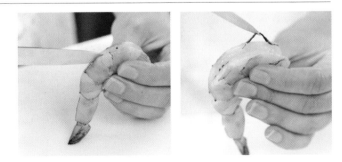

Italian Sausage Cocktail Meatballs

Serves 6 to 8   **Cooking Time** 1 to 2 hours on Low   **Slow Cooker Size** 3½ to 7 quarts

✔️ **WHY THIS RECIPE WORKS:** Slow-cooker cocktail meatballs are an easy way to feed a crowd—a big batch can gently simmer away before guests arrive, then be served warm right out of the slow cooker. We wanted a classic Italian-inspired meatball and marinara dish that would be easy to prepare and would deliver on flavor, with a tangy tomato sauce and tender meatballs. For bold flavor with little effort, we replaced the traditional meatloaf mix with Italian sausage, which already included seasonings like oregano, basil, coriander, and fennel. Using a mix of prepared pesto and panko bread crumbs as a binder reinforced the Italian flavors and kept the meatballs moist and tender. Microwaving the meatballs before adding them to the sauce helped to render any excess fat and firmed the meatballs just enough so they wouldn't fall apart in the moist environment of the slow cooker. Since the meatballs lent their flavor to the sauce as they cooked, a can of crushed tomatoes and a little oregano and garlic were all we needed to create a bold marinara with long-simmered flavor.

1	**pound hot or sweet Italian sausage, casings removed**
½	**cup prepared basil pesto**
½	**cup panko bread crumbs**
	Salt and pepper
1	**(28-ounce) can crushed tomatoes**
1	**teaspoon dried oregano**
2	**teaspoons minced garlic**

1. Mix sausage, pesto, panko, and ⅛ teaspoon pepper together in bowl using hands until uniform. Pinch off and roll mixture into tablespoon-size meatballs (about 30 meatballs total) and arrange on large plate. Microwave meatballs until fat renders and meatballs are firm, about 5 minutes.

2. Combine tomatoes, oregano, garlic, and ½ teaspoon salt in slow cooker. Transfer microwaved meatballs to slow cooker, discarding rendered fat. Cover and cook until meatballs are tender, about 1 hour on high.

3. Using large spoon, skim excess fat from surface of sauce. Season with salt and pepper to taste and serve. (Meatballs can be held on warm or low setting for up to 2 hours; loosen sauce with hot water 2 tablespoons at a time as needed.)

QUICK PREP TIP **REMOVING SAUSAGE FROM ITS CASING**
Italian sausage is sold in several forms, including links (which are most common), bulk-style tubes, and patties. If using links, remove the meat from the casing before cooking so that it can be crumbled into small pieces. To remove sausage from its casing, hold the sausage firmly on one end and squeeze the sausage out of the opposite end.

Tangy Mango Cocktail Meatballs

Serves 6 to 8   **Cooking Time** 1 to 2 hours on Low   **Slow Cooker Size** 3½ to 7 quarts

✔ **WHY THIS RECIPE WORKS:** Sweet and sour meatballs are always a hit, but we wanted to give ours a little twist. For the sweet element, we wanted a bright and fruity flavor. Mango chutney proved perfect; it had a bold, lightly spiced sweet flavor, and its thick, sticky texture clung perfectly to the meatballs. For a balancing savory note, we added a can of tomato sauce. A teaspoon of garam masala, stirred into the meatloaf mix, added warmth and complexity and paired nicely with the mango sauce. A quick stint in the microwave helped to remove excess fat from the raw meatballs and firm them up before they were added to the slow cooker, where they needed to simmer gently for only an hour until they were tender and flavorful. Meatloaf mix is a prepackaged mix of ground beef, pork, and veal; if it's unavailable, use 8 ounces each of ground pork and 85 percent lean ground beef.

1	pound meatloaf mix
½	cup panko bread crumbs
¼	cup milk
1	teaspoon garam masala
1	teaspoon minced garlic
	Salt and pepper
1¼	cups mango chutney
1	(15-ounce) can tomato sauce
2	scallions, sliced thin

1. Using hands, mix meatloaf mix, panko, milk, garam masala, garlic, ¼ teaspoon salt, and ¼ teaspoon pepper together in bowl until uniform. Pinch off and roll mixture into tablespoon-size meatballs (about 30 meatballs total) and arrange on large plate. Microwave meatballs until fat renders and meatballs are firm, about 5 minutes.

2. Combine chutney and tomato sauce in slow cooker. Transfer meatballs to slow cooker, discarding rendered fat. Cover and cook until meatballs are tender, about 1 hour on high.

3. Using large spoon, skim excess fat from surface of sauce. Gently stir in scallions and season with salt and pepper to taste. Serve. (Meatballs can be held on warm or low setting for up to 2 hours; loosen sauce with hot water 2 tablespoons at a time as needed.)

QUICK PREP TIP **KEEPING SCALLIONS FRESH**

Too often, scallions go limp after just a few days in the fridge. We found that if we stand them in an inch of water in a tall container (covering them loosely with a zipper-lock bag and refreshing the water every three days), our scallions last for well over a week with very little loss in quality.

Asian Glazed Wings

Serves 4 to 6   **Cooking Time** 3 to 4 hours on Low   **Slow Cooker Size** 5½ to 7 quarts

✓ **WHY THIS RECIPE WORKS:** We love the making wings in the slow cooker where the low, slow heat renders their fat and leaves them meltingly tender. First we built flavor with a dry rub of brown sugar and ground ginger, then we cooked the wings in the slow cooker until tender. Finally we broiled the wings, glazing them partway through, until browned and caramelized. For a tasty Asian-inspired glaze, we used thick, sweet hoisin sauce, balancing its sweetness with some rice vinegar and a tablespoon of spicy Sriracha. We prefer to buy split chicken wings, but you can purchase 4¼ pounds of whole wings and split them yourself (see page 30).

1	tablespoon packed brown sugar
1	tablespoon ground ginger
1½	teaspoons granulated garlic
	Salt and pepper
4	pounds split chicken wings
1	cup hoisin sauce
3	tablespoons rice vinegar
1	tablespoon Sriracha sauce

1. Mix sugar, ginger, garlic, 1 teaspoon salt, and ½ teaspoon pepper together in bowl, then rub mixture evenly over chicken; transfer to slow cooker. Cover and cook until chicken is tender, 3 to 4 hours on low.

2. Adjust oven rack 10 inches from broiler element and heat broiler. Place wire rack inside aluminum foil–lined rimmed baking sheet and spray with vegetable oil spray. Transfer chicken to prepared sheet; discard cooking liquid. Broil until lightly charred and crisp, about 10 minutes, flipping halfway through cooking.

3. Meanwhile, combine hoisin, vinegar, and Sriracha in bowl. Brush wings with one-third of sauce and continue to broil until wings are browned and sticky, about 10 minutes, flipping and brushing wings with one-third more sauce halfway through cooking. Brush wings with remaining sauce and serve.

QUICK PREP TIP **MAKING GLAZED WINGS**
Cook spice-rubbed wings in slow cooker until tender, then set on wire rack set inside rimmed baking sheet. Broil, brushing twice with sauce, until wings are browned and sticky. Brush with remaining sauce and serve.

Smoky Honey-Lime Glazed Wings

Serves 4 to 6   **Cooking Time** 3 to 4 hours on Low   **Slow Cooker Size** 5½ to 7 quarts

✔ **WHY THIS RECIPE WORKS:** For another flavor-packed variation on our easy slow-cooker glazed wings, we wanted a sweet and tangy sauce with just a little spice. We started with a simple rub of brown sugar, coriander, and cumin before the wings went into the slow cooker, then we moved on to the glaze. After trying several tacks, we hit on using honey as the base; it clung perfectly to our wings and offered a well-rounded sweetness. Chipotle chiles added smoky flavor and complex heat, and lime zest contributed just the right amount of bright tang. For an ultracrisp, intensely flavored crust, we finished the wings under the broiler, glazing them partway through. Now our wings were disappearing from the plate as fast as we could make them. We prefer to buy split chicken wings, but you can purchase 4¼ pounds of whole wings and split them yourself.

1	**tablespoon packed brown sugar**
2	**teaspoons ground coriander**
2	**teaspoons ground cumin**
	Salt and pepper
4	**pounds split chicken wings**
1	**cup honey**
1½	**tablespoons grated lime zest (3 limes)**
1	**tablespoon minced chipotle chile**

1. Mix sugar, coriander, cumin, 1 teaspoon salt, and ½ teaspoon pepper together in bowl, then rub mixture evenly over chicken; transfer to slow cooker. Cover and cook until chicken is tender, 3 to 4 hours on low.

2. Adjust oven rack 10 inches from broiler element and heat broiler. Place wire rack inside aluminum foil–lined rimmed baking sheet and spray with vegetable oil spray. Transfer chicken to prepared sheet; discard cooking liquid. Broil until lightly charred and crisp, about 10 minutes, flipping halfway through cooking.

3. Meanwhile, combine honey, lime zest, chipotle, and ½ teaspoon salt in bowl. Brush wings with one-third of sauce and continue to broil until wings are browned and sticky, about 10 minutes, flipping and brushing wings with one-third more sauce halfway through cooking. Brush wings with remaining sauce and serve.

QUICK PREP TIP
CUTTING UP CHICKEN WINGS
If split wings are not available, you'll need to take a few extra minutes to cut whole wings into pieces yourself. To cut up a wing, simply slice through each of the two joints and discard the wingtip.

Barbecued Cocktail Franks

Serves 8 to 10   **Cooking Time** 1 to 2 hours on Low   **Slow Cooker Size** 3½ to 7 quarts

✓ **WHY THIS RECIPE WORKS:** Cocktail franks are a party favorite and an easy, kid-friendly hors d'oeuvres. We make them even easier by using the slow cooker, where they can gently simmer in a flavorful sauce without worry of scorching. We guarantee this will be your go-to method from now on. We found that sweet and tangy barbecue sauce brought out the subtle smoky flavor of the franks nicely. Since the sauce was the star of the show, we skipped the bottled barbecue and threw together a simple homemade sauce. We started with tangy ketchup and added some molasses for its rich sweetness and Dijon mustard and cider vinegar for a dose of acidity. A combination of chili powder and cayenne added complex but not overwhelming heat. For a spicier barbecue sauce, use the larger amount of cayenne.

1	**cup ketchup**	
½	**cup molasses**	
3	**tablespoons cider vinegar**	
3	**tablespoons Dijon mustard**	
1	**tablespoon packed brown sugar**	
2	**teaspoons chili powder**	
⅛–¼	**teaspoon cayenne pepper**	
1	**pound cocktail franks**	

Combine ketchup, molasses, vinegar, mustard, sugar, chili powder, and cayenne in slow cooker, then stir in cocktail franks. Cover and cook until franks are heated through, about 1 hour on high. Serve. (Cocktail franks can be held on warm or low setting for up to 2 hours; loosen sauce with hot water 2 tablespoons at a time as needed.)

Spicy Mustard Cocktail Franks

Serves 8 to 10   **Cooking Time** 1 to 2 hours on Low   **Slow Cooker Size** 3½ to 7 quarts

✓ **WHY THIS RECIPE WORKS:** For a quick and easy variation on our barbecued cocktail franks, we decided to make a spicy mustard sauce. Yellow mustard had plenty of the bright, tangy flavor we were after, and we added some spice by mixing in a couple tablespoons of hot sauce. To balance the heat with some sweetness, we tried honey, but when heated in the slow cooker it thinned out the sauce and prevented it from clinging to the franks. Instead we turned to apricot preserves, which were sweet, fruity, and flavorful and made our sauce thick and clingy. If you prefer a milder sauce, reduce the amount of hot sauce.

1	**cup yellow mustard**	
½	**cup apricot preserves**	
1	**tablespoon packed brown sugar**	
2	**tablespoons hot sauce**	
1	**pound cocktail franks**	

Combine mustard, preserves, sugar, and hot sauce in slow cooker, then stir in cocktail franks. Cover and cook until franks are heated through, about 1 hour on high. Serve. (Cocktail franks can be held on warm or low setting for up to 2 hours; loosen sauce with hot water 2 tablespoons at a time as needed.)

Shortcut Soups

Hearty Chicken and Garden Vegetable Soup

Serves 8   **Cooking Time** 3 to 4 hours on Low   **Slow Cooker Size** 5½ to 7 Quarts

✅ **WHY THIS RECIPE WORKS:** For a vegetable soup that tasted like it came straight from the garden, we found that the trick was adding the vegetables in stages. Onions, garlic, and diced tomatoes went in at the start so their flavors would deepen and meld into a richly flavored broth. We stirred in zucchini toward the end of cooking so that it would turn tender but not mushy and dull-tasting. For a finishing touch of bright, herbal flavor, we stirred in fresh basil just before serving. We found that pasta shells stirred in along with the zucchini cooked to perfection by the time the soup was done. To ensure that our soup was hearty and filling, we also added plenty of chicken. Bone-in split chicken breasts worked best; the bones and skin helped the chicken to retain its moisture during the long cooking period, giving us juicy, flavorful bites of chicken to complement the soup's fresh vegetable flavor.

2	**cups chopped onions**
2	**tablespoons olive oil**
2	**tablespoons minced garlic**
	Salt and pepper
8	**cups chicken broth**
1	**(14.5-ounce) can diced tomatoes, drained**
3	**(12-ounce) bone-in split chicken breasts, trimmed**
1	**zucchini, quartered lengthwise and sliced ¼ inch thick**
3	**ounces (1 cup) medium shells**
1	**cup chopped fresh basil**

1. Microwave onions, oil, garlic, and ½ teaspoon salt in bowl, stirring occasionally, until onions are softened, about 5 minutes; transfer to slow cooker. Stir in broth and tomatoes. Season chicken with salt and pepper and nestle into slow cooker. Cover and cook until chicken is tender, 3 to 4 hours on low.

2. Transfer chicken to cutting board, let cool slightly, then shred into bite-size pieces, discarding skin and bones. Using large spoon, skim excess fat from surface of soup.

3. Stir in zucchini and pasta. Cover and cook on high until tender, 20 to 30 minutes. Stir in shredded chicken and let sit until heated through, about 5 minutes. Stir in basil and season with salt and pepper to taste. Drizzle individual portions with extra oil before serving.

QUICK PREP TIP
SHREDDING MEAT
To shred poultry, beef, or pork into bite-size pieces, simply insert two forks (tines facing down) into cooked meat and gently pull meat apart.

Asian Chicken Noodle Soup

Serves 8   **Cooking Time** 3 to 4 hours on Low   **Slow Cooker Size** 5½ to 7 Quarts

✔ **WHY THIS RECIPE WORKS:** For a quick but flavorful chicken noodle soup, we decided to give it an Asian-inspired spin. Chicken broth and soy sauce formed the base of our broth in short order. To instill it with deep flavor, we first microwaved onions with some spicy ginger, garlic, and rich toasted sesame oil. For the chicken, we found that gently cooking bone-in chicken breasts in the flavorful broth kept the meat tender and moist and infused it with flavor. Finally, quick-cooking instant ramen noodles and preshredded coleslaw mix stirred in at the end turned tender in minutes. Be sure not to overcook the ramen noodles or else they will become mushy.

2	**cups chopped onions**
3	**tablespoons grated ginger**
2	**tablespoons minced garlic**
1	**tablespoon toasted sesame oil**
8	**cups chicken broth**
2	**tablespoons soy sauce**
3	**(12-ounce) bone-in split chicken breasts, trimmed**
	Salt and pepper
1	**(14-ounce) bag coleslaw mix**
2	**(3-ounce) packages ramen noodles, seasoning discarded**
4	**scallions, sliced thin**

1. Microwave onions, 2 tablespoons ginger, garlic, and oil in bowl, stirring occasionally, until onions are softened, about 5 minutes; transfer to slow cooker. Stir in broth and soy sauce. Season chicken with salt and pepper and nestle into slow cooker. Cover and cook until chicken is tender, 3 to 4 hours on low.

2. Transfer chicken to cutting board, let cool slightly, then shred into bite-size pieces, discarding skin and bones. Using large spoon, skim excess fat from surface of soup.

3. Stir coleslaw and ramen noodles into soup. Cover and cook on high until tender, about 8 minutes. Stir in shredded chicken and remaining 1 tablespoon ginger and let sit until chicken is heated through, about 5 minutes. Stir in scallions and season with extra sesame oil, salt, and pepper to taste. Serve.

QUICK PREP TIP GRATING GINGER
Although we love the floral pungency of fresh ginger, its fibrous texture can be distracting when coarsely grated or minced. What's the best way to avoid ginger's stringy texture? Although fancy kitchen stores sometimes carry porcelain "ginger graters" designed specifically for the job, we prefer to use our rasp-style grater. Its fine blades pulverize the ginger, releasing all of its flavorful juice without any stringy segments. Simply peel a small section of a large piece of ginger, then grate the peeled portion, using the rest of the ginger as a handle. Be sure to work with a large nub of ginger—and watch your knuckles.

Lemony Chicken and Rice Soup

Serves 8   **Cooking Time** 3 to 4 hours on Low   **Slow Cooker Size** 5½ to 7 Quarts

WHY THIS RECIPE WORKS: The classic Greek soup *avgolemono* features chicken and rice in a bright lemony broth enriched with egg yolks. To bring this soup to the slow cooker, we needed to figure out how to add the egg yolks to the soup without them scrambling and forming lumps. We found that first adding a little hot soup to the yolks to raise their temperature (a technique known as tempering) helped stabilize them so they could be stirred into the soup without scrambling, giving our soup a silky texture. For perfectly tender rice, we tried adding it both cooked and raw and found that precooked rice, added at the end of cooking, gave us the best results. For the soup's distinctive lemon flavor, we whisked in a few tablespoons of fresh lemon juice at the end. Do not combine the egg yolks and lemon juice ahead of time or else the yolks will curdle. Feel free to use either leftover rice or store-bought precooked rice.

2	**cups chopped onions**
3	**carrots, peeled and sliced ½ inch thick**
1	**tablespoon minced garlic**
1	**tablespoon vegetable oil**
8	**cups chicken broth**
3	**(12-ounce) bone-in split chicken breasts, trimmed**
	Salt and pepper
4	**large egg yolks**
3	**tablespoons lemon juice**
1	**cup cooked rice**

1. Microwave onions, carrots, garlic, and oil in bowl, stirring occasionally, until vegetables are softened, about 5 minutes; transfer to slow cooker. Stir in broth. Season chicken with salt and pepper and nestle into slow cooker. Cover and cook until chicken is tender, 3 to 4 hours on low.

2. Transfer chicken to cutting board, let cool slightly, then shred into bite-size pieces, discarding skin and bones. Using large spoon, skim excess fat from surface of soup.

3. Whisk egg yolks and lemon juice together in bowl, then slowly whisk 3 tablespoons hot broth into yolk mixture. Whisk yolk mixture into soup and cook on high, whisking constantly, until it thickens slightly, about 1 minute. Stir shredded chicken and rice into soup and let sit until heated through, about 5 minutes. Season with salt and pepper to taste and serve.

QUICK PREP TIP
TEMPERING THE EGGS WITH THE SOUP
Whisking constantly, pour several tablespoons of hot broth into beaten egg yolk mixture in slow, steady stream. Once broth is fully incorporated, slowly pour warm egg yolk mixture back into soup, again whisking constantly.

Spicy Chipotle Chicken and Chickpea Soup

Serves 8   **Cooking Time** 3 to 4 hours on Low   **Slow Cooker Size** 5½ to 7 Quarts

✓ WHY THIS RECIPE WORKS: This hearty south-of-the-border soup features a spicy, tomatoey broth with bites of tender shredded chicken and chickpeas. We started with a little onion, garlic, and tomato paste plus canned chipotle chiles—dried, smoked jalapeños in a chile sauce—for smokiness and heat. We stirred this mixture into the slow cooker along with chicken broth to make a delicious spicy broth. As the chicken gently cooked in this flavorful liquid, it was slowly infused with the broth's bold flavor. Creamy canned chickpeas bulked up the soup, and some bright cilantro and a couple of fresh tomatoes, chopped and stirred in at the end, nicely balanced the spicy broth. Serve with sour cream, shredded Monterey Jack cheese, diced avocado, and/or lime wedges.

2	**cups chopped onions**
4	**teaspoons minced chipotle chile**
1	**tablespoon minced garlic**
1	**tablespoon tomato paste**
1	**tablespoon vegetable oil**
8	**cups chicken broth**
2	**(14-ounce) cans chickpeas, rinsed**
3	**(12-ounce) bone-in split chicken breasts, trimmed**
	Salt and pepper
2	**tomatoes, cored and chopped**
½	**cup minced fresh cilantro**

1. Microwave onions, chipotle, garlic, tomato paste, and oil in bowl, stirring occasionally, until onions are softened, about 5 minutes; transfer to slow cooker. Stir in broth and chickpeas. Season chicken with salt and pepper and nestle into slow cooker. Cover and cook until chicken is tender, 3 to 4 hours on low.

2. Transfer chicken to cutting board, let cool slightly, then shred into bite-size pieces, discarding skin and bones. Using large spoon, skim excess fat from surface of soup.

3. Stir in shredded chicken and tomatoes and let sit until heated through, about 5 minutes. Stir in cilantro and season with salt and pepper to taste. Serve.

SMART SHOPPING CHIPOTLE CHILES IN ADOBO

Canned chipotle chiles are jalapeños that have been ripened until red, then smoked and dried. They are sold as is, ground to a powder, or packed in a tomato-based sauce. We prefer the latter because the chiles are already reconstituted by the sauce, making them easier to use. Most recipes don't require an entire can, but these chiles will keep for 2 weeks in the refrigerator, or they can be frozen. To freeze, puree the chiles and quick-freeze teaspoonfuls on a plastic wrap–covered plate. Once the teaspoons of chiles are hard, peel them off the plastic and transfer them to a zipper-lock freezer bag. The chiles can be stored this way for up to 2 months. Thaw what you need before use.

ALL ABOUT Broths

Granted, nothing compares with the flavor of homemade broth, but few of us ever have time to make it from scratch. Fortunately, we've found a few good stand-ins at the supermarket that will deliver richly flavored yet speedy soups, stews, and more. Below you'll find the brands we prefer.

Chicken Broth

We frequently reach for chicken broth for the bulk of the liquid in our slow-cooker soups. While searching for the best-tasting commercial broth, we discovered a few critical characteristics that made a big difference in quality. First, look for a sodium content between 400 and 700 milligrams per serving. When combined with other salty ingredients such as canned beans and tomatoes, soy sauce, and ham hocks, too-salty chicken broth can easily ruin a dish, but we found that broth with less than 400 milligrams tasted bland. Also, look for a mass-produced broth. We tasted several broths with rancid off-flavors caused by fat oxidation, and the worst offenders were those made by smaller companies. Last, look for a short ingredient list that includes vegetables like carrots, celery, and onions. Our pick? **Swanson Chicken Broth**, which tastes rich and meaty thanks to its relatively high percentage of meat-based protein.

Vegetable Broth

For vegetarian dishes and vegetable dishes that might be overwhelmed by the flavor of chicken broth, we turn to vegetable broth. We sometimes use a mix of chicken and vegetable broths as vegetable broth can be too sweet when used alone. In our search for the best vegetable broth, we tested 10 brands and found that our favorite brands listed vegetable content first on the ingredients list and included a hefty amount of salt. Our winner? **Swanson Vegetarian Vegetable Broth**.

Beef Broth

In the past we've found beef broth to be light on beefy flavor, but making beef broth from scratch is far from convenient. Wanting to find out if supermarket offerings had improved, we gathered 13 top-selling beef broths, stocks, and bases and rated them on beef flavor, aroma, saltiness, and overall appeal. The top eight brands (five were eliminated) were then tasted in gravy and French onion soup. Ultimately, our top two broths delivered on rich, beefy flavor—but using very different ingredients. The runner-up, College Inn, relies on beef, beef derivatives, and glutamate-rich additives (such as yeast extract and tomato paste) for flavor and other additives for body. The winning brand, **Rachael Ray Stock-in-a-Box All-Natural Beef Flavored Stock** (made by Colavita), has a shorter but less foreign ingredient list that starts with concentrated beef stock, which means this stock has more fresh, real meat than the other brands. Also, this broth contained no processed additives except for yeast extract, but it still tasted really beefy. Tasters praised it as "steak-y" and "rich" with "thick, gelatin-like body."

Clam Juice

When we need bold clam flavor for a seafood chowder or stew in our slow cooker, we reach for some clam juice, made by briefly steaming fresh clams in salted water and filtering the resulting broth before bottling. We tested three brands; one tasted "too strong" and "too clammy," possibly because its sodium content was more than double that of the other two. Our winner, **Bar Harbor Clam Juice**, hails from clam country in Maine and brings a "bright" and "mineral-y" flavor to seafood dishes.

Mexican-Style Pork and Vegetable Soup

Serves 8 to 10   **Cooking Time** 6 to 7 hours on Low or 4 to 5 hours on High
Slow Cooker Size 5½ to 7 Quarts

✔ **WHY THIS RECIPE WORKS:** Hearty pork and hominy soup is classic Mexican fare, and we knew it would translate perfectly to the slow cooker, where the long cooking time would gently braise the pork until it was fall-apart tender. Pork shoulder is the traditional cut of meat for this soup, but it required too much extra work to trim the fat and cut the raw meat into pieces. After testing several different cuts of pork, we found the perfect substitute: boneless country-style pork ribs, which could be added straight to the slow cooker and contained a good amount of intramuscular fat to keep the meat moist during the long cooking time. To make our soup even heartier, we added some red potatoes along with the hominy. For a fresh vegetable, we added some zucchini toward the end of cooking so that it would cook until just tender. Cilantro, stirred in at the end, brightened up the soup and provided a nice balance to a new classic.

1	pound red potatoes, cut into ½-inch pieces
1	cup chopped onion
2	tablespoons minced garlic
2	tablespoons tomato paste
1	tablespoon vegetable oil
2	teaspoons minced chipotle chile
8	cups chicken broth
1	(15-ounce) can hominy, rinsed
1½	pounds boneless country-style pork ribs, trimmed
	Salt and pepper
2	zucchini, quartered lengthwise and sliced ¼ inch thick
½	cup minced fresh cilantro

1. Microwave potatoes, onion, garlic, tomato paste, oil, and chipotle in bowl, stirring occasionally, until onion is softened, about 5 minutes; transfer to slow cooker. Stir in broth, and hominy. Season pork with salt and pepper and nestle into slow cooker. Cover and cook until pork is tender, 6 to 7 hours on low or 4 to 5 hours on high.

2. Transfer pork to cutting board, let cool slightly, then shred into bite-size pieces. Using large spoon, skim excess fat from surface of soup.

3. Stir in zucchini, cover, and cook on high until tender, 20 to 30 minutes. Stir in shredded pork and let sit until heated through, about 5 minutes. Stir in cilantro and season with salt and pepper to taste. Serve.

SMART SHOPPING COUNTRY-STYLE RIBS
Country-style ribs aren't actually ribs at all. They're well-marbled pork chops cut from the upper side of the rib cage, from the fatty blade end of the loin. Because they contain a good amount of intramuscular fat, they are a favorite for braising or smoking. Butchers usually cut them into individual ribs and package several together.

Asian Beef Noodle Soup

Serves 6 to 8   **Cooking Time** 9 to 10 hours on Low or 6 to 7 hours on High
Slow Cooker Size 5½ to 7 Quarts

✓ **WHY THIS RECIPE WORKS:** To make Asian-style beef and noodle soup in the slow cooker, we'd need a way to add lots of flavor without a laundry list of ingredients. Spicy ginger and aromatic onions and garlic lent bold, rich flavor to store-bought beef broth. For hearty bites of beef without any prep work, we chose sirloin steak tips over traditional cuts like chuck roast, which required trimming and cutting into pieces. Flavorful ramen noodles needed just a few minutes on high to become tender. For freshness and crunch, we stirred in edamame and water chestnuts at the end and simply let the soup sit until everything was heated through. Be sure not to overcook the ramen noodles or else they will become mushy.

2	**cups chopped onions**
3	**tablespoons grated ginger**
2	**tablespoons minced garlic**
1	**tablespoon toasted sesame oil**
8	**cups beef broth**
2	**tablespoons soy sauce**
1½	**pounds sirloin steak tips, trimmed**
	Salt and pepper
2	**(3-ounce) packages ramen noodles, seasoning discarded**
1	**cup shelled frozen edamame**
1	**(8-ounce) can sliced water chestnuts, rinsed**

1. Microwave onions, 2 tablespoons ginger, garlic, and oil in bowl, stirring occasionally, until onions are softened, about 5 minutes; transfer to slow cooker. Stir in broth and soy sauce. Season beef with salt and pepper and nestle into slow cooker. Cover and cook until beef is tender, 9 to 10 hours on low or 6 to 7 hours on high.

2. Transfer beef to cutting board, let cool slightly, then shred into bite-size pieces. Using large spoon, skim excess fat from surface of soup.

3. Stir ramen noodles into soup; cover, and cook on high until tender, 4 to 8 minutes. Stir in shredded beef, edamame, water chestnuts, and remaining 1 tablespoon ginger and let sit until heated through, about 5 minutes. Season with extra sesame oil, salt, and pepper to taste. Serve.

SMART SHOPPING RAMEN NOODLES

Though inexpensive instant ramen noodles are a favorite among college students, we don't like their salty, stale-tasting seasoning. However, we do like to use plain ramen noodles in our own Asian-inspired recipes; we just discard the seasoning packet and add our own flavorings. Ramen noodles are typically fried in oil then dried, so the noodles both are flavorful and take only a few minutes to cook, making them more convenient than many other dried noodles.

Russian Beef and Cabbage Soup

Serves 6 to 8   **Cooking Time** 9 to 10 hours on Low or 6 to 7 hours on High
Slow Cooker Size 5½ to 7 Quarts

☑ **WHY THIS RECIPE WORKS:** In Russia, beef and cabbage soup is classic comfort food; the crisp, tangy cabbage is a perfect partner for chunks of tender beef. For our version of this tasty soup, we started with the cabbage. In search of a way to avoid prepping fresh cabbage, we tried substituting sauerkraut. Not only was the sauerkraut an easy addition, but tasters loved the tangy flavor it contributed. For the beef, we chose prep-free sirloin steak tips for convenience. We thought that dumplings would make a nice addition, but we weren't willing to make them from scratch. We found that bite-size store-bought gnocchi, though not traditional, worked perfectly and were happily prep-free. Stirred in during the final 30 minutes of cooking time, the gnocchi cooked until just tender. Vacuum-packed gnocchi can be found in the pasta aisle; do not substitute refrigerated or frozen gnocchi, which will turn gummy in the soup. Be sure to rinse the sauerkraut well; otherwise it will make the soup too sour.

2	**cups chopped onions**
2	**tablespoons minced garlic**
2	**tablespoons tomato paste**
1	**tablespoon vegetable oil**
½	**teaspoon dried thyme**
8	**cups beef broth**
2	**cups sauerkraut, rinsed**
1½	**pounds sirloin steak tips, trimmed**
	Salt and pepper
1	**pound vacuum-packed gnocchi**
2	**tablespoons minced fresh dill**
	Sour cream

1. Microwave onions, garlic, tomato paste, oil, and thyme in bowl, stirring occasionally, until onions are softened, about 5 minutes; transfer to slow cooker. Stir in broth and 1 cup sauerkraut. Season beef with salt and pepper and nestle into slow cooker. Cover and cook until beef is tender, 9 to 10 hours on low or 6 to 7 hours on high.

2. Transfer beef to cutting board, let cool slightly, then shred into bite-size pieces. Using large spoon, skim excess fat from surface of soup.

3. Stir in gnocchi, cover, and cook on high until tender, about 30 minutes. Stir in shredded beef and remaining 1 cup sauerkraut and let sit until heated through, about 5 minutes. Stir in dill and season with salt and pepper to taste. Serve with sour cream.

SMART SHOPPING SAUERKRAUT

To find the best sauerkraut available at the supermarket, we tasted eight national contenders—in jars, cans, and vacuum-sealed bags—both plain and on a Reuben sandwich. Right off the bat, tasters panned the heavily processed, long-cooked canned brands as "flavorless" and "flat." Jarred and bagged brands are cooked less, and these generally had more crunch and flavor. Our winning sauerkraut, **Boar's Head Sauerkraut**, is a bagged variety that was praised for its "chewy-crisp" texture and "fresh, vinegary kick." Great Lakes Kraut Co. Krrrrisp Kraut was our runner-up.

Old-Fashioned Beef Oxtail Soup

Serves 6 to 8   **Cooking Time** 9 to 10 hours on Low or 6 to 7 hours on High
Slow Cooker Size 5½ to 7 Quarts

✓ **WHY THIS RECIPE WORKS:** Oxtail soup rarely shows up on the dinner table these days. While it offers deep flavor, rich body, and fall-apart-tender meat (thanks to a significant amount of gelatin), it requires hours of gentle simmering to extract the flavor of the marrow inside the bones and to break down the collagen. We wanted to put the slow cooker to work and put oxtail soup back on the menu. All the oxtails needed was some salt and pepper and plenty of hands-off time in the slow cooker to become meltingly tender. To complement the rich meat, we chose hearty, earthy carrots and parsnips for our vegetables. To round out the soup, we added store-bought beef broth and a combination of onions, tomato paste, garlic, and thyme. A sprinkle of fresh parsley before serving added an herbal flavor. If parsnips are large, cut them in half lengthwise.

2   **cups chopped onions**

2   **tablespoons tomato paste**

1   **tablespoon minced garlic**

1   **tablespoon vegetable oil**

½   **teaspoon dried thyme**

8   **cups beef broth**

3   **carrots, peeled and sliced
     ½ inch thick**

3   **parsnips, peeled and sliced
     ½ inch thick**

2   **bay leaves**

3   **pounds oxtails**

     Salt and pepper

2   **tablespoons minced fresh parsley**

1. Microwave onions, tomato paste, garlic, oil, and thyme in bowl, stirring occasionally, until onions are softened, about 5 minutes; transfer to slow cooker. Stir in broth, carrots, parsnips, and bay leaves. Season oxtails with salt and pepper and nestle into slow cooker. Cover and cook until oxtails are tender, 9 to 10 hours on low or 6 to 7 hours on high.

2. Transfer oxtails to cutting board, let cool slightly, then shred into bite-size pieces, discarding fat and bones. Using large spoon, skim excess fat from surface of soup. Discard bay leaves.

3. Stir in shredded beef and let sit until heated through, about 5 minutes. Stir in parsley and season with salt and pepper to taste. Serve.

SMART SHOPPING BUYING OXTAILS

Depending on which part of the tail they come from, oxtail pieces can vary in diameter from ¾ inch to 4 inches. (Thicker pieces are cut close to the body; thinner pieces come from the end of the tail.) Try to buy oxtail packages with pieces approximately 2 inches thick and between 2 and 4 inches in diameter; they will yield more meat for the soup. Thicker pieces also lend more flavor to the broth. It's fine to use a few small pieces; just don't rely on them exclusively. Oxtails are often found in the freezer section of the grocery store; if using frozen oxtails, be sure to thaw them completely before using.

Garden Vegetable Tortellini Soup

Serves 6   **Cooking Time** 4 to 5 hours on Low or 3 to 4 hours on High
Slow Cooker Size 5½ to 7 Quarts

✓ **WHY THIS RECIPE WORKS:** To make a simple vegetable soup with clean vegetable flavor, we had to pare down our ingredient list so that the individual flavors could shine through. We loved the deep sweetness of carrots; a quick zap in the microwave ensured that they got perfectly tender in the low heat of the slow cooker. To develop a complexly flavored broth, we cooked onions, garlic, and a bit of tomato paste with the carrots, then added it all to the slow cooker along with chicken broth. Toward the end of cooking, we stirred in cheesy fresh tortellini as well as hearty, healthy Swiss chard and frozen peas, which gave the soup garden-fresh vegetable flavor. You can substitute one 9-ounce package of fresh tortellini for the dried tortellini.

2	**cups chopped onions**
2	**carrots, peeled and sliced ½ inch thick**
2	**tablespoons minced garlic**
1	**tablespoon extra-virgin olive oil**
1	**tablespoon tomato paste**
8	**cups chicken broth**
5	**ounces dried cheese tortellini**
10	**ounces Swiss chard, stemmed and sliced into ½-inch-wide strips**
1	**cup frozen peas**
	Salt and pepper
	Grated Parmesan cheese

1. Microwave onions, carrots, garlic, oil, and tomato paste in bowl, stirring occasionally, until vegetables are softened, about 5 minutes; transfer to slow cooker. Stir in broth, cover, and cook until flavors meld and carrots are tender, 4 to 5 hours on low.

2. Stir in tortellini, cover, and cook on high until tender, 15 to 20 minutes. Stir in Swiss chard, 1 handful at a time, then stir in peas; let sit until chard is wilted and peas are heated through, about 5 minutes. Season with salt and pepper to taste. Drizzle individual portions with extra oil and serve with Parmesan.

QUICK PREP TIP
PREPARING HEARTY GREENS
To prepare kale, Swiss chard, and collard greens, cut away leafy green portion from either side of stalk or stem using chef's knife. Stack several leaves on top of one another and either slice leaves crosswise or cut them into pieces as directed in recipe. After they are cut, wash leaves and dry using salad spinner.

Tomato Florentine Soup

Serves 6 to 8   **Cooking Time** 4 to 5 hours on Low or 3 to 4 hours on High
Slow Cooker Size 5½ to 7 Quarts

✓ **WHY THIS RECIPE WORKS:** For a bright tomato Florentine soup that would taste fresh from the garden any time of year, we started by combining canned crushed tomatoes and aromatics (onions, garlic, and thyme) in the slow cooker and cooking them until the flavors melded. Simmering a Parmesan rind in the soup gave it a subtle meatiness and more complex flavor, and stirring in grated Parmesan cheese just before serving helped to thicken the soup and added salty, nutty flavor. We added the pasta to the soup during the last 20 minutes of cooking so it would cook until just al dente. Fistfuls of baby spinach stirred in at the end added color and fresh vegetable flavor. Be sure to use a small pasta shape, such as ditalini, tubettini or mini elbows.

1	**cup chopped onion**
2	**tablespoons minced garlic**
1	**tablespoon extra-virgin olive oil**
1	**teaspoon dried thyme**
8	**cups chicken broth**
1	**(28-ounce) can crushed tomatoes**
1	**Parmesan cheese rind (optional)**
4	**ounces (1 cup) small pasta**
6	**ounces (6 cups) baby spinach**
1	**cup grated Parmesan cheese**
	Salt and pepper

1. Microwave onion, garlic, oil, and thyme in bowl, stirring occasionally, until onion is softened, about 5 minutes; transfer to slow cooker. Stir in broth, tomatoes, and Parmesan rind, if using. Cover and cook until flavors meld, 4 to 5 hours on low.

2. Discard Parmesan rind. Stir in pasta, cover, and cook on high until tender, 20 to 30 minutes. Stir in spinach, 1 handful at a time, and let sit until wilted, about 5 minutes. Stir in Parmesan and season with salt and pepper to taste. Drizzle individual portions with extra oil and serve with extra Parmesan.

SMART SHOPPING PREGRATED PARMESAN

We weren't surprised when freshly grated cheese won out over the store-bought pregrated variety in a recent tasting, but we were surprised by the "strong, pungent" taste of the pregrated cheese. We learned this had less to do with the quality of the cheese than it did with its weight. In the test kitchen we generally use a rasp-style grater to grate Parmesan cheese into thin, fluffy wisps. Supermarket pregrated Parmesan is typically pulverized into a dense, heavy powder. Thus, an equal weight of the pregrated cheese has only about half as much volume as the fluffy rasp-grated cheese. So if you choose to use pregrated Parmesan, start by adding half the volume of cheese the recipe calls for, then add more to taste if desired.

No-Fuss New England Clam Chowder

Serves 4 to 6   **Cooking Time** 4 to 5 hours on Low or 3 to 4 hours on High
Slow Cooker Size 5½ to 7 Quarts

✓ **WHY THIS RECIPE WORKS:** Slow cooker chowders usually end up either thin and watery or overly thickened and grainy. Getting the proper rich and creamy consistency for our New England chowder took some ingenuity. In the end we came up with a twofold solution. First, a combination of condensed cream of celery soup, clam juice, and water created a rich and creamy base with nicely balanced flavor. Second, we swapped the usual fresh potatoes for frozen diced potatoes, which partially broke down while cooking and helped to thicken the chowder to the proper consistency—plus they cut down on prep work. Simmering bacon in the chowder infused the broth with smoky, meaty flavor; we simply added whole slices and discarded them before serving. Stirring in canned clams at the end allowed them to just heat through without turning tough. Frozen diced potatoes come in several styles; we've had the best results using cubed hash browns here (they are sometimes labeled "Southern style").

20	ounces frozen diced potatoes
1	(11-ounce) can condensed cream of celery soup
1	(8-ounce) bottle clam juice
1	cup water
4	slices bacon
½	teaspoon dried thyme
4	(6.5-ounce) cans minced clams
	Salt and pepper

1. Combine potatoes, condensed soup, clam juice, water, bacon, and thyme in slow cooker. Cover and cook until flavors meld and potatoes are tender, 4 to 5 hours on low.

2. Discard bacon. Stir clams and their juice into chowder and let sit until heated through, about 5 minutes. Season with salt and pepper to taste and serve.

SMART SHOPPING BACON
Premium bacon can cost double or triple the price of ordinary bacon. Is it worth it? To find out, we bought six artisanal mail-order bacons and two high-end grocery store bacons. We were amazed to find that two of the four highest-rated bacons were supermarket brands. **Applegate Farms Uncured Sunday Bacon** and **Farmland/Carando Apple Cider Cured Bacon, Applewood Smoked** were a step up from the usual mass-produced bacon, straddling the gap between artisanal and more mainstream supermarket styles. Although these bacons didn't receive quite the raves of the two top-ranked premium bacons, tasters praised them both for good meaty flavor and mild smokiness—plus they were far more convenient than ordering bacon by mail.

Cajun Shrimp and Corn Chowder

Serves 6 to 8 **Cooking Time** 4 to 5 hours on Low or 3 to 4 hours on High
Slow Cooker Size 5½ to 7 Quarts

✔ **WHY THIS RECIPE WORKS:** Achieving fresh corn flavor in a chowder can be a challenge, but we were determined to develop a foolproof recipe for corn chowder in a slow cooker. We started with frozen corn, which was convenient and available any time of year. We found that the trick to getting fresh corn flavor from frozen corn was to puree a portion of the corn in a blender before adding it to the soup. Not only did this amplify the corn's flavor, but the starch released by the pureed corn helped to thicken the chowder. We added the remaining corn at the end of cooking for color and a satisfying crunch. To give our chowder a Cajun feel, we added shrimp, andouille sausage, bell pepper, and Cajun seasoning. Stirring the shrimp in at the end of cooking allowed us to monitor them closely and ensure they did not overcook.

6	**cups frozen corn, thawed**
3	**cups chicken broth**
12	**ounces red potatoes, cut into ½-inch pieces**
8	**ounces andouille sausage, cut into ¼-inch pieces**
2	**teaspoons minced garlic**
1½	**teaspoons Cajun seasoning**
1	**red bell pepper, cored and chopped**
1	**pound small shrimp (51 to 60 per pound), peeled and deveined**
½	**cup heavy cream**
	Salt and pepper

1. Process 4 cups corn and 2 cups broth in blender until smooth, about 1 minute; transfer to slow cooker.

2. Microwave potatoes, andouille, garlic, and Cajun seasoning in bowl, stirring occasionally, until vegetables are softened, about 5 minutes; transfer to slow cooker. Stir in remaining 1 cup broth and bell pepper. Cover and cook until flavors meld and potatoes are tender, 4 to 5 hours on low.

3. Stir in remaining 2 cups corn and shrimp. Cover and cook on high until shrimp are opaque throughout, 15 to 20 minutes. Stir in cream and let sit until heated through, about 5 minutes. Season with salt and pepper to taste and serve.

SMART SHOPPING ANDOUILLE

Traditional andouille (pronounced an-DOO-ee) sausage from Louisiana is made from ground pork, salt, and garlic, seasoned with plenty of black pepper, then slowly smoked over pecan wood and sugarcane for up to 14 hours. Used in a wide range of Louisiana dishes such as gumbo, jambalaya, and red beans and rice, it bolsters any dish with intense smoky, spicy, and earthy flavor. We tasted four brands in search of the right combination of smokiness and heat with a traditionally chewy but dry texture. Not surprisingly, a sausage straight from Louisiana, **Jacob's World Famous Andouille**, won the contest with the smokiest and spiciest flavors in the lineup.

Creamy Potato, Cheddar, and Ale Soup

Serves 4 to 6   **Cooking Time** 4 to 5 hours on Low or 3 to 4 hours on High
Slow Cooker Size 5½ to 7 Quarts

✔ **WHY THIS RECIPE WORKS:** This hearty pub classic is surprisingly easy to make in a slow cooker. We started by microwaving the potatoes along with garlic and thyme to jump-start their cooking and help infuse the soup with flavor. Then we added chicken broth, beer, and a little dry mustard (to complement the cheddar flavor) and let the soup cook hands-off. Once the potatoes were tender and all of the flavors had melded, we transferred the soup to a blender and pureed it smooth. The starchy potatoes thickened the broth for an incredibly velvety, rich soup. Finally, we whisked in the cheddar (preshredded for ease) at the end of cooking to ensure that it did not break and curdle. A little heavy cream and a sprinkling of scallions were an elegant finish for our rustic soup. We prefer the milder flavor of American lagers here; darker beers can be bitter and distracting.

1½	**pounds russet potatoes, peeled and cut into ½-inch pieces**
1	**cup chopped onion**
2	**tablespoons vegetable oil**
2	**teaspoons minced garlic**
½	**teaspoon dried thyme**
1	**teaspoon dry mustard**
	Salt and pepper
4	**cups chicken broth**
1	**cup beer**
2	**cups shredded cheddar cheese**
½	**cup heavy cream**
3	**scallions, sliced thin**

1. Microwave potatoes, onion, oil, garlic, thyme, mustard, and ½ teaspoon salt in bowl, stirring occasionally, until vegetables are softened, about 5 minutes; transfer to slow cooker. Stir in broth and beer. Cover and cook until potatoes are tender, 4 to 5 hours on low.

2. Working in batches, process soup in blender until smooth, about 2 minutes. Return soup to slow cooker. Whisk in cheddar until evenly melted, then whisk in cream. Let soup sit until heated through, about 5 minutes. (Adjust consistency with extra hot broth as needed.) Season with salt and pepper to taste. Sprinkle individual portions with scallions and extra cheddar before serving.

QUICK PREP TIP WHEN POTATOES TURN GREEN
When potatoes are stored on the counter, over time they turn slightly green under the skin. It turns out that when potatoes are exposed to light for prolonged periods, they produce chlorophyll in the form of a green ring under their skin. While the chlorophyll is tasteless and harmless, it can signal the potential presence of solanine, a toxin that can cause gastrointestinal distress. Since solanine develops on or just under the skin of the potato, discarding the peel greatly reduces the risk of becoming ill from a slightly green spud. We've found that potatoes stored in a well-ventilated, dark, dry, cool place stay solanine-free for up to a month, while potatoes left on the counter will begin to exhibit signs of solanine in as little as a week.

Creamy Roasted Tomato Soup

Serves 6   **Cooking Time** 4 to 5 hours on Low or 3 to 4 hours on High
Slow Cooker Size 5½ to 7 Quarts

✔ **WHY THIS RECIPE WORKS:** The problem with most cream-based tomato soups is that too much rich cream dulls the bright, acidic tomato flavor. Our solution to getting a creamy tomato soup without using a lot of cream was an unusual addition: bread. We tore a few slices of bread into pieces and simmered them in the soup for just 10 minutes, then blended the soup until smooth. As the bread broke down into the soup, it thickened the soup to a satisfying creaminess and tempered the acidity of the tomatoes without muting their flavor. Because perfectly ripe tomatoes are available just a few weeks out of the year, we turned to our trusty standby, canned diced tomatoes, which are consistent in quality and prep-free. For even more flavor, we swapped the plain tomatoes for fire-roasted diced tomatoes, which infused the soup with a subtle charred flavor. Adding a little brown sugar boosted the tomato flavor further and added a nicely caramelized note, and onion, garlic, and red pepper flakes rounded out the flavors. To finish, we only needed a little heavy cream to enrich our smooth soup and a sprinkling of minced chives to give it a hit of fresh flavor.

2	cups chopped onions
2	tablespoons minced garlic
1	tablespoon extra-virgin olive oil
⅛	teaspoon red pepper flakes
2	(28-ounce) cans fire-roasted diced tomatoes
2	cups chicken broth
1	tablespoon packed brown sugar
3	slices white bread, crusts removed, torn into 1-inch pieces
½	cup heavy cream
¼	cup minced fresh chives
	Salt and pepper

1. Microwave onions, garlic, oil, and pepper flakes in bowl, stirring occasionally, until onions are softened, about 5 minutes; transfer to slow cooker. Stir in tomatoes and their juice, broth, and sugar. Cover and cook until flavors meld, 4 to 5 hours on low.

2. Stir in bread, cover, and cook on high until bread is saturated and begins to break down, 10 to 15 minutes. Working in batches, process soup in blender until smooth, about 2 minutes. Return soup to slow cooker. Stir in cream and let sit until heated through, about 5 minutes. (Adjust soup consistency with extra hot broth as needed.) Stir in chives and season with extra sugar, salt, and pepper to taste. Drizzle individual portions with extra oil before serving.

ON THE SIDE FOOLPROOF GREEN SALAD
Whisk 1 tablespoon vinegar (red wine, white wine, or champagne), 1½ teaspoons minced shallot, ½ teaspoon mayonnaise, ½ teaspoon Dijon mustard, ⅛ teaspoon salt, and pinch pepper together in small bowl until mixture is smooth and looks milky. Very slowly drizzle in 3 tablespoons extra-virgin olive oil while whisking constantly until emulsified. Toss with 10 cups lightly packed greens. Serves 4 to 6.

Creamy Pumpkin-Chai Soup

Serves 6   **Cooking Time** 4 to 5 hours on Low or 3 to 4 hours on High
Slow Cooker Size 5½ to 7 Quarts

✓ WHY THIS RECIPE WORKS: For a warming soup perfect for chilly fall days, we streamlined traditional spiced pumpkin soup in several ways. Since fresh pumpkin is rarely in season and requires significant prep work, we kept things simple by using readily available canned pumpkin puree. Some softened onion and garlic provided a good base of aromatics, and a little brown sugar brought out the flavor of the pumpkin and added a touch of sweetness. To give our soup a complex warmth that would complement the pumpkin flavor, we found that chai tea was a perfect one-stop source for a multitude of warm spices. We simply simmered a chai tea bag in the soup to infuse it with subtle chai flavor. Pureeing the soup at the end gave it a velvety texture, and some heavy cream added just the right amount of richness. You can substitute ¼ teaspoon of ground cinnamon, ¼ teaspoon of ground ginger, ¼ teaspoon of ground cardamom, and ¼ teaspoon of ground cloves for the chai tea bag.

1 **cup chopped onion**
1 **tablespoon minced garlic**
1 **tablespoon vegetable oil**
6 **cups chicken broth**
1 **(29-ounce) can unsweetened pumpkin puree**
½ **cup packed brown sugar**
1 **chai-flavored tea bag**
½ **cup heavy cream**
Salt and pepper

1. Microwave onion, garlic, and oil in bowl, stirring occasionally, until onion is softened, about 5 minutes; transfer to slow cooker. Stir in broth, pumpkin, sugar, and tea bag. Cover and cook until flavors meld, 4 to 5 hours on low.

2. Discard tea bag. Working in batches, process soup in blender until smooth, about 2 minutes. Return soup to slow cooker, stir in cream, and let sit until heated through, about 5 minutes. (Adjust soup consistency with extra hot broth as needed.) Season with salt and pepper to taste and serve.

QUICK PREP TIP PUREEING SOUPS SAFELY
To prevent getting sprayed or burned by an exploding blender top when pureeing hot soup, fill blender jar as directed, making sure it is never more than two-thirds full. Hold lid in place with folded dish towel and pulse rapidly a few times before blending continuously.

Curried Lentil Soup

Serves 6 to 8   **Cooking Time** 6 to 7 hours on Low or 4 to 5 hours on High
Slow Cooker Size 5½ to 7 Quarts

✔ **WHY THIS RECIPE WORKS:** For an Indian-inspired lentil soup, we paired lentils with curry powder and ginger. Microwaving the ginger and curry powder along with onion and garlic and some tomato paste helped their flavors to bloom, giving us the base for a richly flavored broth. For the vegetables, we simmered some sliced carrots along with the lentils and stirred in fresh tomatoes at the end of cooking. To ensure that the spicy ginger flavor wasn't lost after hours of cooking, we added a little more ginger just before serving. A dollop of plain yogurt added a cool, creamy contrast to the warm, rich flavors of the soup. We prefer French green lentils, or *lentilles du Puy*, for this recipe, but it will work with any type of lentil except red or yellow.

2	cups chopped onions
2	tablespoons grated ginger
2	tablespoons tomato paste
2	tablespoons vegetable oil
4	teaspoons curry powder
8	cups chicken broth
3	carrots, peeled and sliced ½ inch thick
1	cup lentils, picked over and rinsed
2	tomatoes, cored and chopped
¼	cup minced fresh cilantro
	Salt and pepper
	Plain yogurt

1. Microwave onions, 1 tablespoon ginger, tomato paste, oil, and curry powder in bowl, stirring occasionally, until onions are softened, about 5 minutes; transfer to slow cooker. Stir in broth, carrots, and lentils. Cover and cook until lentils are tender, 6 to 7 hours on low or 4 to 5 hours on high.

2. Stir in tomatoes and remaining 1 tablespoon ginger and let sit until heated through, about 5 minutes. Stir in cilantro and season with salt and pepper to taste. Serve with yogurt.

SMART SHOPPING CURRY POWDER
Though blends vary dramatically, curry powders come in two basic styles: mild or sweet and a hotter version called Madras. The former combines as many as 20 different ground spices, herbs, and seeds. We tasted six curry powders, mixed into a simple rice pilaf and in a plain vegetable curry. Our favorite was **Penzeys Sweet Curry Powder**, though Durkee Curry Powder came in a close second.

U.S. Senate Navy Bean Soup

Serves 6   **Cooking Time** 9 to 10 hours on Low or 6 to 7 hours on High
Slow Cooker Size 5½ to 7 Quarts

✔ **WHY THIS RECIPE WORKS:** This simple ham and bean soup is a long-standing tradition on the U.S. Senate lunch menu, but it doesn't always live up to its reputation. Often the beans are tough or overcooked, the ham flavor is weak, and the broth is thin. We wondered if we could add more heft to this humble soup. To give the soup more robust ham flavor, we found that a combination of ham hock and ham steak was ideal for both a nice smoky flavor and lots of meaty bites of ham. To keep the soup's saltiness under control, we rinsed the ham hock before cooking and replaced some of the chicken broth with water. We added dried navy beans straight to the slow cooker, where the gentle simmering heat helped them cook through evenly. By the time the ham hock was tender, the beans were perfectly cooked. Carrots made our soup even heartier, and onions and garlic deepened its flavor. A splash of red wine vinegar added just before serving helped to balance the rich, meaty soup with a little acidity.

2	**cups chopped onions**
2	**tablespoons minced garlic**
1	**tablespoon vegetable oil**
½	**teaspoon dried thyme**
1	**pound (2½ cups) dried navy beans, picked over and rinsed**
7	**cups chicken broth**
2	**cups water**
8	**ounces ham steak, chopped**
3	**carrots, peeled and sliced ½ inch thick**
1	**smoked ham hock, rinsed**
1	**teaspoon red wine vinegar**
	Salt and pepper

1. Microwave onions, garlic, oil, and thyme in bowl, stirring occasionally, until onions are softened, about 5 minutes; transfer to slow cooker. Stir in beans, broth, water, ham steak, carrots, and ham hock. Cover and cook until beans are tender, 9 to 10 hours on low or 6 to 7 hours on high.

2. Transfer ham hock to cutting board, let cool slightly, then shred meat into bite-size pieces, discarding skin and bones. Stir shredded meat into soup and let sit until heated through, about 5 minutes. Stir in vinegar and season with salt, pepper, and extra vinegar to taste. Serve.

SMART SHOPPING SMOKED HAM HOCKS

Ham hocks add a deep, smoky, meaty flavor to our U.S. Senate Navy Bean Soup. Cut from the ankle joint of the hog's leg, hocks contain a great deal of bone, fat, and connective tissue, which lend a complex flavor and a rich, satiny texture to a soup or sauce. Though ham hocks can contain quite a bit of meat, they must be braised or slow-cooked for long periods of time to break down the connective tissue, making them perfect for the slow cooker. Once cooked, the ham hock meat can be easily removed from the bone, shredded, then returned to the dish. Ham hocks can be quite salty, however, so be sure to rinse them before cooking.

Southern Black-Eyed Pea Soup

Serves 6   **Cooking Time** 9 to 10 hours on Low or 6 to 7 hours on High
Slow Cooker Size 5½ to 7 Quarts

✔ **WHY THIS RECIPE WORKS:** The slow cooker is the perfect environment for turning dried beans into a creamy, flavorful soup. We wanted to take advantage of this with a classic Southern-style black-eyed pea soup. To give our soup plenty of kick, we added Cajun seasoning and kielbasa sausage. We used the microwave to bloom the seasoning for more flavor and to jump-start the kielbasa as well as the onions, then we dumped them into the slow cooker to simmer away with the beans and a combination of chicken broth and water. The only prep the black-eyed peas needed was to be quickly picked over (to remove any small stones or debris) and rinsed. Then we added them right into the slow cooker where they gently simmered, absorbing the flavors of the sausage, aromatics, and seasonings, until they were perfectly cooked. Collard greens, stirred in during the final 30 minutes of cooking so they'd be just tender, and wild rice stirred in at the end, added color and heft. Feel free to use leftover rice or precooked rice from the supermarket. Because kielbasa can be quite salty, be careful when seasoning the soup with additional salt.

2	**cups chopped onions**
8	**ounces kielbasa sausage, halved and sliced ½ inch thick**
1	**tablespoon minced garlic**
1	**teaspoon Cajun seasoning**
8	**ounces dried black-eyed peas, picked over and rinsed**
5	**cups chicken broth**
2	**cups water**
1	**pound collard greens, stemmed and cut into 1-inch pieces**
1	**cup cooked wild rice**
1	**teaspoon hot sauce**
	Salt and pepper

1. Microwave onions, kielbasa, garlic, and Cajun seasoning in bowl, stirring occasionally, until onions are softened, about 5 minutes; transfer to slow cooker. Stir in beans, broth, and water. Cover and cook until beans are tender, 9 to 10 hours on low or 6 to 7 hours on high.

2. Stir in collard greens, cover, and cook on high until tender, 20 to 30 minutes. Stir in rice and let sit until heated through, about 5 minutes. Stir in hot sauce and season with salt, pepper, and extra hot sauce to taste. Serve.

QUICK PREP TIP
SORTING DRIED BEANS
Before cooking any dried beans, you should pick them over for any small stones or debris and then rinse them. The easiest way to check for small stones is to spread the beans out over a large plate or rimmed baking sheet.

Sicilian Chickpea and Escarole Soup

Serves 6   **Cooking Time** 10 to 11 hours on Low or 7 to 8 hours on High
Slow Cooker Size 5½ to 7 Quarts

✓ WHY THIS RECIPE WORKS: While most Italian soups usually feature cannellini beans, in Sicily, chickpeas are the favored legume for soup. To create a Sicilian-style bean soup in our slow cooker, we started with some classic flavors of the region: onions, garlic, oregano, and red pepper flakes. Fennel, which grows wild throughout much of the Mediterranean and is common in Sicilian cooking, made a great addition; its mild anise bite complemented the nutty chickpeas. A couple of minced anchovies added a subtle meatiness (without adding fishiness). We also incorporated a leftover Parmesan rind, simmering it in the broth so that it could lend a richness and complexity that bolstered the broth's flavor. We preferred dried chickpeas over canned; by the time the flavors of the soup had melded, the chickpeas were just tender. Escarole, stirred in at the end, perfectly rounded out our Sicilian soup, adding freshness and a nice light crunch.

2	**fennel bulbs, cored and chopped**
1	**tablespoon extra-virgin olive oil**
1	**tablespoon minced garlic**
½	**teaspoon dried oregano**
2	**anchovy fillets, rinsed and minced**
¼	**teaspoon red pepper flakes**
8	**ounces dried chickpeas, picked over and rinsed**
7	**cups chicken broth**
1	**Parmesan cheese rind (optional)**
½	**head escarole, chopped coarse**
	Salt and pepper
	Grated Parmesan cheese

1. Microwave fennel, oil, garlic, oregano, anchovies, and pepper flakes in bowl, stirring occasionally, until fennel is softened, about 5 minutes; transfer to slow cooker. Stir in chickpeas, broth, and Parmesan rind, if using. Cover and cook until chickpeas are tender, 10 to 11 hours on low or 7 to 8 hours on high.

2. Discard Parmesan rind. Stir in escarole, cover, and cook on high until tender, about 15 minutes. Season with salt and pepper to taste. Drizzle individual portions with extra oil and serve with Parmesan.

QUICK PREP TIP
TRIMMING AND SLICING FENNEL
After cutting off stems and feathery fronds, cut off thin slice from base of bulb. Remove any tough or blemished layers and cut bulb in half through base. Using small, sharp knife, remove pyramid-shaped core, then either slice each half into thin strips with chef's knife or cut them into pieces (as directed in recipe).

Hearty Stews, Curries, and Chilis

Provençal-Style Chicken Stew

Serves 6 to 8   **Cooking Time** 4 to 5 hours on Low   **Slow Cooker Size** 5½ to 7 Quarts

✓ **WHY THIS RECIPE WORKS:** This French-inspired dish with sun-dried tomatoes, chickpeas, and fall-apart-tender chunks of chicken may taste like you spent hours at the stove, but it can be assembled in the slow cooker and ready for dinner with little effort. We created an easy, flavorful base for our stew by microwaving chopped onions, sun-dried tomatoes, garlic, and herbes de Provence, which we then added to the slow cooker with chicken broth. Canned chickpeas added heartiness, and a little instant tapioca thickened the stew to the proper consistency. To keep our prep work to a minimum, we chose boneless, skinless chicken thighs, which remained moist and tender during cooking and could be simply seasoned and stirred into the stew right out of the package. Once tender, we shredded them into bite-size pieces. A handful of parsley and some briny kalamata olives stirred in at the end brightened the flavors of the stew.

2	cups chopped onions
1	cup oil-packed sun-dried tomatoes, rinsed and chopped
2	tablespoons minced garlic
1	tablespoon olive oil
2	teaspoons herbes de Provence
4	cups chicken broth
1	(14-ounce) can chickpeas, rinsed
3	tablespoons instant tapioca
4	pounds boneless, skinless chicken thighs, trimmed
	Salt and pepper
1	cup pitted kalamata olives, halved
¼	cup minced fresh parsley or basil

1. Microwave onions, tomatoes, garlic, oil, and herbes de Provence in bowl, stirring occasionally, until onions are softened, about 5 minutes; transfer to slow cooker. Stir in broth, chickpeas, and tapioca. Season chicken with salt and pepper and nestle into slow cooker. Cover and cook until chicken is tender, 4 to 5 hours on low.

2. Using large spoon, skim excess fat from surface of stew. Break chicken into about 1-inch pieces with tongs. Stir in olives and let sit until heated through, about 2 minutes. (Adjust stew consistency with extra hot broth as needed.) Stir in parsley and season with salt and pepper to taste. Serve.

SMART SHOPPING CANNED CHICKPEAS
Think all brands of canned chickpeas taste the same? So did we—until we tried six brands in a side-by-side taste test. Once we drained and rinsed the beans, we found that many of them were incredibly bland or, worse yet, had bitter and metallic flavors. Tasters preferred those that were well seasoned and had a creamy yet "al dente" texture. **Pastene Chickpeas** came out on top for their clean flavor and firm yet tender texture.

Spanish Chicken and Saffron Stew

Serves 6 to 8   **Cooking Time** 4 to 5 hours on Low   **Slow Cooker Size** 5½ to 7 Quarts

WHY THIS RECIPE WORKS: For an easy weeknight meal with an exotic edge, we took inspiration from the classic saffron-infused sauces used in Spanish dishes to make a hearty stew. To start, we microwaved saffron with paprika, onion, and garlic to intensify their flavors. We added this flavorful mixture to the slow cooker along with chicken broth, boneless chicken thighs, and canned diced tomatoes. After hours of cooking, the spices infused the stew with rich flavor. For the final touch, we made a version of a Spanish *picada*, traditionally a mixture of ground toasted almonds, garlic, and herbs. Our stew already had plenty of garlic flavor, so we simply added chopped toasted almonds and fresh parsley just before serving.

2	cups chopped onions
2	tablespoons minced garlic
1	tablespoon olive oil
1	tablespoon paprika
¼	teaspoon saffron, crumbled
4	cups chicken broth
1	(14.5-ounce) can diced tomatoes, drained
3	tablespoons instant tapioca
4	pounds boneless, skinless chicken thighs, trimmed
	Salt and pepper
¼	cup chopped almonds, toasted
¼	cup minced fresh parsley

1. Microwave onions, garlic, oil, paprika, and saffron in bowl, stirring occasionally, until onions are softened, about 5 minutes; transfer to slow cooker. Stir in broth, tomatoes, and tapioca. Season chicken with salt and pepper and nestle into slow cooker. Cover and cook until chicken is tender, 4 to 5 hours on low.

2. Using large spoon, skim excess fat from surface of stew. Break chicken into about 1-inch pieces with tongs. (Adjust stew consistency with extra hot broth as needed.) Stir in almonds and parsley and season with salt and pepper to taste. Serve.

SMART SHOPPING SAFFRON
Sometimes known as "red gold," saffron is the world's most expensive spice. Luckily, a little saffron goes a long way, and we have found that brand isn't important as long as the recipe has other strong flavors, as this one does. Look for bottles that contain dark red threads—saffron is graded, and the richly hued, high-grade threads yield more flavor than the lighter, lesser-grade threads.

Spicy Chicken and Chorizo Stew

Serves 6 to 8   **Cooking Time** 4 to 5 hours on Low   **Slow Cooker Size** 5½ to 7 Quarts

✓ **WHY THIS RECIPE WORKS:** This Southwestern-style recipe is not only hearty and satisfying but also quick, thanks to chorizo sausage, canned crushed tomatoes, and frozen corn. Boldly spiced chorizo lent complex flavor, aroma, and plenty of meatiness to the stew, saving us from reaching for multiple jars of dried spices. Microwaving the sausage along with some chopped onions and garlic helped to render some of its fat and bring out its flavor. For added kick and a boost of smoky flavor, we stirred in spicy canned chipotle chiles. Adding the frozen corn to the stew at the end of cooking ensured that it remained tender and fresh-tasting. A final sprinkling of minced cilantro added brightness and rounded out the dish.

12 **ounces chorizo sausage, cut into ½-inch pieces**

2 **cups chopped onions**

2 **tablespoons minced garlic**

1 **tablespoon minced chipotle chile**

1 **(28-ounce) can crushed tomatoes**

1 **cup chicken broth**

2 **tablespoons instant tapioca**

4 **pounds boneless, skinless chicken thighs, trimmed**

   Salt and pepper

1 **cup frozen corn**

¼ **cup minced fresh cilantro**

1. Microwave chorizo, onions, garlic, and chipotle in bowl, stirring occasionally, until onions are softened, about 5 minutes; transfer to slow cooker. Stir in tomatoes, broth, and tapioca. Season chicken with salt and pepper and nestle into slow cooker. Cover and cook until chicken is tender, 4 to 5 hours on low.

2. Using large spoon, skim excess fat from surface of stew. Break chicken into about 1-inch pieces with tongs. Stir in corn and let sit until heated through, about 5 minutes. (Adjust stew consistency with extra hot broth as needed.) Stir in cilantro and season with salt and pepper to taste. Serve.

SMART SHOPPING CHORIZO

When shopping for chorizo, you may come across several different styles, including Spanish, Colombian/Argentinean, and Mexican. Though they all will work in this recipe, they have distinctly different flavors and textures. The dry-cured Spanish chorizo has a coarsely ground texture and a smoky flavor from the inclusion of smoked paprika; depending on the paprika, the chorizo can be sweet (*dulce*) or hot (*picante*). Colombian/Argentinean chorizo can be either raw or cooked; it is very coarsely ground and seasoned with garlic and herbs (much like Italian sausage). Mexican chorizo is raw and made from either pork or beef. It is very finely ground and has a spicy tanginess from chili powder and vinegar.

SPANISH   COLOMBIAN/ARGENTINEAN   MEXICAN

Pork Vindaloo

Serves 6 to 8   **Cooking Time** 6 to 7 hours on Low or 4 to 5 hours on High
Slow Cooker Size 5½ to 7 Quarts

✔ **WHY THIS RECIPE WORKS:** This classic Indian dish of tender, slowly simmered pork in a richly spiced tomato-based sauce is a perfect match for the slow cooker and a great option for a weeknight meal. While pork shoulder is the most common choice for slow-cooked pork, using it in a stew requires extra work to trim the fat and cut the meat into pieces. Instead we used boneless country-style pork ribs, which contained plenty of intramuscular fat to keep the meat moist during the extended cooking time and could be added whole right into the slow cooker. Once fully cooked and tender, we could easily break the meat into chunks with a pair of tongs. A variety of spices, including black pepper, cinnamon, coriander, cardamom, and dried chiles, are key to the complex flavor of this dish, but we found we could easily replace the laundry list of spices with garam masala, a classic Indian spice blend. We just added a good amount of paprika for sweetness and a dash of cayenne for heat, then bloomed the spices with the onions in the microwave to deepen their flavors. Some bright red wine vinegar and fresh cilantro balanced the rich flavors of the dish.

3	cups chopped onions
3	tablespoons paprika
2	tablespoons vegetable oil
1	tablespoon garam masala
	Salt and pepper
¼	teaspoon cayenne pepper
1	(28-ounce) can crushed tomatoes
½	cup chicken broth
2	tablespoons red wine vinegar
2	tablespoons instant tapioca
4	pounds boneless country-style pork ribs, trimmed
¼	cup minced fresh cilantro

1. Microwave onions, paprika, oil, garam masala, ½ teaspoon salt, and cayenne in bowl, stirring occasionally, until onions are softened, about 5 minutes; transfer to slow cooker. Stir in tomatoes, broth, vinegar, and tapioca. Season pork with salt and pepper and nestle into slow cooker. Cover and cook until pork is tender, 6 to 7 hours on low or 4 to 5 hours on high.

2. Using large spoon, skim excess fat from surface of stew. Break pork into about 1-inch pieces with tongs. (Adjust stew consistency with extra hot broth as needed.) Stir in cilantro and season with salt, pepper, and extra vinegar to taste. Serve.

ON THE SIDE EASY RICE PILAF
Rinse 1½ cups long-grain white rice. Heat 2 tablespoons olive oil in large saucepan over medium heat until shimmering. Add ½ cup finely chopped onion and 1 teaspoon salt and cook until softened, 5 to 7 minutes. Stir in rice and cook until edges begin to turn translucent, about 3 minutes. Stir in 2¼ cups water and bring to simmer. Cover, reduce heat to low, and continue to simmer until rice is tender and liquid is absorbed, 16 to 20 minutes. Off heat, lay clean folded dish towel underneath lid and let rice rest for 10 minutes. Fluff rice with fork and season with salt and pepper to taste. Serves 4. (To double recipe, increase rice to 2½ cups, oil to 3 tablespoons, onion to 1 cup, and water to 3¾ cups; cook as directed.)

Italian Pork and White Bean Stew

Serves 6 to 8   **Cooking Time** 6 to 7 hours on Low or 4 to 5 hours on High
Slow Cooker Size 5½ to 7 Quarts

✔ **WHY THIS RECIPE WORKS:** For a real stick-to-your-ribs stew, we used a classic Italian white bean stew as a starting point and incorporated meaty pork and earthy spinach. As in our Pork Vindaloo (page 69), boneless country-style pork ribs required no prep work, and thanks to plenty of intramuscular fat, they were moist and fall-apart tender after several hours in the slow cooker. Dried beans were still undercooked by the time the pork was done, but canned white beans cooked through perfectly in the same amount of time and required little preparation. To boost the fresh flavor of the stew and complement the rich pork and beans, we added half a cup of prepared basil pesto with the spinach. Delicate baby spinach needed to cook for just a few minutes at the end to warm through and wilt into the stew. The spinach may seem like a lot at first, but it wilts down substantially.

2	cups chopped onions
4	teaspoons minced garlic
1	tablespoon olive oil
½	teaspoon dried rosemary
4	cups chicken broth
2	(15-ounce) cans cannellini beans, rinsed
3	tablespoons instant tapioca
4	pounds boneless country-style pork ribs, trimmed
	Salt and pepper
½	cup prepared basil pesto
4	ounces (4 cups) baby spinach

1. Microwave onions, garlic, oil, and rosemary in bowl, stirring occasionally, until onions are softened, about 5 minutes; transfer to slow cooker. Stir in broth, beans, and tapioca. Season pork with salt and pepper and nestle into slow cooker. Cover and cook until pork is tender, 6 to 7 hours on low or 4 to 5 hours on high.

2. Using large spoon, skim excess fat from surface of stew. Break pork into about 1-inch pieces with tongs. Stir in pesto, then stir in spinach, 1 handful at a time, and let sit until spinach is wilted, about 5 minutes. (Adjust stew consistency with extra hot broth as needed.) Season with salt and pepper to taste and serve.

QUICK PREP TIP STORING BABY SPINACH
Baby spinach is sold in bags and plastic containers of various sizes. If you happen to have leftover spinach, store it either in its original bag with the open end folded over and taped shut, or in its original plastic container, as long as it has holes that allow air to pass through. These specially designed breathable bags and containers keep the spinach fresh as long as possible; if you transfer the spinach to a sealed airtight bag or container, it will spoil prematurely.

Moroccan-Spiced Beef Stew

Serves 6 to 8   **Cooking Time** 9 to 10 hours on Low or 6 to 7 hours on High
Slow Cooker Size 5½ to 7 Quarts

✔ **WHY THIS RECIPE WORKS:** This stew gets its exotic flavor from a combination of paprika, cayenne, and garam masala (a classic Indian blend of warm spices). We knew we didn't want to have to trim and cut up a whole chuck roast. Luckily, sirloin steak tips were much easier to prep; they come in strips or chunks with minimal excess fat, so they were a snap to cut into pieces for the stew. Plus, once cooked, they were just as tender and flavorful as chuck meat. Chickpeas, with their slightly nutty flavor and creamy texture, paired well with the steak tips. For a vegetable that could hold up to the long cooking time, we opted for hearty carrots. Dried figs rounded out the stew and accentuated its Moroccan roots. We added the figs both at the beginning of cooking, so that their flavor permeated the sauce, and at the end, so that some pieces retained their texture in the finished stew.

2	**cups chopped onions**
3	**tablespoons paprika**
2	**tablespoons vegetable oil**
1	**tablespoon garam masala**
¼	**teaspoon cayenne pepper**
1	**(14-ounce) can chickpeas, rinsed**
3	**cups beef broth**
1	**pound carrots, peeled and sliced ½ inch thick**
1	**cup dried figs, chopped coarse**
2½	**tablespoons instant tapioca**
4	**pounds sirloin steak tips, trimmed and cut into 1½-inch pieces**
	Salt and pepper

1. Microwave onions, paprika, oil, garam masala, and cayenne in bowl, stirring occasionally, until onions are softened, about 5 minutes; transfer to slow cooker. Stir chickpeas, broth, carrots, half of figs, and tapioca into slow cooker.

2. Season beef with salt and pepper and stir into slow cooker. Cover and cook until beef is tender, 9 to 10 hours on low or 6 to 7 hours on high.

3. Using large spoon, skim excess fat from surface of stew. Stir in remaining figs and let sit until heated through and softened, about 5 minutes. (Adjust stew consistency with extra hot broth as needed.) Season with salt and pepper to taste and serve.

SMART SHOPPING PAPRIKA

"Paprika" is a generic term for a spice made from ground dried red peppers that is available in several forms. Sweet paprika (also called "Hungarian paprika," or simply "paprika") is the most common. Typically made from a combination of mild red peppers, it is prized more for its deep scarlet hue than for its very subtle flavor. Smoked paprika, a Spanish favorite, is produced by drying sweet or hot peppers over smoldering oak embers. We don't recommend using this variety for all paprika applications; it is best for seasoning grilled meats or adding a smoky aroma to boldly flavored dishes. Hot paprika, most often used in chilis, curries, and stews, can range from slightly spicy to punishingly assertive. Although hot paprika shouldn't be substituted for sweet paprika in cooking, sweet paprika can be substituted for hot by adding cayenne pepper.

ALL ABOUT Spice Blends

We use a generous amount of spices in our slow-cooker dishes to prevent their flavors from becoming muted over the long cooking times. To keep things easy, we rely on spice blends where we can—that way, we don't have to keep our spice rack stocked to the gills, and we can keep prep time to a minimum. To increase their flavor, we often bloom the spices in oil in the microwave. Here are a few spice blends we keep on hand.

Garam Masala

We like to keep a jar of good garam masala in our pantry to add its warm, complex flavor to curries and stews. It comes in many variations but consistently includes black pepper, cinnamon, coriander, cardamom, and dried chiles. It may also have cumin, cloves, fennel, mace, or nutmeg. It's useful for replicating the varied spice mixes in traditional dishes from India to Morocco—we put it to use in both our Pork Vindaloo (page 69) and our Moroccan-Spiced Beef Stew (page 72). Garam masala also makes a quick, tasty spice rub for our Spiced Pork Tenderloin with Couscous (page 133). To find the best supermarket brand, we tested five widely available brands. One of the more traditional mixtures, **McCormick Gourmet Collection Garam Masala**, was the favorite, winning praise for its "mellow," "well-balanced" aroma. To make 1 tablespoon of your own, combine 2 teaspoons ground coriander, ½ teaspoon ground black pepper, and ¼ teaspoon each ground cardamom and ground cinnamon.

Herbes de Provence

Herbes de Provence is a mixture of the herbs used most frequently in the south of France. Usually a combination of basil, fennel seeds, lavender, marjoram, rosemary, sage, summer savory, and thyme, it is a great one-stop source for bold herbal flavor. We use it to season our Provençal-Style Chicken Stew (page 65) and other Mediterranean dishes. If you can't find herbes de Provence, you can make your own by combining 2 teaspoons each dried marjoram and dried thyme, 1 teaspoon each dried basil, dried sage, and crumbled dried rosemary, and ⅛ teaspoon ground fennel.

Spice Storage

Don't store spices on the counter close to the stove since heat, light, and moisture shorten their shelf life. Keep them in a cool, dark, dry place in well-sealed containers.

Taco Seasoning

Look at your favorite chili recipe and you will see a long list of spices. That's why when we are looking for a quick and easy way to season chili, we skip rummaging through our spice cabinet and simply grab a packet of taco seasoning. Not just for taco night anymore, it has the chili powder, cumin, oregano, and other Southwestern spices that are key to a great chili, like our Easy Barbecue Turkey Chili (page 82), and other Tex-Mex greats.

Chili Powder

There is no single recipe for chili powder, but it is most commonly a blend of roasted dried chiles, garlic powder, oregano, ground cumin, and sometimes salt. We use it to add bold flavor and plenty of spicy kick to our classic chilis and to spice rubs and marinades. When shopping for chili powder, be careful not to confuse it with chile powder (also often spelled chili powder), which is made solely from chiles without additional seasoning. The volatile oils in chiles lose potency within a few months, so be sure to replace your chili powder regularly. For information on the test kitchen's favorite brand of chili powder, see page 83.

Cajun Seasoning

Cajun seasoning can vary quite a bit, but generally these blends are boldly flavored and include garlic, onions, chiles, black pepper, mustard, and celery. They reflect the flavor profiles found in Cajun cuisine, which originated with French immigrants in Louisiana and incorporates both French and Southern influences. Since mixing up our own Cajun spice blend can be time-consuming and costly, we turn to the spice aisle at our supermarket for a premade blend.

Easiest-Ever Beef and Potato Stew

Serves 6 to 8   **Cooking Time** 9 to 10 hours on Low or 6 to 7 hours on High
Slow Cooker Size 5½ to 7 Quarts

✔ **WHY THIS RECIPE WORKS:** By the time you've trimmed, cubed, and browned the meat and chopped all the vegetables, beef stew can feel like more of a hassle than it's worth. We wanted a stew with maximum flavor without all the labor. To start, we skipped the traditional chuck roast in favor of convenient steak tips, which were far easier to trim and cut into pieces. For the vegetables, we stuck to the classics: potatoes and peas. We chose small Yukon Gold potatoes so that we could dump them right into the slow cooker without any peeling or chopping. Frozen peas could be stirred in before serving until just warmed through. In lieu of building a flavorful broth from scratch with chopped onion, garlic, and herbs and spices, we turned to condensed French onion soup. This prep-free convenience product boasted thick, beefy broth with lots of aromatic flavor; bolstered with tomato paste and a little thyme, it gave us a flavorful, *umami*-rich base for our stew without the need for browning the meat. Look for small Yukon Gold potatoes measuring 1 to 2 inches in diameter; if your potatoes are larger, cut them into 1-inch pieces to ensure they cook through.

2 **(10.5-ounce) cans condensed French onion soup**

1 **cup water**

¼ **cup tomato paste**

2½ **tablespoons instant tapioca**

1 **teaspoon dried thyme**

2 **pounds small Yukon Gold potatoes**

4 **pounds sirloin steak tips, trimmed and cut into 1½-inch pieces**
   Salt and pepper

2 **cups frozen peas**

1. Whisk soup, water, tomato paste, tapioca, and thyme together in slow cooker; stir in potatoes. Season beef with salt and pepper and stir into slow cooker. Cover and cook until beef is tender, 9 to 10 hours on low or 6 to 7 hours on high.

2. Using large spoon, skim excess fat from surface of stew. Stir in peas and let sit until heated through, about 5 minutes. (Adjust stew consistency with extra hot broth as needed.) Season with salt and pepper to taste and serve.

ON THE SIDE QUICK DINNER ROLLS
Cut 1 pound pizza dough into 8 equal pieces and roll into balls. Arrange on well-oiled baking sheet, brush lightly with olive oil, and sprinkle with salt and pepper. Bake in 400-degree oven until golden, about 20 minutes. Let cool for 5 minutes before serving. Makes 8 rolls.

Lamb Curry

Serves 6 to 8   **Cooking Time** 9 to 10 hours on Low or 6 to 7 hours on High
Slow Cooker Size 5½ to 7 Quarts

WHY THIS RECIPE WORKS: Indian curry, a traditionally slow-simmered dish, is perfect for the slow cooker, where the spices can meld with the other ingredients to create a deeply flavorful and complex dish. We started with the star of the show, boneless leg of lamb, which remained tender and juicy during the extended cooking time. Next, curry powder and ginger were givens; we microwaved them along with chopped onions and tomato paste to compound their flavor, then rounded out the curry base with chicken broth. A little tapioca helped to thicken the broth. Tender chunks of cauliflower, added toward the end so they wouldn't overcook, worked well with the flavors of the curry. We also stirred in some frozen peas and a little extra fresh ginger to lend a pop of color and flavor to the finished dish.

3   **tablespoons grated ginger**

2   **tablespoons curry powder**

1   **tablespoon tomato paste**

1   **tablespoon vegetable oil**

2   **cups chicken broth**

3   **tablespoons instant tapioca**

5   **pounds boneless leg of lamb, trimmed and cut into 1-inch pieces**
    Salt and pepper

2   **cups canned coconut milk**

1   **pound cauliflower florets**

2   **cups frozen peas**

1. Microwave 2 tablespoons ginger, curry powder, tomato paste, and oil in bowl, stirring occasionally, until fragrant, about 1 minute; transfer to slow cooker. Stir in broth and tapioca.

2. Season lamb with salt and pepper and stir into slow cooker. Cover and cook until lamb is tender, 9 to 10 hours on low or 6 to 7 hours on high.

3. Using large spoon, skim excess fat from surface of curry. Microwave coconut milk and cauliflower in bowl, stirring occasionally, until cauliflower is tender, 10 to 12 minutes; stir into slow cooker. Stir in peas and remaining 1 tablespoon ginger and let sit until heated through, about 5 minutes. (Adjust curry consistency with extra hot broth as needed.) Season with salt and pepper to taste and serve.

QUICK PREP TIP
CUTTING LAMB FOR STEW
A boneless leg of lamb roast is made up of several different muscles held together with fat and sinew. To cut it into pieces for stew meat, pull roast apart at its major seams (delineated by lines of fat and silverskin), using sharp knife if necessary. Trim off excess fat and silverskin, then cut meat into 1-inch pieces.

Thai-Style Shrimp Curry

Serves 6 to 8   **Cooking Time** 4 to 5 hours on Low or 3 to 4 hours on High
Slow Cooker Size 5½ to 7 Quarts

✔ **WHY THIS RECIPE WORKS:** Thai curries usually get their complex flavor from a laundry list of aromatic ingredients—lemon grass, ginger, garlic, chiles, and other spices. To achieve the same great flavor without the hassle of gathering and preparing all those ingredients, we found a single ingredient that could substitute for them all: green curry paste. The curry paste contained all the ingredients of classic Thai curries and added big flavor and depth to this dish in record time. All it needed was a little lime juice and fish sauce to round out the flavors. A combination of chicken broth and coconut milk gave us a rich, creamy base for our curry. To ensure that the delicate shrimp didn't overcook, we stirred them in at the end of cooking. For snow peas that were perfectly crisp-tender, we microwaved them with a little oil, then added them to the finished curry. The sweet potatoes become very tender in this dish; be sure to stir the curry gently to prevent the potatoes from breaking up too much. Serve over rice.

2   **cups chicken broth**
2   **tablespoons Thai green curry paste**
2   **tablespoons instant tapioca**
1½   **pounds sweet potatoes, peeled and cut into 1-inch pieces**
2   **cups canned coconut milk**
2   **tablespoons lime juice**
1   **tablespoon fish sauce**
2   **pounds large shrimp (26 to 30 per pound), peeled and deveined**
8   **ounces snow peas, trimmed and cut into 1-inch pieces**
1   **tablespoon vegetable oil**
½   **cup fresh cilantro leaves**
     Salt and pepper

1. Whisk broth, curry paste, and tapioca together in slow cooker, then stir in potatoes. Cover and cook until flavors meld and potatoes are tender, 4 to 5 hours on low.

2. Microwave coconut milk in bowl until hot, about 2 minutes; stir into curry with lime juice and fish sauce. Stir in shrimp, cover, and cook on high until opaque throughout, about 30 minutes.

3. Microwave snow peas and oil in bowl, stirring occasionally, until tender, 3 to 5 minutes; stir into curry. (Adjust curry consistency with extra hot broth as needed.) Stir in cilantro and season with salt and pepper to taste. Serve.

QUICK PREP TIP
TRIMMING SNOW PEAS
Using paring knife and your thumb, snip off tip of pea and pull along flat side of pod to remove string at same time.

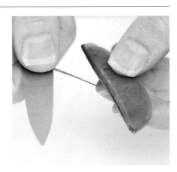

Hearty Fisherman's Stew

Serves 6   **Cooking Time** 4 to 5 hours on Low or 3 to 4 hours on High
Slow Cooker Size 5½ to 7 Quarts

✔ **WHY THIS RECIPE WORKS:** To make a slow-cooker fish stew with tender and moist cod and shrimp, a full-flavored broth, spicy chorizo, and hearty potatoes, the key was to allow the stew to simmer and build flavor, then add the fish and shrimp at the end and poach them gently just until they were done. For the broth, we started with white wine, clam juice, and diced tomatoes. We simmered onion, garlic, chorizo, and chunks of red potatoes in the broth until the potatoes were tender and the broth was richly flavored. Then we added the seafood and gently cooked it in the flavorful broth for 30 minutes. All the stew needed was a sprinkle of fresh parsley to finish. Serve with Paprika Mayonnaise.

1	**pound red potatoes, cut into ½-inch pieces**
1	**cup chopped onion**
8	**ounces chorizo sausage, cut into ¼-inch pieces**
4	**teaspoons minced garlic**
2	**(8-ounce) bottles clam juice**
1	**(14.5-ounce) can diced tomatoes, drained**
¼	**cup dry white wine**
1½	**pounds skinless cod fillets**
8	**ounces large shrimp (26 to 30 per pound), peeled and deveined**
	Salt and pepper
2	**tablespoons minced fresh parsley**

1. Microwave potatoes, onions, chorizo, and garlic in bowl, stirring occasionally, until vegetables are softened, about 5 minutes; transfer to slow cooker. Stir in clam juice, tomatoes, and wine. Cover and cook until flavors meld and potatoes are tender, 4 to 5 hours on low.

2. Cut cod into 2- to 3-inch pieces. Season cod and shrimp with salt and pepper and gently stir into stew. Cover and cook on high until shrimp are opaque throughout and cod flakes apart when gently prodded with paring knife, about 30 minutes. Sprinkle with parsley and season with salt and pepper to taste. Serve.

ON THE SIDE PAPRIKA MAYONNAISE
Whisk ½ cup mayonnaise, 1½ teaspoons lemon juice, 1 teaspoon minced garlic, and ½ teaspoon paprika together in bowl. Season with salt and pepper to taste. Makes about ½ cup.

Tomatillo Chicken Chili

Serves 6 to 8   **Cooking Time** 4 to 5 hours on Low   **Slow Cooker Size** 5½ to 7 Quarts

✔ **WHY THIS RECIPE WORKS:** To achieve a great chicken chili in the slow cooker, we needed to build flavor every step of the way. We started by choosing convenient boneless, skinless chicken thighs. They could be added to the slow cooker whole, then easily broken into pieces once fully cooked, and they stayed juicy in the slow cooker. For the base of our chili, we used canned hominy, pureeing some of the hominy with chicken broth to give the chili an appealing texture and a hearty corn flavor. Microwaving onion and garlic along with a combination of cumin and coriander also added a richer, deeper flavor. Finally, adding store-bought tomatillo salsa—a zesty combination of green tomatoes, chiles, and cilantro—was a quick and easy way to give our chili a boost of fresh flavor. Jarred tomatillo salsa is also called "salsa verde." Serve with your favorite chili garnishes.

2	**(15-ounce) cans hominy, rinsed**
4	**cups chicken broth**
2	**cups chopped onions**
2	**tablespoons minced garlic**
2	**tablespoons olive oil**
4	**teaspoons ground cumin**
2	**teaspoons ground coriander**
4	**pounds boneless, skinless chicken thighs, trimmed**
	Salt and pepper
3	**poblano chiles, stemmed, seeded, and minced**
1	**cup jarred tomatillo salsa**
¼	**cup minced fresh cilantro**

1. Process half of hominy and 2 cups broth in blender until smooth, about 1 minute; transfer to slow cooker.

2. Microwave onions, garlic, 1 tablespoon oil, cumin, and coriander in bowl, stirring occasionally, until onions are softened, about 5 minutes; transfer to slow cooker. Stir in remaining hominy and remaining 2 cups broth. Season chicken with salt and pepper and nestle into slow cooker. Cover and cook until chicken is tender, 4 to 5 hours on low.

3. Using large spoon, skim excess fat from surface of stew. Break chicken into about 1-inch pieces with tongs.

4. Microwave poblanos and remaining 1 tablespoon oil in bowl, stirring occasionally, until tender, about 8 minutes. Stir poblanos and salsa into chili and let sit until heated through, about 2 minutes. Stir in cilantro and season with salt and pepper to taste. Serve.

SMART SHOPPING HOMINY

Hominy is made from dried corn kernels that have been soaked (or cooked) in an alkaline solution (commonly lime water or calcium hydroxide) to remove the germ and hull. It has a slightly chewy texture and toasted corn flavor and is widely used in soups, stews, and chilis throughout southern North America and Central and South America. Given its sturdy texture, hominy can easily withstand hours of simmering and is perfectly suited for the slow cooker. It is sold both dried and canned; however, we prefer the convenience of canned hominy, which requires only a quick rinse before using.

Easy Barbecue Turkey Chili

Serves 6 to 8   **Cooking Time** 4 to 5 hours on Low   **Slow Cooker Size** 5½ to 7 Quarts

✔ **WHY THIS RECIPE WORKS:** Turkey chili is a great alternative to classic beef chili, providing a leaner meal that's still packed with flavor thanks to a variety of spices. However, turkey does present one major challenge: Because it's much leaner than beef, it can quickly turn dry and grainy. To prevent our ground turkey from drying out, it was important to cook the chili on low. We also found that microwaving the turkey for a few minutes firmed it up enough to break it into coarse crumbles that did not turn grainy during cooking. With the turkey sorted out, we moved on to the seasoning. We wanted this chili to be as easy as possible, so we skipped rummaging through the spice cabinet. Instead we simply opened a store-bought packet of taco seasoning, which was a flavor-packed mix of all the Southwestern spices we needed. Microwaving the taco seasoning with the turkey helped to bloom the spices, deepening their flavor. To complement the spices and give our chili a sweet and smoky flavor, we stirred in a cup of barbecue sauce. For the bulk of the chili, we used canned crushed tomatoes, kidney beans, and frozen corn; the convenient no-prep ingredients made our turkey chili as easy as it was flavorful. Be sure to use ground turkey, not ground turkey breast (also labeled 99 percent fat free), in this recipe. Serve with your favorite chili garnishes.

2	**pounds ground turkey**
1	**(1-ounce) packet taco seasoning**
2	**(28-ounce) cans crushed tomatoes**
2	**(15-ounce) cans kidney beans, rinsed**
1	**cup barbecue sauce**
2	**cups frozen corn**
	Salt and pepper

1. Microwave ground turkey and taco seasoning in bowl, stirring occasionally, until turkey is no longer pink, about 10 minutes.

2. Transfer mixture to slow cooker, breaking up any large pieces of turkey. Stir in tomatoes, beans, and barbecue sauce. Cover and cook until turkey is tender, 4 to 5 hours on low.

3. Using large spoon, skim excess fat from surface of chili. Break up any remaining large pieces of turkey with spoon. Stir in corn and let sit until heated through, about 5 minutes. Season with salt and pepper to taste and serve.

SMART SHOPPING BOTTLED BARBECUE SAUCE
Homemade barbecue sauce is a project requiring a lengthy list of ingredients and a good chunk of time. No wonder bottled barbecue sauce is so popular—in just one local supermarket, we found more than 30 varieties! To make sense of all these options, we conducted a blind taste test of eight leading national brands. We chose tomato-based sauces that were labeled "original" and tasted each sauce on its own, broiled on chicken thighs, and as a dip for chicken nuggets. Although tasters' personal preferences varied, our winner was **Bull's-Eye Original Barbecue Sauce**, which tasters found "robust" and "spicy."

Smoky Ranch Chili

Serves 6 to 8   **Cooking Time** 9 to 10 hours on Low or 6 to 7 hours on High
Slow Cooker Size 5½ to 7 Quarts

✅ **WHY THIS RECIPE WORKS:** Just like classic cowboy chili simmered over an open fire under a starry sky, this chili is packed with chunks of rich pork and stewed beans with Southwestern spices and smoky flavor. For this traditional chili, we wanted to use pork butt; its superior fat marbling produced supremely tender chunks of meat. To limit the amount of preparation, we cut the raw roast into five large pieces instead of cutting it into cubes, then placed it in the slow cooker. Once the pork was fully tender, we could easily break it into smaller pieces with tongs. For the rest of the chili, we used convenient canned crushed tomatoes and kidney beans plus some chopped onions. We kept the spices simple and classic: chili powder, cumin, oregano, and lots of garlic. A quick stint in the microwave helped to soften the onions and bloom the spices for deeper flavor. A dash of liquid smoke added authentic campfire flavor. Serve with your favorite chili garnishes.

2	**cups chopped onions**
¼	**cup chili powder**
2	**tablespoons minced garlic**
2	**tablespoons vegetable oil**
1	**tablespoon ground cumin**
1	**teaspoon dried oregano**
2	**(28-ounce) cans crushed tomatoes**
2	**(15-ounce) cans kidney beans, rinsed**
1	**teaspoon liquid smoke**
4	**pounds boneless pork butt roast**
	Salt and pepper

1. Microwave onions, chili powder, garlic, oil, cumin, and oregano in bowl, stirring occasionally, until onions are softened, about 5 minutes; transfer to slow cooker. Stir in tomatoes, beans, and liquid smoke.

2. Slice pork roast crosswise into 5 equal pieces, trim excess fat, and season with salt and pepper. Nestle pork into slow cooker, cover, and cook until pork is tender, 9 to 10 hours on low or 6 to 7 hours on high.

3. Using large spoon, skim excess fat from surface of chili. Break pork into about 1-inch pieces with tongs. Season with salt and pepper to taste and serve.

SMART SHOPPING CHILI POWDER
To see what the difference was among the various brands of chili powder found at the market, we gathered up seven widely available brands and pitted them against one another in a taste-off. To focus on the flavor of the chili powders, we tasted them sprinkled over potatoes and cooked in beef-and-bean chili. Many included unusual ingredients, but our top picks stuck with classic flavorings: cumin, oregano, and garlic. We also liked the addition of paprika, which gave our top two picks a nice complexity. In the end, tasters concluded that **Morton & Bassett Chili Powder** was the clear winner. Tasters found that it had a deep, roasty, complex flavor; subtle sweetness; and just the right amount of heat.

Beef and Three-Bean Chili

Serves 6 to 8   **Cooking Time** 6 to 7 hours on Low or 4 to 5 hours on High
Slow Cooker Size 5½ to 7 Quarts

✔ **WHY THIS RECIPE WORKS:** For a super easy, family-friendly slow-cooker chili, we started by choosing only the essential aromatics: onions, chili powder, and oregano. Ground beef was convenient, but it had a tendency to turn gritty after hours of slow cooking. We found that the solution was to microwave it for a few minutes first so that it became firm enough to break into coarse crumbles that did not turn grainy during cooking. Canned tomatoes and beans (we chose a mix of black, pinto, and kidney beans for more complex flavor and visual appeal) eliminated prep work and were full of flavor after hours of gentle simmering with the spices and aromatics. Along with the ground beef, we quickly microwaved the onions and spices before adding them to the slow cooker to ensure that the onions cooked through in time and to bring out the flavor of the chili powder and oregano. Serve with your favorite chili garnishes.

2	pounds 85 percent lean ground beef
2	cups chopped onions
¼	cup chili powder
1	teaspoon dried oregano
	Salt and pepper
1	(15-ounce) can black beans, rinsed
1	(15-ounce) can pinto beans, rinsed
1	(15-ounce) can kidney beans, rinsed
2	(28-ounce) cans crushed tomatoes
2	tablespoons packed brown sugar

1. Microwave ground beef, onions, chili powder, oregano, ½ teaspoon salt, and ½ teaspoon pepper in bowl, stirring occasionally, until beef is no longer pink, about 10 minutes.

2. Transfer mixture to slow cooker, breaking up any large pieces of beef. Stir in beans, tomatoes, and sugar. Cover and cook until beef is tender, 6 to 7 hours on low or 4 to 5 hours on high.

3. Using large spoon, skim excess fat from surface of chili. Break up any remaining large pieces of beef with spoon. Season with salt and pepper to taste and serve.

ON THE SIDE **GOLDEN NORTHERN CORNBREAD**
Whisk together 2 large eggs, ⅔ cup buttermilk, and ⅔ cup milk in bowl. In separate large bowl, whisk together 1 cup yellow cornmeal, 1 cup all-purpose flour, 2 teaspoons baking powder, ½ teaspoon baking soda, 4 teaspoons sugar, and ½ teaspoon salt. Make well in cornmeal mixture, add egg mixture, and stir together until just combined. Stir in 2 tablespoons melted unsalted butter. Transfer batter to greased 9-inch square baking pan. Bake in 425-degree oven until top is golden brown and lightly cracked and edges have pulled away from sides of pan, about 25 minutes. Transfer to wire rack to cool slightly, 5 to 10 minutes. Serves 6 to 8.

Easy Chicken Dinners

Easy Cherry-Sage Glazed Chicken

Serves 4   **Cooking Time** 2 to 3 hours on Low   **Slow Cooker Size** 5½ to 7 Quarts

✔ **WHY THIS RECIPE WORKS:** When slow-cooking boneless, skinless chicken breasts, the biggest challenge is getting moist, tender meat despite the long cooking time. To keep the lean chicken juicy and tender, we found that using the low heat setting and minding our time range were essential. We also cooked the breasts in a flavorful liquid to even out the heat and to infuse the meat with flavor. Next, we needed to perfect the glaze, which we would use to coat the chicken before serving. Instead of turning to the stovetop to thicken a sauce, we used cherry preserves, which gave our sauce a thick, fruity base from the start. To ramp up the fruity flavor even more, we added dried cherries, which we softened in the microwave with some of the braising liquid. Sage reinforced the savory flavor of our chicken and added depth to our flavorful glaze.

½ **cup chicken broth**

2 **(2-inch) strips orange zest**

1 **teaspoon minced garlic**

1 **teaspoon dried sage**

4 **(6- to 8-ounce) boneless, skinless chicken breasts, trimmed**

    Salt and pepper

½ **cup dried cherries**

1 **cup cherry preserves**

1. Combine broth, orange zest, garlic, and sage in slow cooker. Season chicken with salt and pepper and nestle into slow cooker. Cover and cook until chicken is tender, 2 to 3 hours on low.

2. Transfer chicken to plate and tent with aluminum foil. Microwave ¼ cup braising liquid and cherries in bowl until cherries are soft, about 2 minutes; stir in preserves until well combined.

3. Season glaze with salt and pepper to taste. Dip chicken into glaze to coat and transfer to clean platter. Pour remaining glaze over top and serve.

SMART SHOPPING **BONELESS, SKINLESS CHICKEN BREASTS**

Americans cook a lot of chicken breasts—the lean cut accounts for 60 percent of the chicken sold in stores, and the vast majority are boneless and skinless. To find out which brand tastes best, we gathered eight popular brands and tasted them all side by side. Tasters' comments made clear that texture was paramount (the flavor was more or less the same across the board). The clear winner, **Bell & Evans Air-Chilled Boneless, Skinless, Chicken Breasts**, was described as juicy and tender. The key is in the processing; Bell & Evans age their chicken breasts in chilled containers for as long as 12 hours before removing the bones and skin; this prevents the muscles from contracting, which results in more tender meat. This process takes more time, but the texture suffered in brands that skip this step to save money.

Easy Apricot-Ginger Glazed Chicken

Serves 4   **Cooking Time** 2 to 3 hours on Low   **Slow Cooker Size** 5½ to 7 Quarts

WHY THIS RECIPE WORKS: Following the success of our Easy Cherry-Sage Glazed Chicken, we turned to apricot preserves to create a flavorful base for a second glazed chicken dish. We chose spicy fresh ginger to complement and balance the sweet preserves. We cooked the chicken in ginger-spiked broth to ensure that it would be tender and moist and to provide our chicken with a flavor boost from the start. The apricot preserves gave us a head start on our simple glaze. Apple cider vinegar balanced the sweetness of the preserves and a little rosemary added a warm, earthy background note. More fresh ginger stirred in at the end gave the sauce a subtle spicy bite.

½   **cup chicken broth**

4   **teaspoons grated ginger**

4   **(6- to 8-ounce) boneless, skinless chicken breasts, trimmed**
     Salt and pepper

½   **cup dried apricots, chopped**

1   **tablespoon cider vinegar**

2   **teaspoons minced fresh rosemary**

1   **cup apricot preserves**

1. Combine broth and 2 teaspoons ginger in slow cooker. Season chicken with salt and pepper and nestle into slow cooker. Cover and cook until chicken is tender, 2 to 3 hours on low.

2. Transfer chicken to plate and tent with aluminum foil. Measure out ¼ cup braising liquid and combine with apricots, vinegar, rosemary, and remaining 2 teaspoons ginger in bowl. Microwave until apricots are soft, about 2 minutes; stir in preserves until well combined.

3. Season glaze with salt and pepper to taste. Dip chicken into glaze to coat and transfer to clean platter. Pour remaining glaze over top. Serve.

QUICK PREP TIP **CHOPPING DRIED FRUIT**
Dried fruits, especially apricots (or dates), very often stick to the knife when you try to chop them. To avoid this problem, coat the blade with a thin film of vegetable oil spray just before you begin chopping any dried fruit. The chopped fruit won't cling to the blade, and the knife will stay relatively clean.

Chicken Pomodoro

Serves 4   **Cooking Time** 2 to 3 hours on Low   **Slow Cooker Size** 5½ to 7 Quarts

✔ **WHY THIS RECIPE WORKS:** Classic chicken pomodoro features tender chicken braised in a rich tomato sauce; gently simmering the chicken in the sauce helps it to remain moist while enriching the flavors of both. It should be a perfect dish for the slow cooker, but most slow-cooker recipes result in a dull, waterlogged tomato sauce. For a pomodoro recipe with assertive tomato flavor, we'd need to perfect the sauce. Fresh tomatoes and canned diced tomatoes both released too much liquid during cooking. Compounded with the juices from the chicken, they created a thin, dull sauce. Switching to tomato paste proved to be the answer; the thick, concentrated paste, thinned with a little heavy cream and the chicken's juices, gave our sauce the perfect consistency and bold tomato flavor. Finishing the sauce with Parmesan gave our dish a creamy, nutty flavor, and a sprinkling of fresh basil tied it all together. Serve over egg noodles or rice.

1	**cup chopped onion**
½	**cup tomato paste**
4	**teaspoons minced garlic**
1	**tablespoon vegetable oil**
½	**teaspoon dried oregano**
	Salt and pepper
⅛	**teaspoon red pepper flakes**
⅓	**cup heavy cream**
4	**(6- to 8-ounce) boneless, skinless chicken breasts, trimmed**
½	**cup grated Parmesan cheese**
¼	**cup chopped fresh basil**

1. Microwave onion, tomato paste, garlic, oil, oregano, ¼ teaspoon salt, and pepper flakes in bowl, stirring occasionally, until onion is softened, about 5 minutes; transfer to slow cooker. Whisk in cream. Season chicken with salt and pepper and nestle into slow cooker. Cover and cook until chicken is tender, 2 to 3 hours on low.

2. Sprinkle chicken with Parmesan, cover, and cook on high until cheese is melted, about 5 minutes.

3. Transfer chicken to serving dish and sprinkle with 2 tablespoons basil. Stir remaining 2 tablespoons basil into sauce and season with salt and pepper to taste. Serve with chicken.

ON THE SIDE BROCCOLI RABE WITH BALSAMIC VINAIGRETTE
Stir 1½ pounds broccoli rabe, trimmed and cut into 1-inch pieces, into large pot of salted boiling water. Cook until wilted and tender, 2 to 3 minutes. Drain. Submerge broccoli rabe in bowl of cold water, drain, and pat dry. Whisk together 6 tablespoons extra-virgin olive oil, 2 tablespoons balsamic vinegar, 1 tablespoon maple syrup, 1 minced shallot, and ¼ teaspoon dry mustard in large bowl. Season with salt and pepper to taste. Add broccoli rabe and toss to combine. Serves 4.

Chicken Pizzaiola

Serves 4   **Cooking Time** 2 to 3 hours on Low   **Slow Cooker Size** 5½ to 7 Quarts

✔ **WHY THIS RECIPE WORKS:** For the ultimate easy, family-friendly dinner, we wanted to translate the flavors of pizza to a simple chicken dinner. We nestled boneless, skinless chicken breasts into the slow cooker and surrounded them with flavorful jarred marinara sauce to help them cook gently and retain their juices. We layered the pepperoni over the chicken so it would season the chicken and sauce as its fat rendered. We set the slow cooker on low so the chicken would cook through gently. After a few hours, we had moist, tender chicken and rich sauce to spoon over pasta. For the finishing touch, we sprinkled on mozzarella to give each piece of chicken a rich, cheesy coating. Victoria Marinara Sauce is the test kitchen's favorite brand; see page 174. You will need an oval slow cooker for this recipe. Serve over pasta or egg noodles.

2   **cups jarred marinara sauce**

4   **(6- to 8-ounce) boneless, skinless chicken breasts, trimmed**
     Salt and pepper

2   **ounces thinly sliced pepperoni**

1   **cup shredded mozzarella cheese**

1. Spread marinara sauce in slow cooker. Season chicken with salt and pepper and nestle into slow cooker. Lay pepperoni in even layer over chicken. Cover and cook until chicken is tender, 2 to 3 hours on low.

2. Sprinkle chicken with mozzarella, cover, and cook on high until cheese is melted, about 5 minutes.

3. Transfer chicken to serving dish. Using large spoon, skim excess fat from surface of sauce. Stir sauce to recombine and season with salt and pepper to taste. Serve with chicken.

ON THE SIDE SOFT AND CHEESY BREADSTICKS
Roll out 1 pound pizza dough on lightly floured counter into 12 by 6-inch rectangle. Cut dough crosswise into 1-inch-wide strips and lay on well-oiled rimmed baking sheet. Brush with 1½ tablespoons olive oil, sprinkle with ¼ cup grated Parmesan cheese, and season with salt and pepper. Bake in 400-degree oven until golden, about 20 minutes. Serve warm. Makes 12. (This recipe can be doubled.)

Unstuffed Chicken Cordon Bleu

Serves 4   **Cooking Time** 2 to 3 hours on Low   **Slow Cooker Size** 5½ to 7 Quarts

✔ **WHY THIS RECIPE WORKS:** Traditional recipes for chicken cordon bleu require carefully stuffing bone-in breasts, but we wanted an easier approach. To streamline the method and adapt it to the slow cooker, we wrapped boneless chicken breasts in thin slices of deli ham, nestled them in the slow cooker, then topped them with Swiss cheese for a no-fuss approach that kept prep work to a minimum. Poaching the breasts in a flavorful mixture of broth, mustard, and aromatics seasoned the chicken and allowed it to cook more gently. Once the chicken was cooked through, we whisked some cream into the braising liquid to make an easy mustard cream sauce. Our slow-cooker version had all the classic flavors of chicken cordon bleu—the only thing we lost was the fussy technique. You will need an oval slow cooker for this recipe. Serve over egg noodles or rice.

½	**cup chicken broth**
2	**tablespoons Dijon mustard**
1	**tablespoon instant tapioca**
1	**teaspoon minced garlic**
¼	**teaspoon dried thyme**
	Salt and pepper
4	**(6- to 8-ounce) boneless, skinless chicken breasts, trimmed**
8	**thin slices deli ham**
4	**slices deli Swiss cheese**
¼	**cup heavy cream**

1. Combine broth, mustard, tapioca, garlic, thyme, and ½ teaspoon pepper in slow cooker. Season chicken with salt and pepper. Working with 1 breast at a time, stack 2 slices of ham on counter, slightly overlapped; lay chicken in center of slices. Fold ham around chicken and arrange in slow cooker. Cover and cook until tender, 2 to 3 hours on low.

2. Top each chicken breast with 1 slice cheese. Cover and cook on high until cheese is melted, about 5 minutes.

3. Transfer chicken to serving dish. Whisk cream into braising liquid and cook on high, whisking constantly, until smooth, about 1 minute. Season with salt and pepper to taste. Serve chicken with sauce.

QUICK PREP TIP

UNSTUFFING CHICKEN CORDON BLEU
For simpler Chicken Cordon Bleu, we skip stuffing the chicken. Instead, we wrap it with ham and top it with cheese. To wrap chicken, stack 2 slices of ham on counter, slightly overlapped, and place chicken breast in center of slices. Fold ham ends neatly over chicken breast and press on overlapping ends to adhere.

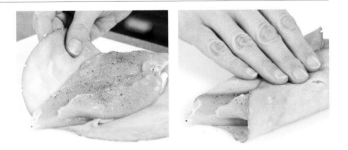

Chicken and Vegetable "Stir-Fry"

Serves 4　　**Cooking Time** 2 to 3 hours on Low　　**Slow Cooker Size** 5½ to 7 Quarts

✓ **WHY THIS RECIPE WORKS:** Making a stir-fry usually means quick, last-minute cooking in a skillet that's splattering hot oil. Surprisingly, we found a way to replicate this dish in the slow cooker for an easy, make-ahead, and mess-free dinner. First we poached boneless, skinless chicken breasts in a flavorful cooking liquid, which later doubled as a sauce. A combination of chicken broth, soy sauce, and ginger was a good start. Hot pepper jelly helped to thicken the sauce and contributed a great sweet and spicy flavor. To get perfectly crisp-tender vegetables from the slow cooker, the key was using a steamer basket. Placing the steamer basket on top of the chicken allowed the vegetables to steam gently throughout the cooking time. We finished the dish with fresh ginger to give it a nice spicy bite and stirred in water chestnuts at the end for appealing freshness and crunch. Serve with rice.

½　cup chicken broth

½　cup hot pepper jelly

3　tablespoons soy sauce

2　tablespoons grated ginger

2　tablespoons instant tapioca

4　(6- to 8-ounce) boneless, skinless chicken breasts, trimmed

1　teaspoon five-spice powder
　　Salt and pepper

2　red bell peppers, cored and cut into ¼-inch-wide strips

1　(15-ounce) can baby corn, rinsed

1　(8-ounce) can sliced water chestnuts, rinsed

3　scallions, sliced thin

1. Combine broth, pepper jelly, soy sauce, 1 tablespoon ginger, and tapioca in slow cooker. Season chicken with five-spice powder, salt, and pepper and nestle into slow cooker. Place steamer basket on top of chicken and place bell peppers and baby corn in basket. Cover and cook until chicken is tender, 2 to 3 hours on low.

2. Remove steamer basket and transfer vegetables to bowl. Transfer chicken to cutting board, let cool slightly, and slice into bite-size pieces.

3. Whisk braising liquid to recombine. Stir in vegetables, sliced chicken, water chestnuts, and remaining 1 tablespoon ginger. Let sit until heated through, about 5 minutes. Sprinkle with scallions and serve.

QUICK PREP TIP
CUTTING BELL PEPPER
To cut bell pepper, slice off top and bottom, remove core, then slice down through side of pepper. Lay pepper flat on cutting board, cut away any remaining ribs, then cut pepper into pieces as directed in recipe.

ALL ABOUT Chicken in the Slow Cooker

It's hard enough to cook chicken properly on the stovetop or in the oven, where you have complete control of the temperature, but in a slow cooker it's even trickier to ensure moist, flavorful chicken at the end of a long cooking time. We've seen soups and stews full of dry shredded chicken and braised breasts and thighs that were bland and unappealing. Here is what we've learned about getting juicy, flavorful chicken from a slow cooker.

Cooking Times for Chicken

We found that the only way to cook chicken in a slow cooker is on the low setting, which takes longer to get to the maximum heat level and allows the chicken time to gradually cook through without overcooking. Different cuts also require different cooking times to keep from overcooking.

TYPE OF CHICKEN	COOKING TIME *
Boneless, Skinless Chicken Breasts	2 to 3 hours on Low
Bone-In Chicken Breasts	3 to 4 hours on Low
Chicken Thighs	4 to 5 hours on Low
Drumsticks and Wings	3 to 4 hours on Low
Ground Chicken	2 to 3 hours on Low

*Note that cooking times vary in our Cooking for Two chapter

Boneless, Skinless Chicken Breasts

Convenient and easy to prep, this lean cut is great for quick weeknight meals, but it's also the most likely to overcook and turn dry. To keep our breasts juicy and tender, we found that keeping the heat level low and minding our time range were essential. We also cook them in a flavorful liquid to keep the heat gentle and even and to infuse the meat with flavor.

Bone-In Chicken Breasts

Bone-in breasts work well in the slow cooker because the bone helps to insulate the lean meat, preventing it from drying out during the longer cooking time. We cook the breasts with the skin on so that its fat can help keep the meat juicy and infuse it with flavor, but the moist environment of the slow cooker leaves it flabby and pale, so we remove it before serving. A paper towel is useful to help grip the skin more easily.

Chicken Thighs

Chicken thighs work well in the slow cooker; even after hours of simmering, they stay tender thanks to their fat and connective tissue. For stews and curries, we like boneless thighs; once cooked, they can easily be shredded into bite-size pieces. For hearty dishes where we want whole pieces of chicken, we like bone-in thighs. To keep the fatty skin from making the dish too greasy, we remove it before cooking, using a paper towel to provide extra grip.

Drumsticks and Wings

We found that the low, steady heat of the slow cooker is ideal for breaking down collagen for exceptionally tender drumsticks and wings. For crisp, browned skin, we simply pass them under the broiler for a few minutes, basting them with a thick, flavorful glaze partway through.

Ground Chicken

We found that ground chicken turns grainy in the slow cooker. To solve this problem, we microwave it for a few minutes, until it is just firm enough to break into coarse crumbles. It was also important to use ground chicken, not ground chicken breast, which was too lean and consistently overcooked.

Pesto Chicken with Fennel and Tomato Couscous

Serves 4   **Cooking Time** 3 to 4 hours on Low   **Slow Cooker Size** 5½ to 7 Quarts

✔ **WHY THIS RECIPE WORKS:** For a simple braised chicken dinner with fresh Italian flavors, we combined easy boneless chicken breasts with fennel and bright cherry tomatoes. Store-bought chicken broth flavored with garlic, salt, and pepper made a simple braising liquid that seasoned the chicken as it simmered and helped it to cook gently and evenly. Once the chicken was cooked, we used the flavorful braising liquid, enriched with the chicken's juices, to cook couscous for a quick and easy side dish. Finally, we stirred a little reserved braising liquid into store-bought pesto to make a fresh, herbal sauce. Be sure to use regular (or fine-grain) couscous; large-grain couscous, often labeled "Israeli-style," takes much longer to cook and won't work in this recipe. For more information on how to prep fennel, see page 60.

1	**fennel bulb, cored and sliced thin**
1	**tablespoon olive oil**
2	**teaspoons minced garlic**
½	**cup chicken broth**
	Salt and pepper
4	**(12-ounce) bone-in split chicken breasts, trimmed**
8	**ounces cherry tomatoes, halved**
1	**cup couscous**
½	**cup prepared basil pesto**

1. Microwave fennel, oil, and garlic in bowl, stirring occasionally, until fennel is tender, about 5 minutes; transfer to slow cooker. Stir in broth, ½ teaspoon salt, and ½ teaspoon pepper. Season chicken with salt and pepper and nestle into slow cooker. Sprinkle tomatoes over chicken, cover, and cook until chicken is tender, 3 to 4 hours on low.

2. Transfer chicken to serving dish, remove skin, and tent with aluminum foil. Strain braising liquid into fat separator and let sit for 5 minutes; reserve strained vegetables and 1½ cups defatted liquid. Return 1 cup defatted liquid and vegetables to now-empty slow cooker. Stir in couscous, cover, and cook on high until tender, about 15 minutes.

3. Combine remaining ½ cup reserved liquid and pesto in bowl and season with salt and pepper to taste. Pour sauce over chicken. Serve with couscous.

SMART SHOPPING COUSCOUS

Although couscous looks like a grain, it is technically a pasta. This starch is made from durum semolina, a high-protein wheat flour that is also used to make Italian pasta. Traditional Moroccan couscous is made by rubbing coarse-ground durum semolina and water between the hands to form small, coarse granules. The couscous is then dried and cooked over a simmering stew in a steamer called a *couscoussière*, which is essentially a stockpot fitted with a small-holed colander. The couscous sits in the colander and plumps in the steam produced by the pot's contents. The boxed couscous found in most supermarkets is a precooked version of traditional couscous. About the size of bread crumbs, the precooked couscous needs only a few minutes of steeping in hot liquid to be fully cooked.

Mediterranean Chicken with Potatoes, Fennel, and Olives

Serves 4   **Cooking Time** 3 to 4 hours on Low   **Slow Cooker Size** 5½ to 7 Quarts

WHY THIS RECIPE WORKS: For a hearty chicken dinner with bright flavor, we chose Mediterranean-inspired ingredients: fennel, rosemary, and olives. Microwaving the fennel and potatoes, along with aromatics, ensured that our vegetables would be fully tender when the chicken finished cooking. Bone-in chicken breasts stayed moist during the long cooking time, thanks to the insulation provided by the bones, plus they worked well in our rustic dish. Dried rosemary and bright, citrusy orange zest infused the braising liquid with flavor, seasoning the chicken as it cooked. We added the olives at the end so their briny flavor wouldn't become muted, and a healthy dose of fresh parsley rounded out the dish. For more information on how to prep fennel, see page 60.

1	**pound Yukon Gold potatoes, cut into ½-inch pieces**
1	**fennel bulb, cored and sliced thin**
1	**cup chopped onion**
3	**tablespoons unsalted butter**
1	**tablespoon minced garlic**
1	**teaspoon dried rosemary**
½	**cup chicken broth**
2	**teaspoons grated orange zest**
	Salt and pepper
4	**(12-ounce) bone-in split chicken breasts, trimmed**
½	**cup pitted salt-cured black olives, rinsed and halved**
¼	**cup minced fresh parsley**

1. Microwave potatoes, fennel, onion, 1 tablespoon butter, garlic, and rosemary in bowl, stirring occasionally, until vegetables are softened, about 5 minutes; transfer to slow cooker. Stir in broth, orange zest, ½ teaspoon salt, and ½ teaspoon pepper. Season chicken with salt and pepper and nestle into slow cooker. Cover and cook until chicken is tender, 3 to 4 hours on low.

2. Transfer chicken to serving dish and remove skin. Stir olives, parsley, and remaining 2 tablespoons butter into vegetables and season with salt and pepper to taste. Serve.

SMART SHOPPING OLIVES

Jarred olives come in three basic types at the supermarket: brine-cured green (left), brine-cured black (middle), and salt-cured black (right). Curing is the process that removes the bitter compound oleuropein from olives to make them suitable for eating. Brine-cured olives are soaked in a salt solution; salt-cured olives are packed in salt and left to sit until nearly all their liquid has been extracted, then covered in oil to replump. Both processes traditionally take weeks or even months. For canned California olives, on the other hand, producers use lye, which "ripens" the olives artificially in a matter of days, then further process the olives to turn their green flesh black.

Lemony Chicken with Artichokes and Capers

Serves 4   **Cooking Time** 3 to 4 hours on Low   **Slow Cooker Size** 5½ to 7 Quarts

✔ **WHY THIS RECIPE WORKS:** For an easy braise with bright citrus flavor, we used the slow cooker to gently simmer chicken and artichokes with strips of lemon zest. As the chicken cooked, the lemon zest infused the meat and the sauce with bright flavor. Bone-in chicken breasts stayed moist and juicy even after hours of simmering. Some onion and garlic gave the dish additional depth and savory flavor. For the sauce, we loved the combination of bold, briny capers with the bright lemon and hearty artichokes. A squeeze of fresh lemon juice added at the end reinforced the citrus flavor, and a little heavy cream thickened and enriched the sauce. Serve over egg noddles or rice.

1   cup chopped onion

1   tablespoon vegetable oil

2   teaspoons minced garlic

18   ounces frozen artichoke hearts, thawed and patted dry

¼   cup chicken broth

1   tablespoon instant tapioca

2   (2-inch) strips lemon zest plus 2 tablespoons juice
     Salt and pepper

4   (12-ounce) bone-in split chicken breasts, trimmed

½   cup heavy cream

2   tablespoons capers, rinsed

1. Microwave onion, oil, and garlic in bowl, stirring occasionally, until onion is softened, about 5 minutes; transfer to slow cooker. Stir in artichokes, broth, tapioca, lemon zest, ½ teaspoon salt, and ½ teaspoon pepper. Season chicken with salt and pepper and nestle into slow cooker. Cover and cook until chicken is tender, 3 to 4 hours on low.

2. Transfer chicken to serving dish and remove skin. Discard lemon zest. Stir cream, capers, and lemon juice into braising liquid and heat through for 2 minutes. Season with salt and pepper to taste, pour over chicken, and serve.

SMART SHOPPING CAPERS

An ideal caper has the perfect balance of saltiness, sweetness, acidity, and crunch. These sun-dried, pickled flower buds have a strong flavor that develops as they are cured, either immersed in a salty brine or packed in salt. From previous tastings we knew we preferred the compact size and slight crunch of tiny nonpareil capers, so we tasted six nationally available supermarket brands, evaluating them on their sharpness, saltiness, and overall appeal. The winner, **Reese Non-Pareil Capers**, had a bold, salty flavor that tasters loved.

Thai Chicken with Asparagus and Mushrooms

Serves 4   **Cooking Time** 3 to 4 hours on Low   **Slow Cooker Size** 5½ to 7 Quarts

✔ WHY THIS RECIPE WORKS: Thai dishes are known for their complex, long-simmered flavor. A few shortcut ingredients and the slow cooker were all we needed to create a boldly flavored, but easy-to-prepare, Thai chicken dinner. Thai red curry paste was an easy swap for an overwhelming list of traditional seasonings. We enriched it with coconut milk to deepen the flavor of our sauce. Stirring in a portion of the coconut milk just before serving helped to deepen the coconut flavor, which otherwise can taste washed out after several hours in the slow cooker. A little instant tapioca helped to thicken the sauce to a currylike consistency that went perfectly with rice. Bone-in chicken breasts stayed moist and tender as the sauce simmered and the rich flavors melded. We liked light, fresh asparagus and delicate shiitakes in this dish, but they turned to mush in the slow cooker. Luckily, just 5 minutes in the microwave was enough to turn them tender, then we added them to the dish at the end. We finished the sauce with lime juice, fish sauce, and fresh cilantro to brighten its rich flavors. Serve with rice.

1	cup canned coconut milk
2	tablespoons Thai red curry paste
1	tablespoon instant tapioca
	Salt and pepper
4	(12-ounce) bone-in split chicken breasts, trimmed
1	pound asparagus, trimmed and cut into 1-inch lengths
1	pound shiitake mushrooms, stemmed and sliced ½ inch thick
1	tablespoon vegetable oil
2	tablespoons lime juice
1	tablespoon fish sauce
¼	cup minced fresh cilantro

1. Whisk ½ cup coconut milk, curry paste, tapioca, ½ teaspoon salt, and ½ teaspoon pepper together in slow cooker. Season chicken with salt and pepper and nestle into slow cooker. Cover and cook until chicken is tender, 3 to 4 hours on low.

2. Transfer chicken to serving dish, remove skin, and tent with aluminum foil. Microwave asparagus, mushrooms, and oil in bowl, stirring occasionally, until tender, about 5 minutes.

3. Stir microwaved vegetables, remaining ½ cup coconut milk, lime juice, and fish sauce into braising liquid and let heat through for 5 minutes. Stir in cilantro and pour sauce over chicken. Serve.

SMART SHOPPING CURRY PASTE

Curry pastes, which can be either green or red, are a key ingredient for adding deep, well-rounded flavor to Thai curries. They are made from a mix of lemon grass, kaffir lime leaves, shrimp paste, ginger, garlic, chiles (fresh green Thai chiles for green curry paste and dried red Thai chiles for red curry paste), and other spices. So it's not surprising that making curry paste at home can be quite a chore. We have found that the store-bought variety does a fine job and saves significant time in terms of both shopping and prep. It is usually sold in small jars next to other Thai ingredients at the supermarket. Be aware that these pastes can vary in spiciness depending on the brand, so use more or less as desired.

Rustic Braised Chicken with Mushrooms

Serves 4   **Cooking Time** 3 to 4 hours on Low   **Slow Cooker Size** 5½ to 7 Quarts

✓ **WHY THIS RECIPE WORKS:** A combination of sliced cremini mushrooms, diced tomatoes, and bacon made a great start to a rustic sauce for bone-in chicken breasts, but it still needed some work. We wanted a sauce that would cling to the chicken and lightly coat a bed of noodles or rice. Instead, by the end of cooking, the mushrooms, tomatoes, and chicken had released so much liquid that the sauce was thin, watery, and dull. To cut back on moisture, first we switched from diced tomatoes to tomato paste, which still gave us great simmered tomato flavor but added a lot less moisture. Next, we briefly microwaved the mushrooms and bacon along with the aromatics to release their moisture and render the bacon fat. Finally, we stirred in some instant tapioca to give our sauce just the right amount of cling. A handful of fresh parsley added at the end contributed a bright note and rounded out the hearty flavors of this rustic meal. Serve over egg noodles or rice.

8 **ounces sliced cremini mushrooms**

6 **slices bacon, chopped coarse**

1 **cup chopped onion**

¼ **cup tomato paste**

4 **teaspoons minced garlic**

½ **teaspoon dried thyme**

¼ **cup dry white wine**

2 **tablespoons instant tapioca**
   Salt and pepper

4 **(12-ounce) bone-in split chicken breasts, trimmed**

¼ **cup minced fresh parsley**

1. Microwave mushrooms, bacon, onion, tomato paste, garlic, and thyme in bowl, stirring occasionally, until vegetables are softened, about 5 minutes; transfer to slow cooker. Stir in wine, tapioca, ½ teaspoon salt, and ½ teaspoon pepper. Season chicken with salt and pepper and nestle into slow cooker. Cover and cook until chicken is tender, 3 to 4 hours on low.

2. Transfer chicken to serving dish and remove skin. Stir parsley into braising liquid, season with salt and pepper to taste, and pour sauce over chicken. Serve.

ON THE SIDE PARSLEY EGG NOODLES
Cook 8 ounces egg noodles in salted boiling water, drain, and toss with 2 tablespoons unsalted butter and 1 tablespoon chopped fresh parsley. Season with salt and pepper to taste. Serves 4.

Chicken Thighs with Swiss Chard and Mustard

Serves 4   **Cooking Time** 4 to 5 hours on Low   **Slow Cooker Size** 5½ to 7 Quarts

✔ **WHY THIS RECIPE WORKS:** Tender chicken, spicy mustard, and earthy Swiss chard are a great combination for a warming winter supper. Quick-cooking Swiss chard may not seem like a good match for the slow cooker, but by adding it for just the last 30 minutes of cooking, we were able to get it perfectly crisp-tender without dirtying an extra pot. To complement the slightly bitter chard, we wanted a rich, mustardy sauce. We found that a combination of dry and whole-grain mustard was the key to getting the right amount of mustard flavor. Dry mustard added to the slow cooker at the beginning of cooking infused the chicken with a subtle flavor, and finishing the sauce with bold whole-grain mustard punched up its acidity. Onion, garlic, and some dried thyme rounded out the dish's flavor.

1   **cup chopped onion**

4   **teaspoons minced garlic**

1   **tablespoon vegetable oil**

1   **teaspoon dry mustard**

½   **teaspoon dried thyme**
     Salt and pepper

8   **(5- to 7-ounce) bone-in chicken thighs, skin removed**

2   **pounds Swiss chard, stemmed and cut into 1-inch pieces**

2   **tablespoons whole-grain mustard**

1. Microwave onion, garlic, oil, dry mustard, thyme, ½ teaspoon salt, and ½ teaspoon pepper in bowl, stirring occasionally, until onion is softened, about 5 minutes; transfer to slow cooker. Season chicken with salt and pepper and nestle into slow cooker. Cover and cook until chicken is tender, 4 to 5 hours on low.

2. Transfer chicken to serving dish and tent with aluminum foil. Stir Swiss chard and whole-grain mustard into liquid in slow cooker, cover, and cook on high until chard is wilted, 20 to 30 minutes.

3. Return chicken and any accumulated juices to slow cooker and season with salt and pepper to taste. Let chicken heat through, about 5 minutes. Serve.

SMART SHOPPING WHOLE-GRAIN MUSTARD

Mustard aficionados argue that the coarse-grained version of this condiment improves any ham sandwich or grilled sausage, and we also rely on it in myriad recipes to contribute spiciness, tanginess, and a pleasant pop of seeds. After sampling 11 brands, tasters agreed that they disliked those with superfluous ingredients such as xanthan gum, artificial flavors, and garlic and onion powders. But the more noteworthy factor turned out to be salt. Mustards with a meager amount ranked low, while the winners had roughly twice as much of this flavor amplifier. Our co-winners—the classic, moderately coarse **Grey Poupon Country Dijon** (left) and the newer, "poppier" product, **Grey Poupon Harvest Coarse Ground Mustard** (right)—make good pantry staples.

Chicken Adobo

Serves 4   **Cooking Time** 4 to 5 hours on Low   **Slow Cooker Size** 5½ to 7 Quarts

✔ **WHY THIS RECIPE WORKS:** Chicken adobo is a popular Filipino dish made by slowly simmering chicken in a mixture of vinegar, soy sauce, garlic, bay leaves, and black pepper. The beauty of this dish is that it features a short ingredient list and requires very little prep work, while still delivering tender, moist chicken and a boldly flavored sauce. In traditional recipes the chicken is marinated, then the marinade is reduced to create a thick sauce. Since we would be cooking the chicken thighs for a full five hours, we skipped the marinade and simply cooked the chicken directly in the sauce. So that we wouldn't have to reduce the sauce over the stove, we scaled it down and added a little tapioca to thicken it as it cooked. Some creamy coconut milk helped to balance the tart and salty flavors of the sauce. Stirring in a portion of the coconut milk just before serving helped to deepen the coconut flavor, which can taste dull after several hours in the slow cooker. Serve with rice.

½ **cup canned coconut milk**

2 **tablespoons cider vinegar**

2 **tablespoons soy sauce**

2 **teaspoons minced garlic**

1 **tablespoon instant tapioca**

2 **bay leaves**

   Salt and pepper

8 **(5- to 7-ounce) bone-in chicken thighs, skin removed**

2 **scallions, sliced thin**

1. Combine ¼ cup coconut milk, vinegar, soy sauce, garlic, tapioca, bay leaves, and 1 teaspoon pepper in slow cooker. Season chicken with salt and pepper and nestle into slow cooker. Cover and cook until chicken is tender, 4 to 5 hours on low.

2. Transfer chicken to serving dish. Discard bay leaves. Stir remaining ¼ cup coconut milk into braising liquid and season with salt and pepper to taste. Pour sauce over chicken and sprinkle with scallions. Serve.

SMART SHOPPING COCONUT MILK

Coconut milk is not the thin liquid found inside the coconut itself (that is called coconut water). Coconut milk is made by steeping equal parts shredded coconut meat in either warm milk or water. The meat is pressed or mashed to release as much liquid as possible, the mixture is strained, and the result is coconut milk. We tasted seven nationally available brands (five regular and two light) in coconut rice, a Thai-style chicken soup, chicken curry, and coconut pudding. In the savory recipes, tasters preferred **Chaokoh**, which boasted an incredibly smooth texture. When it came to the sweet recipes, tasters liked **Ka-Me** coconut milk best.

Chicken Mole

Serves 4   **Cooking Time** 4 to 5 hours on Low   **Slow Cooker Size** 5½ to 7 Quarts

WHY THIS RECIPE WORKS: A great mole (a rich Mexican chile sauce) requires hours of slow cooking to develop the deep, complex flavors for which it is so well known, making it a perfect match for the slow cooker. For our mole, we chose meaty bone-in chicken thighs, which paired well with the spicy sauce. We cooked the chicken directly in the mole so it would absorb that smoky-sweet flavor, and after 5 hours in the slow cooker it was fall-off-the-bone tender. Traditionally mole boasts an extensive list of ingredients, but we streamlined the recipe by relying on pantry staples, including chili powder, cocoa powder, and peanut butter, for complex flavor without the work. Canned diced tomatoes added acidity, and raisins gave us just the right sweetness; finishing with cilantro brightened things up. Serve with rice.

1	**(14.5-ounce) can diced tomatoes**
⅓	**cup raisins**
2	**tablespoons cocoa powder**
2	**tablespoons peanut butter**
1	**tablespoon chili powder**
1	**tablespoon minced garlic**
	Salt and pepper
8	**(5- to 7-ounce) bone-in chicken thighs, skin removed**
¼	**cup minced fresh cilantro**

1. Drain tomatoes, reserving ½ cup juice. Combine tomatoes, tomato juice, raisins, cocoa, peanut butter, chili powder, garlic, ½ teaspoon salt, and ½ teaspoon pepper in slow cooker. Season chicken with salt and pepper and nestle into slow cooker. Cover and cook until chicken is tender, 4 to 5 hours on low.

2. Transfer chicken to serving dish. Process braising liquid in blender until smooth, about 20 seconds. Season sauce with salt and pepper to taste, pour over chicken, and sprinkle with cilantro. Serve.

ON THE SIDE CILANTRO RICE
Process 3 cups chicken broth and 1½ cups fresh cilantro leaves in blender or food processor until mostly smooth, about 15 seconds. Bring cilantro mixture, 1½ cups long-grain white rice, and 1 teaspoon salt to boil over medium-high heat in large saucepan and cook until no liquid is visible, 5 to 8 minutes. Cover and continue to cook over low heat until rice is tender, about 15 minutes. Serves 4.

Fig-Balsamic Glazed Chicken Drumsticks

Serves 4 to 6   **Cooking Time** 3 to 4 hours on Low   **Slow Cooker Size** 5½ to 7 Quarts

WHY THIS RECIPE WORKS: Following our success with slow-cooker chicken wings, we wanted to use our easy method to make tender, slow-cooked drumsticks with a delicious, sticky-sweet glaze. The method translated perfectly to the drumsticks; we simply seasoned them with salt, pepper, and a little aromatic rosemary and cooked them until tender. Then we set them on a wire rack and broiled them until the skin was crisp and browned, glazing them partway through. For the glaze, we decided on the classic Italian combination of figs and balsamic vinegar. To keep our glaze as simple as possible, we relied on fig preserves, which had great flavor and an ideal thick consistency. We simply added some balsamic vinegar and orange zest to round out the flavor. These drumsticks cook up charred and sticky after a short time under the broiler. Be sure to coat the drumsticks generously; you won't want any of the glaze to go to waste.

2	**teaspoons dried rosemary**
4	**pounds chicken drumsticks**
	Salt and pepper
¾	**cup fig preserves**
3	**tablespoons balsamic vinegar**
1½	**teaspoons orange zest**

1. Crumble rosemary into fine pieces. Season drumsticks with rosemary, salt, and pepper and place in slow cooker. Cover and cook until chicken is tender, 3 to 4 hours on low.

2. Adjust oven rack 10 inches from broiler element and heat broiler. Place wire rack inside aluminum foil–lined rimmed baking sheet and spray with vegetable oil spray. Transfer drumsticks to prepared sheet; discard cooking liquid. Broil until lightly charred and crisp, about 10 minutes, flipping halfway through cooking.

3. Meanwhile, combine preserves, vinegar, orange zest, 1 teaspoon pepper, and ½ teaspoon salt in bowl. Brush drumsticks with one-third of sauce and continue to broil until drumsticks are browned and sticky, about 10 minutes, flipping and brushing drumsticks with more sauce halfway through cooking. Brush drumsticks with remaining sauce. Serve.

SMART SHOPPING BALSAMIC VINEGAR

We were curious about the differences among the various brands of balsamic vinegar found at the supermarket, so we bought a bunch of them (ranging from $5 to $20) and pitted them against one another in a taste test. Right off the bat, we found that the sweetness and viscosity of the vinegars make a difference. A good balsamic vinegar must be sweet and thick, but it should also offer a bit of acidity. In the end, one supermarket vinegar—**Lucini Gran Riserva Balsamico**—impressed us with its nice balance of sweet and tangy.

Caribbean-Style Chicken Drumsticks

Serves 4 to 6   **Cooking Time** 3 to 4 hours on Low   **Slow Cooker Size** 5½ to 7 Quarts

✓ **WHY THIS RECIPE WORKS:** The smoky, spicy, and sweet flavors in Caribbean jerk chicken sounded like a perfect match for tender slow-cooker chicken drumsticks. We started by building flavor with a dry rub of brown sugar and ground allspice—a classic spice in Caribbean cooking—then cooked the chicken in the slow cooker until tender. To get the skin appealingly crisp and browned, the drumsticks just needed a quick trip under the broiler for a lightly charred exterior. To make a flavorful paste to coat the chicken, we combined scallions, thyme, smoky chipotle chile, garlic, and lime zest along with molasses for sweetness and oil to bind everything together. The blender made quick work of mixing the ingredients. We brushed the drumsticks with the paste twice as they broiled until they were well browned and sticky.

1	tablespoon packed brown sugar
2	teaspoons ground allspice
	Salt and pepper
4	pounds chicken drumsticks
6	scallions, chopped coarse
3	tablespoons molasses
3	tablespoons vegetable oil
2	teaspoons dried thyme
1½	tablespoons minced chipotle chile
2	teaspoons minced garlic
2	teaspoons lime zest

1. Mix sugar, allspice, ½ teaspoon salt, and ½ teaspoon pepper together in bowl. Rub mixture evenly over drumsticks; transfer to slow cooker. Cover and cook until chicken is tender, 3 to 4 hours on low.

2. Adjust oven rack 10 inches from broiler element and heat broiler. Place wire rack inside aluminum foil–lined rimmed baking sheet and spray with vegetable oil spray. Transfer drumsticks to prepared sheet; discard cooking liquid. Broil until lightly charred and crisp, about 10 minutes, flipping halfway through cooking.

3. Meanwhile, process scallions, molasses, oil, thyme, chipotle, garlic, lime zest, and ½ teaspoon salt in blender until almost smooth. Brush drumsticks with half of paste and continue to broil until drumsticks are browned and sticky, about 10 minutes, flipping and brushing drumsticks with remaining paste halfway through cooking. Serve.

ON THE SIDE BUTTERMILK COLESLAW
Toss ½ head shredded green cabbage (6 cups) and 1 shredded carrot with 1 teaspoon salt and let drain in colander until wilted, about 1 hour. Rinse cabbage and carrot with cold water, then dry thoroughly with paper towels and transfer to large bowl. Stir in ⅓ cup buttermilk, ¼ cup mayonnaise, 2 tablespoons sour cream, 4 thinly sliced scallions, 1 tablespoon sugar, and ½ teaspoon Dijon mustard. Season with salt and pepper to taste and refrigerate until chilled. Serves 4 to 6.

Sloppy Janes

Serves 4   **Cooking Time** 2 to 3 hours on Low   **Slow Cooker Size** 5½ to 7 Quarts

WHY THIS RECIPE WORKS: Ground chicken is a great alternative to beef for Sloppy Joes—its more delicate flavor is a perfect medium for boldly flavored sauces. Because chicken is leaner than beef, it can quickly turn dry and grainy in the slow cooker. To prevent our ground chicken from drying out, it was important to cook the mixture on low for no more than three hours. We also found that microwaving the chicken for a few minutes made it firm enough to break into coarse crumbles that did not turn grainy during cooking. A combination of ketchup and canned tomato sauce gave our sauce the right balance of light sweetness and strong tomato flavor. We doctored up this simple sauce by adding a little brown sugar, chili powder, and hot sauce until our sandwiches had enough flavor to please both kids and adults. Be sure to use ground chicken, not ground chicken breast (also labeled 99 percent fat free). This recipe can easily be doubled for a crowd.

1	pound ground chicken
1	cup chopped onion
2	teaspoons minced garlic
½	teaspoon chili powder
½	cup canned tomato sauce
½	cup ketchup
1	tablespoon packed brown sugar
¼	teaspoon hot sauce
	Salt and pepper
4	hamburger buns

1. Microwave ground chicken, onion, garlic, and chili powder in bowl, stirring occasionally, until chicken is no longer pink, about 5 minutes. Transfer mixture to slow cooker, breaking up any large pieces of chicken. Stir in tomato sauce, ketchup, sugar, hot sauce, ½ teaspoon salt, and ½ teaspoon pepper. Cover and cook until chicken is tender, 2 to 3 hours on low.

2. Using large spoon, skim excess fat from surface of chicken mixture. Break up any remaining large pieces of chicken with spoon and season with salt and pepper to taste. Spoon chicken mixture onto buns. Serve.

SMART SHOPPING KETCHUP

Since the 1980s, most ketchup has been made with high-fructose corn syrup (HFCS); manufacturers like this ingredient because it's cheap and easy to mix with other ingredients. But in the past few years, many manufacturers have started offering alternatives, such as ketchup made with white sugar. For our recent taste test of eight national brands, we focused on classic tomato ketchups. Tasters tried each plain and with fries. It was clear they wanted ketchup that tasted the way they remembered it: boldly seasoned, with all the flavor elements—salty, sweet, tangy, and tomatoey. Our top three ketchups were all sweetened with sugar; **Heinz Organic Tomato Ketchup** got the top spot.

Tomatillo Chicken Soft Tacos

Serves 4 to 6   **Cooking Time** 4 to 5 hours on Low   **Slow Cooker Size** 5½ to 7 Quarts

✓ WHY THIS RECIPE WORKS: To make great chicken soft tacos, we needed a tender, flavorful chicken filling. Cooking chicken in tomatillo salsa flavored the chicken in a big way without the involved prep of using fresh tomatillos. Fresh poblano chile peppers lent a little heat to the sauce and created a more complex flavor profile than salsa alone. We found that boneless chicken thighs worked best here; after 4 to 5 hours in the slow cooker they were meltingly tender, and they could be shredded easily for the filling. Finishing with a little lime juice and fresh cilantro brightened up this dish. Jarred tomatillo salsa is also called salsa verde. We leave all the braising liquid with the shredded chicken to help season the filling and keep it moist; a slotted spoon works best for serving the filling. Serve the tacos plain or with lime wedges, diced avocado, queso fresco, and/or sour cream.

1	**cup jarred tomatillo salsa**
2	**poblano chiles, stemmed, seeded, and chopped**
¼	**teaspoon dried oregano**
	Salt and pepper
3	**pounds boneless, skinless chicken thighs, trimmed**
¼	**cup minced fresh cilantro**
2	**tablespoons lime juice**
12–18	**(6-inch) flour tortillas, warmed**

1. Combine salsa, poblanos, oregano, ½ teaspoon salt, and ½ teaspoon pepper in slow cooker. Season chicken with salt and pepper and nestle into slow cooker. Cover and cook until chicken is tender, 4 to 5 hours on low.

2. Using tongs, break chicken into bite-size pieces. Stir in cilantro and lime juice and season with salt and pepper to taste. Serve chicken filling with warm tortillas.

QUICK PREP TIP   WARMING TORTILLAS

Warming the tortillas up before serving is crucial for both their flavor and their texture. If your tortillas are very dry, pat each tortilla with a little water before warming them. Toast tortillas, one at a time, directly on cooking grate over medium gas flame until slightly charred around edges, about 30 seconds per side. Or toast tortillas, one at a time, in dry skillet over medium-high heat until softened and speckled brown, 20 to 30 seconds per side. Once warmed, immediately wrap tortillas in aluminum foil or clean dish towel to keep them warm and soft until serving time.

Asian Chicken Lettuce Wraps

Serves 4 to 6   **Cooking Time** 2 to 3 hours on Low   **Slow Cooker Size** 5½ to 7 Quarts

✔ **WHY THIS RECIPE WORKS:** This Sichuan-inspired recipe features seasoned ground chicken spooned into lettuce leaves and eaten like a taco. Packed with flavor and easy to assemble, it's an all-around winner. We found that we could make a sauce and season our chicken all at once by combining soy sauce and hoisin in the slow cooker with the chicken. A little garlic rounded out the sauce, and a chopped red bell pepper added color and a refreshing crunch. To protect the ground chicken from drying out as it cooked, it was important to cook the mixture on low for no more than three hours. We also found that if we microwaved the chicken for a few minutes, it became firm enough to break into coarse crumbles that did not turn grainy during cooking. Once the chicken was cooked, we stirred in some cooked rice. The rice soaked up the extra sauce and bulked up the filling. Finally, we added some scallions and water chestnuts for freshness and crunch. Be sure to use ground chicken, not ground chicken breast (also labeled 99 percent fat free), in this recipe. Feel free to use leftover rice or precooked rice from the supermarket.

2	pounds ground chicken
4	teaspoons minced garlic
1	red bell pepper, cored and chopped fine
½	cup hoisin sauce
2	tablespoons soy sauce
	Salt and pepper
1	(8-ounce) can sliced water chestnuts, rinsed and chopped
1	cup cooked rice
3	scallions, sliced thin
2	heads Bibb lettuce

1. Microwave ground chicken and garlic in bowl, stirring occasionally, until chicken is no longer pink, about 5 minutes. Drain off liquid and transfer mixture to slow cooker. Stir in bell pepper, hoisin, soy sauce, ½ teaspoon salt, and ½ teaspoon pepper. Cover and cook until chicken is tender, 2 to 3 hours on low.

2. Stir in water chestnuts and rice and let sit until heated through, about 5 minutes. Stir in scallions and season with salt and pepper to taste. Separate Bibb lettuce leaves. Serve with chicken filling.

SMART SHOPPING HOISIN SAUCE

Hoisin is a thick, reddish-brown mixture of soybeans, sugar, vinegar, garlic, chiles, and spices, the most predominant of which is five-spice powder. It is used in many classic Chinese dishes, such as Peking duck and kung pao shrimp, and as a table condiment. Our favorite brand is **Kikkoman Hoisin Sauce**; tasters praised its initial "burn," which mellowed into a harmonious blend of sweet and savory flavors.

Braised Chicken Sausage with White Bean Ragout

Serves 4   **Cooking Time** 2 to 3 hours on Low   **Slow Cooker Size** 5½ to 7 Quarts

✔ **WHY THIS RECIPE WORKS:** For this hearty winter braise, a simple combination of sausage, beans, and rosemary is transformed into a rich, warming bean ragout by the gentle simmer of the slow cooker. For the main components of the dish, we chose delicately flavored cannellini beans and Italian chicken sausage, which was full of spices like fennel and caraway that would flavor the dish. We combined broth, wine, minced garlic, and rosemary for a flavorful cooking liquid that would season the beans as they cooked. Cherry tomatoes added a pop of bright color and fresh flavor. Once the sausage was cooked and the beans were tender, we mashed a portion of the beans and tomatoes together to help thicken the ragout. Stirring in some baby spinach right before serving brightened up this comforting dish. Both sweet and hot Italian chicken sausages work well in this recipe.

2	**(15-ounce) cans cannellini beans, rinsed**
¼	**cup chicken broth**
¼	**cup dry white wine**
2	**teaspoons minced garlic**
1	**sprig fresh rosemary**
	Salt and pepper
1½	**pounds Italian chicken sausage**
8	**ounces cherry tomatoes**
4	**ounces (4 cups) baby spinach**
2	**tablespoons extra-virgin olive oil**

1. Combine beans, broth, wine, garlic, rosemary, ½ teaspoon salt, and ½ teaspoon pepper in slow cooker. Nestle sausage into slow cooker and top with tomatoes. Cover and cook until sausage is tender, 2 to 3 hours on low.

2. Transfer sausage to serving dish and tent with aluminum foil. Discard rosemary. Transfer 1 cup bean-tomato mixture to bowl and mash with potato masher until mostly smooth.

3. Stir spinach and mashed bean mixture into slow cooker and let sit until spinach is wilted and mixture is heated through, about 5 minutes. Stir in oil and season with salt and pepper to taste. Serve with sausages.

SMART SHOPPING MILD VERSUS HOT ITALIAN CHICKEN SAUSAGE

When shopping for Italian chicken sausage, either hot or sweet, look first for fresh sausage. Fresh sausage contains meat that has not previously been cured or cooked, so it is important to remember that it must be kept in the refrigerator and be thoroughly cooked before eating. The meat is contained within a thin casing that is edible. Mild Italian chicken sausages (right) contain white meat chicken and fennel seeds as the most prominent flavorings. Hot Italian chicken sausages (left) add red chili pepper flakes for heat and paprika for color. It is not uncommon for garlic to be mixed in for added flavor (though this is not typical for pork sausages). Be aware that hot sausages can range in heat from mildly hot to very hot.

Steaks, Chops, Ribs, and More

Braised Steaks with Horseradish Smashed Potatoes

Serves 4   **Cooking Time** 8 to 9 hours on Low or 5 to 6 hours on High
Slow Cooker Size 5½ to 7 Quarts

✔ **WHY THIS RECIPE WORKS:** Steak and smashed potatoes is a classic pairing that we wanted to bring to the slow cooker. We knew our biggest challenge would be getting the steak and potatoes to cook through in the same amount of time. The key to success turned out to be an unlikely tool: a steamer basket. Placing the potatoes in the steamer basket on top of the steaks elevated them above the braising liquid and allowed them to steam gently. Once they were fully cooked, we smashed the potatoes with milk, cream cheese, butter, fresh chives, and spicy horseradish. We braised blade steaks in a mix of onions, garlic, and tomato paste until they were nearly fall-apart tender. To make the sauce, we simply defatted the braising liquid and served it with the rich steak and creamy, tangy potatoes. Look for small red potatoes measuring 1 to 2 inches in diameter; if your potatoes are larger, cut them into 1-inch pieces to ensure that they cook through properly.

2	cups chopped onions
2	tablespoons minced garlic
2	tablespoons tomato paste
1	tablespoon vegetable oil
4	(8-ounce) beef blade steaks, ¾ to 1 inch thick
	Salt and pepper
1½	pounds small red potatoes
¾	cup milk, warm
2	ounces cream cheese, softened
3	tablespoons unsalted butter, melted
3	tablespoons prepared horseradish
2	tablespoons minced fresh chives

1. Microwave onions, garlic, tomato paste, and oil in bowl, stirring occasionally, until onions are softened, about 5 minutes; transfer to slow cooker. Season steaks with pepper and nestle into slow cooker. Place steamer basket on top of steaks and arrange potatoes in basket. Cover and cook until beef is tender, 8 to 9 hours on low or 5 to 6 hours on high.

2. Transfer potatoes to large bowl. Transfer steaks to serving dish and tent with aluminum foil. Strain sauce into fat separator and let sit for 5 minutes.

3. Meanwhile, break potatoes into large chunks with rubber spatula. Fold in milk, cream cheese, melted butter, horseradish, and chives until incorporated and only small chunks of potato remain. Adjust potatoes' consistency with extra warm milk as needed and season with salt and pepper to taste. Pour defatted sauce over steaks. Serve with potatoes.

SMART SHOPPING BLADE STEAKS

One of our favorite cuts for the slow cooker, this surprisingly tender steak is a small cut from the cow's shoulder, or chuck, where most other cuts are quite tough. Blade steaks are inexpensive because they have a line of gristle that runs down the middle, but when slow cooked, these steaks turn fall-apart tender and the gristle is easily removed, yielding a richly flavored, beefy steak.

Cowboy Steak and Beans

Serves 4   **Cooking Time** 8 to 9 hours on Low or 5 to 6 hours on High
Slow Cooker Size 5½ to 7 Quarts

WHY THIS RECIPE WORKS: To make a meal that would really satisfy, we braised juicy steaks in the slow cooker until they were meltingly tender and paired them with rich, smoky baked beans. We found that blade steaks were ideal for this dish because they have a relatively high and even distribution of fat; after hours of simmering in the slow cooker, the steaks were supremely moist and tender. We got a head start on our beans by using canned baked beans, which already had great sweet and smoky flavor. To give them more depth, we enhanced their flavor with barbecue sauce, molasses, and Dijon. The rich flavors of the meat and the saucy beans melded as they cooked to give us a hearty steak and baked beans supper.

2   **(16-ounce) cans baked beans**

½   **cup barbecue sauce**

3   **tablespoons molasses**

1   **tablespoon Dijon mustard**

4   **(8-ounce) beef blade steaks,**
     ¾ to 1 inch thick

     Salt and pepper

1. Combine beans, barbecue sauce, molasses, and mustard in slow cooker. Season steaks with salt and pepper and nestle into slow cooker. Cover and cook until beef is tender, 8 to 9 hours on low or 5 to 6 hours on high.

2. Transfer steaks to serving dish, tent with aluminum foil, and let rest for 5 minutes. Using large spoon, skim excess fat from surface of beans. Season with salt and pepper to taste and serve.

SMART SHOPPING BAKED BEANS

The slow cooker is great for making slow-simmered baked beans with rich molasses flavor. But for an easy weeknight meal, we wanted to skip the hassle of making baked beans from scratch. Convenient canned baked beans seemed like a great shortcut—but are they any good? To find out, we gathered cans from industry leaders and three vegetarian-style brands for a side-by-side tasting. Tasters' preferences quickly fell into line: They liked sweet, slightly firm beans. The favorite was **B&M Vegetarian Baked Beans**, which tasters applauded for their "very molasses-y" flavor and "firm," "pleasant" texture.

Provençal-Style Braised Steaks

Serves 4   **Cooking Time** 8 to 9 hours on Low or 5 to 6 hours on High
Slow Cooker Size 5½ to 7 Quarts

✔ **WHY THIS RECIPE WORKS:** We wanted to complement rich, tender braised steaks with a bright, aromatic tomato sauce with Italian flavors. Blade steaks, a reasonably priced cut that turns meltingly tender when slow-cooked, had lots of meaty flavor. For a flavor-packed base for our sauce, we microwaved onions, tomato paste, garlic, anchovy, and red pepper flakes to bring out their flavors. We added this potent mixture to the slow cooker with the steaks; as the steaks cooked, their juices melded with the aromatics to create a deeply flavorful sauce. Once the meat was tender, we simply strained the sauce and stirred in briny olives and capers and plenty of fresh parsley for a bright sauce that perfectly balanced the rich steak. Serve over egg noodles.

2	**cups chopped onions**
2	**tablespoons minced garlic**
2	**tablespoons tomato paste**
1	**tablespoon vegetable oil**
1	**anchovy fillet, rinsed and minced**
⅛	**teaspoon red pepper flakes**
4	**(8-ounce) beef blade steaks,**
	¾ to 1 inch thick
	Salt and pepper
½	**cup pitted kalamata olives,**
	halved
¼	**cup minced fresh parsley**
2	**tablespoons capers, rinsed**

1. Microwave onions, garlic, tomato paste, oil, anchovy, and pepper flakes in bowl, stirring occasionally, until onions are softened, about 5 minutes; transfer to slow cooker. Season steaks with pepper and nestle into slow cooker. Cover and cook until beef is tender, 8 to 9 hours on low or 5 to 6 hours on high.

2. Transfer steaks to serving dish and tent with aluminum foil. Strain sauce into fat separator, let sit for 5 minutes, then pour defatted sauce into bowl. Stir in olives, parsley, and capers and season with salt and pepper to taste. Pour sauce over steaks. Serve.

SMART SHOPPING ANCHOVY FILLETS VERSUS PASTE
Since most recipes call for only a small amount of anchovies, we wondered whether a tube of anchovy paste might be a more convenient option. Made from pulverized anchovies, vinegar, salt, and water, anchovy paste promises all the flavor of oil-packed anchovies without the mess. We tested the paste and jarred or canned anchovies side by side in recipes calling for an anchovy or two. Tasters found little difference, though a few astute tasters felt that the paste had a "saltier" and "slightly more fishy" flavor. You can substitute ¼ teaspoon of the paste for each fillet. However, when a recipe calls for more than a couple of anchovies, stick with jarred or canned as the paste's more intense flavor will be overwhelming. Our favorite brand of canned anchovies is **Ortiz Oil-Packed Anchovies**.

Harvest Pork Chops with Kale and Apples

Serves 4   **Cooking Time** 2 to 3 hours on Low   **Slow Cooker Size** 5½ to 7 Quarts

✔ **WHY THIS RECIPE WORKS:** For a simple dinner with the flavors of fall, we combined juicy pork chops and apples with hearty, healthy kale. When developing other recipes for pork chops, we've found that the best cut of pork chop for the slow cooker is the blade chop. This cut, from the shoulder end of the loin, typically contains a good amount of fat and connective tissue, helping it to remain juicy after several hours in a slow cooker. But when we tried adding everything straight to the slow cooker, the pork chops cooked through before the apples and kale were done. The solution was to jump-start the kale and apples in the microwave along with the aromatics so that they were evenly cooked by the time the pork chops were tender. To reinforce the apple flavor, we used apple cider for the braising liquid. A little sage rounded out the flavors. Very often, blade chops aren't labeled specifically as such. Just look for bone-in chops with a good streak of dark meat running through the center of the chop or for chops with as much dark meat as possible. The kale may seem like a lot at first, but it wilts down substantially.

12 ounces kale, stemmed and sliced into ½-inch-wide strips

2 apples, peeled, cored, and quartered

1 cup chopped onion

½ cup apple cider

2 teaspoons dried sage

4 (8-ounce) bone-in blade-cut pork chops, ¾ inch thick
   Salt and pepper

1. Microwave kale, apples, onion, apple cider, and sage in covered bowl, stirring occasionally, until vegetables are almost tender, about 5 minutes; transfer to slow cooker. Cut 2 slits, about 2 inches apart, through outer layer of fat and silverskin on each chop. Season chops with salt and pepper and nestle into slow cooker. Cover and cook until pork is tender, 2 to 3 hours on low.

2. Transfer chops to serving dish, tent with aluminum foil, and let rest for 5 minutes. Season kale and apple mixture with salt and pepper to taste. Serve.

QUICK PREP TIP PREVENTING CURLED PORK CHOPS
As pork chops cook, the fat and silverskin around the edges contract and will cause the chops to bow or curl. To prevent this and ensure more even cooking, use sharp knife to cut 2 slits, about 2 inches apart, into fat and silverskin of each chop.

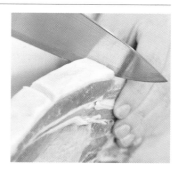

Sweet and Spicy Pork Chops with Bok Choy and Shiitakes

Serves 4   **Cooking Time** 2 to 3 hours on Low   **Slow Cooker Size** 5½ to 7 Quarts

✔ **WHY THIS RECIPE WORKS:** For this Asian-inspired dish, we built on the success of our Harvest Pork Chops, swapping out the apples and kale for bok choy and shiitakes. We created an easy, flavorful braising liquid by combining Asian sweet chili sauce and soy sauce. Tapioca helped thicken the braising liquid so that it would coat the vegetables lightly. We briefly microwaved the shiitakes to ensure that they would be tender by the time the pork chops were done. The sturdy bok choy stalks maintained a nice crunch throughout the cooking time; we stirred in the more delicate green leaves at the end to provide fresh flavor and color. Very often, blade chops aren't labeled specifically as such. Just look for bone-in chops with a good streak of dark meat running through the center of the chop or for chops with as much dark meat as possible. Serve with rice.

8   **ounces shiitake mushrooms, stemmed and quartered**

1   **tablespoon vegetable oil**

½   **cup Asian sweet chili sauce**

1   **tablespoon soy sauce**

1   **tablespoon instant tapioca**

1½   **pounds bok choy, stems and greens separated, both sliced ½ inch thick**

4   **(8-ounce) bone-in blade-cut pork chops, ¾ inch thick**
     Salt and pepper

1. Microwave mushrooms and oil in bowl, stirring occasionally, until softened, about 5 minutes; drain mushrooms and transfer to slow cooker. Stir in chili sauce, soy sauce, and tapioca. Stir in bok choy stems. Cut 2 slits, about 2 inches apart, through outer layer of fat and silverskin on each chop. Season chops with salt and pepper and nestle into slow cooker. Cover and cook until pork is tender, 2 to 3 hours on low.

2. Transfer chops to serving dish and tent with aluminum foil. Stir bok choy greens into slow cooker, cover, and cook on high until wilted, about 5 minutes. Season with salt, pepper, and extra soy sauce to taste. Pour bok choy mixture over chops and serve.

SMART SHOPPING BLADE-CUT PORK CHOPS
Pork chops come from the loin of the pig and can be cut into blade chops, rib chops, center-cut chops, and sirloin chops. Cut from the shoulder end of the loin, blade chops are the toughest cut—but they are also the fattiest, juiciest, and most flavorful. We put the slow cooker to work to gently cook these chops until they are tender. Look for bone-in chops with plenty of dark meat and good marbling.

Easy Barbecued Spareribs

Serves 4 to 6   **Cooking Time** 4 to 5 hours on Low   **Slow Cooker Size** 6½ to 7 Quarts

✓ **WHY THIS RECIPE WORKS:** We wanted to use the low, even heat of the slow cooker to make fall-off-the-bone-tender barbecued pork spareribs with authentic grilled flavor. To start, we covered the ribs with a dry rub of paprika, sugar, cayenne, salt, and pepper for deeper flavor. To fit two racks of spareribs into the slow cooker, we stood the racks upright around the perimeter of the slow cooker, spiraling them toward the center. We found that leaving the membrane coating the underside of the ribs attached helped hold the racks together as they cooked (and, as a bonus, shortened our prep time). Once the ribs were fully tender, we transferred them to a wire rack set in a baking sheet and broiled them to develop an authentic crispy, lightly charred exterior. As they broiled, we brushed them with barbecue sauce every few minutes until they were sticky and caramelized. Avoid buying racks of ribs labeled only "spareribs"; their large size and irregular shape make them unwieldy in a slow cooker. St. Louis–style spareribs are smaller and more uniform in size and will fit nicely in a standard 6½-quart or larger slow cooker. You will need an oval slow cooker for this recipe.

3	**tablespoons paprika**
2	**tablespoons packed brown sugar**
¼	**teaspoon cayenne pepper**
	Salt and pepper
2	**(2½- to 3-pound) racks St. Louis–style spareribs**
1	**cup barbecue sauce**

1. Mix paprika, sugar, cayenne, 1 tablespoon salt, and 1 tablespoon pepper together in bowl and rub evenly over ribs. Arrange ribs upright in slow cooker with meaty sides facing outward. Cover and cook until ribs are tender, 4 to 5 hours on low.

2. Adjust oven rack 10 inches from broiler element and heat broiler. Place wire rack in aluminum foil–lined rimmed baking sheet and spray with vegetable oil spray. Transfer ribs, meaty side up, to prepared sheet. Brush ribs with some of barbecue sauce, then broil until browned and sticky, 10 to 15 minutes, flipping and brushing with additional sauce every few minutes. Serve ribs with remaining sauce.

QUICK PREP TIP ARRANGING RIBS IN A SLOW COOKER
To ensure that ribs cook evenly, stand racks up along perimeter of slow cooker with wide end down and meatier side of ribs facing slow-cooker insert wall.

Fiery Mustard Baby Back Ribs

Serves 4 to 6   **Cooking Time** 4 to 5 hours on Low   **Slow Cooker Size** 6½ to 7 Quarts

WHY THIS RECIPE WORKS: For those who like it spicy (and a little bit messy), we set out to make slow-cooker ribs that boasted tender, juicy meat and a sauce with a serious kick. We coated baby back ribs in a mixture of chili powder, salt, and pepper before placing them in the slow cooker. Once the ribs were tender, we got to work on a thick, spicy sauce to coat our ribs. We started with ½ cup of yellow mustard. Pickled banana peppers added tartness, and a minced habanero chile really brought home the heat. A little brown sugar lent a balancing sweetness. Finally, some chili sauce gave our sauce multidimensional flavor. A few minutes under the intense heat of the broiler while we periodically basted the ribs with our fiery mustard sauce built up flavor and gave our ribs the perfect sticky, charred exterior. Avoid racks of baby back ribs that are larger than 2 pounds as they will be difficult to maneuver into the slow cooker. Chili sauce (we used Heinz Chili Sauce here) is a lightly spiced condiment made with tomatoes, chiles or chili powder, onions, green peppers, vinegar, sugar, and spices. Don't confuse it with the chile sauces used in Asian cuisine. You will need an oval slow cooker for this recipe.

3	tablespoons chili powder
	Salt and pepper
2	(1½- to 2-pound) racks baby back ribs
½	cup yellow mustard
¼	cup jarred banana pepper rings, chopped fine, plus 2 tablespoons pickling juice
¼	cup packed brown sugar
¼	cup chili sauce
1	habanero chile, minced

1. Mix chili powder, 1 tablespoon salt, and 1 tablespoon pepper together in bowl and rub evenly over ribs. Arrange ribs upright in slow cooker with meaty sides facing outward. Cover and cook until ribs are tender, 4 to 5 hours on low.

2. Adjust oven rack 10 inches from broiler element and heat broiler. Place wire rack in aluminum foil–lined rimmed baking sheet and spray with vegetable oil spray. Whisk mustard, banana peppers and pickling juice, sugar, chili sauce, and habanero together in bowl. Transfer ribs, meaty side up, to prepared sheet. Brush ribs with some of sauce, then broil until browned and sticky, 10 to 15 minutes, flipping and brushing with additional sauce every few minutes. Serve ribs with remaining sauce.

QUICK PREP TIP WORKING WITH HABANEROS
Hotter than jalapeños and even serranos, habaneros are very spicy chiles and require proper handling. While working with habaneros, wear gloves to avoid direct contact with the oils that supply heat. If you don't wear gloves, make absolutely sure to wash your hands thoroughly immediately after handling the chile. Also wash your knife and cutting board well once you are finished prepping.

Porter-Braised Beef Short Ribs

Serves 4   **Cooking Time** 8 to 9 hours on Low or 5 to 6 hours on High
Slow Cooker Size 5½ to 7 Quarts

WHY THIS RECIPE WORKS: Beer-braised short ribs are classic pub fare, but when they're made in the slow cooker, the beer tends to turn bitter and the dish falls flat. To bring it back to life, we added some aromatics, including onions, garlic, tomato paste, and Worcestershire sauce. This combination gave our sauce rich flavor and a velvety texture. To make sure that the beer flavor came through, we chose full-bodied porter and added part of the beer at the end of cooking so that its flavor wouldn't be dulled by the long cooking time. A couple of tablespoons of instant tapioca helped to maintain a perfectly thick consistency. The well-marbled short ribs were fall-apart tender when they came out of the slow cooker, but we found that they shrank substantially as their fat rendered, so we started with large 10-ounce ribs to compensate. Look for boneless short ribs that are well marbled and measure about 2 inches wide and 1 inch thick. Serve over egg noodles or rice.

2	**cups chopped onions**
2	**tablespoons minced garlic**
2	**tablespoons tomato paste**
1	**tablespoon vegetable oil**
¾	**cup porter beer, such as Guinness or Newcastle**
2	**tablespoons instant tapioca**
2	**teaspoons Worcestershire sauce**
4	**(10-ounce) boneless beef short ribs**
	Salt and pepper
2	**tablespoons minced fresh parsley**

1. Microwave onions, garlic, tomato paste, and oil in bowl, stirring occasionally, until onions are softened, about 5 minutes; transfer to slow cooker. Stir in ½ cup beer, tapioca, and Worcestershire. Trim fat from top and bottom of short ribs, season with salt and pepper, and nestle into slow cooker. Cover and cook until beef is tender, 8 to 9 hours on low or 5 to 6 hours on high.

2. Transfer short ribs to serving dish and tent with aluminum foil. Strain braising liquid into fat separator, let sit for 5 minutes, then pour 1 cup defatted braising liquid into now-empty slow cooker; discard extra braising liquid. Stir in remaining ¼ cup beer and let sit until heated through, about 5 minutes. Stir in parsley and season with salt and pepper to taste. Pour sauce over short ribs. Serve.

QUICK PREP TIP **TRIMMING SHORT RIBS**
Short ribs are notoriously fatty and need to be trimmed well before cooking. Using sharp knife, trim away large piece of fat on top and, if necessary, any fat on bottom of each rib.

Rustic Italian Braised Beef Short Ribs

Serves 4 **Cooking Time** 8 to 9 hours on Low or 5 to 6 hours on High
Slow Cooker Size 5½ to 7 Quarts

✓ **WHY THIS RECIPE WORKS:** For braised beef short ribs with an Italian spin, we made a flavorful braise with classic Italian ingredients. Starting with the aromatics, we softened onions and bloomed tomato paste, garlic, oil, oregano, and red pepper flakes in the microwave. We added this flavor-packed mixture to the slow cooker with a can of whole peeled tomatoes. As the short ribs simmered, the tomatoes broke down and melded with the aromatic ingredients and meaty short ribs to create a hearty tomato sauce reminiscent of a traditional Sunday gravy. Once the short ribs were meltingly tender, we defatted the sauce, then stirred it back into the tomatoes, breaking the tomatoes into large chunks. A generous sprinkling of fresh basil finished the dish on a bright note. Look for boneless short ribs that are well marbled and measure about 2 inches wide and 1 inch thick.

2	**cups chopped onions**
10	**garlic cloves, sliced thin**
3	**tablespoons tomato paste**
1	**tablespoon olive oil**
1	**teaspoon dried oregano**
½	**teaspoon red pepper flakes**
1	**(28-ounce) can whole peeled tomatoes, drained**
4	**(10-ounce) boneless beef short ribs**
	Salt and pepper
¼	**cup chopped fresh basil**

1. Microwave onions, garlic, tomato paste, oil, oregano, and pepper flakes in bowl, stirring occasionally, until onions are softened, about 5 minutes; transfer to slow cooker. Stir in tomatoes. Trim fat from top and bottom of short ribs, season with salt and pepper, and nestle into slow cooker. Cover and cook until beef is tender, 8 to 9 hours on low or 5 to 6 hours on high.

2. Transfer short ribs to serving dish and tent with aluminum foil. Strain sauce into fat separator, reserving tomatoes, and let sit for 5 minutes. Add reserved tomatoes to now-empty slow cooker and break into large chunks with back of wooden spoon. Stir in defatted sauce and season with salt and pepper to taste. Pour sauce over short ribs and sprinkle with basil. Serve.

ON THE SIDE CHEESY POLENTA
Bring 2 cups water and 2 cups milk to boil in large saucepan. Slowly whisk in 1 cup instant polenta. Cook, stirring constantly, until polenta is thickened, about 3 minutes. Stir in ¾ cup grated Parmesan cheese and season with salt and pepper to taste. Serves 4.

Spiced Pork Tenderloin with Couscous

Serves 4   **Cooking Time** 1 to 2 hours on Low   **Slow Cooker Size** 5½ to 7 Quarts

✔ **WHY THIS RECIPE WORKS:** We wanted to make tender pork tenderloin with warm spices and an easy side dish—all in the slow cooker. First, we seasoned the pork with a fragrant spice rub. In place of a laundry list of spices, we used garam masala (an Indian spice blend) for complex flavor. Once the pork was cooked, we used the potent cooking liquid to make couscous. We simply stirred the couscous into the slow cooker along with some raisins and almonds, and 15 minutes later we had a richly flavored couscous salad. An easy fresh parsley vinaigrette rounded out the flavors of the spiced pork and couscous. Be sure to use regular (or fine-grain) couscous; large-grain couscous, often labeled Israeli-style, takes much longer to cook and won't work here. Because it is cooked gently and not browned, the tenderloin will be rosy throughout even once it registers 145 degrees. Check the tenderloins' temperature after 1 hour of cooking and continue to monitor until they register 145 degrees. You will need an oval slow cooker for this recipe.

1	cup chicken broth
4	teaspoons minced garlic
2	(12- to 16-ounce) pork tenderloins, trimmed
2	teaspoons garam masala Salt and pepper
1	cup couscous
½	cup raisins
¼	cup sliced almonds, toasted
½	cup extra-virgin olive oil
½	cup minced fresh parsley
2	tablespoons red wine vinegar

1. Combine broth and 2 teaspoons garlic in slow cooker. Season pork with garam masala, salt, and pepper. Nestle into slow cooker, side by side, alternating thicker end to thinner end. Cover and cook until pork is tender and registers 145 degrees, 1 to 2 hours on low.

2. Transfer pork to carving board and tent with aluminum foil. Strain cooking liquid into fat separator and let sit for 5 minutes. Reserve 1 cup defatted liquid; discard extra cooking liquid. Stir reserved liquid, couscous, and raisins into now-empty slow cooker. Cover and cook on high until couscous is tender, about 15 minutes. Fluff couscous with fork, then stir in almonds.

3. Whisk oil, parsley, vinegar, and remaining 2 teaspoons garlic together in bowl and season with salt and pepper to taste. Slice pork and serve with couscous and parsley vinaigrette.

QUICK PREP TIP **TOASTING NUTS AND SEEDS**
Toasting nuts and seeds maximizes their flavor and takes only a few minutes. To toast 1 cup or less of nuts or seeds, add to dry skillet over medium heat. Shake skillet occasionally to prevent scorching and toast until lightly browned and fragrant, 3 to 8 minutes. Watch nuts closely because they can go from golden to burnt very quickly. To toast more than 1 cup of nuts, spread nuts in single layer in rimmed baking sheet and toast in 350-degree oven. Toast, shaking baking sheet every few minutes, until nuts are lightly browned and fragrant, 5 to 10 minutes.

Hoisin-Glazed Pork Tenderloin

Serves 4   **Cooking Time** 1 to 2 hours on Low   **Slow Cooker Size** 5½ to 7 Quarts

✔ **WHY THIS RECIPE WORKS:** Cooking a lean roast like a pork tenderloin in a slow cooker is tricky because it can quickly turn overcooked and dry. We discovered that nestling two tenderloins side by side, alternating the narrow and thicker ends, helped to insulate the meat and prevented it from overcooking. We also monitored the temperature of the pork after a couple of hours and took it out of the slow cooker as soon as it reached 145 degrees. Once we had the method in hand, we flavored the pork with a sweet Asian-inspired glaze. A combination of chicken broth and ginger created a flavorful cooking liquid, then, once the pork was cooked, we added hoisin sauce and sesame oil to give the glaze additional flavor and body. A sprinkling of thinly sliced fresh scallions was the finishing touch. Because it is cooked gently and not browned, the tenderloin will be rosy throughout even once it registers 145 degrees. Check the tenderloins' temperature after 1 hour of cooking and continue to monitor until they register 145 degrees. You will need an oval slow cooker for this recipe. For a spicier glaze, use the larger amount of chili-garlic sauce. Serve with white rice.

¼ **cup chicken broth**

4 **teaspoons grated ginger**

2 **(12- to 16-ounce) pork tenderloins, trimmed**

Salt and pepper

½ **cup hoisin sauce**

1 **tablespoon toasted sesame oil**

1–2 **teaspoons Asian chili-garlic sauce**

2 **scallions, sliced thin**

1. Combine broth and 1 tablespoon ginger in slow cooker. Season pork with salt and pepper and nestle into slow cooker, side by side, alternating thicker end to thinner end. Cover and cook until pork is tender and registers 145 degrees, 1 to 2 hours on low.

2. Transfer pork to carving board and tent with aluminum foil. Stir remaining 1 teaspoon ginger, hoisin, sesame oil, and chili-garlic sauce into slow cooker and let sit until heated through, about 5 minutes. Season with salt and pepper to taste. Slice pork, drizzle with glaze, and sprinkle with scallions. Serve.

QUICK PREP TIP
PREPPING PORK TENDERLOIN
To remove sinewy silverskin, slip boning knife underneath silverskin, angle blade slightly upward, and use gentle back-and-forth motion to remove it from tenderloin. To ensure that tenderloins cook through evenly, nestle them into slow cooker, side by side, alternating thicker end to thinner end.

Game Day Brats and Beer

Serves 4   **Cooking Time** 2 to 3 hours on Low   **Slow Cooker Size** 5½ to 7 Quarts

✔ **WHY THIS RECIPE WORKS:** Nobody wants to be stuck in the kitchen on game day, so we wanted to develop a recipe for brats and beer that would simmer in the slow cooker while we joined the party. To make sure the bratwurst had plenty of flavor, we stirred a mixture of savory soy sauce, punchy Dijon mustard, caraway seeds, and a little balancing brown sugar into the slow cooker. Onions were also a must; we microwaved them briefly to ensure that they were fully tender by the time the brats were cooked through. We tested a variety of styles of beer to see which worked best. American lager was the winner thanks to its light, clean flavor that held up after hours of cooking. As the bratwurst cooked, the flavors in the pot melded and deepened, giving us rich, juicy sausage and flavorful onions. For the finishing touch, we stirred some tangy sauerkraut into the onion mixture to round out the dish. Light-bodied American lagers, such as Budweiser, work best for this recipe.

1	pound onions, sliced into ½-inch-thick rings
1	tablespoon vegetable oil
1½	pounds bratwurst
1	cup beer
¼	cup Dijon mustard
¼	cup soy sauce
2	tablespoons packed brown sugar
½	teaspoon caraway seeds
1	cup sauerkraut, rinsed and drained
4	(6-inch) sub rolls

1. Microwave onions and oil in bowl, stirring occasionally, until softened, about 8 minutes; transfer to slow cooker. Nestle sausage into slow cooker. Whisk beer, mustard, soy sauce, sugar, and caraway seeds together in bowl and pour over sausage. Cover and cook until sausage is tender, 2 to 3 hours on low.

2. Transfer sausage to cutting board and tent with aluminum foil. Stir sauerkraut into slow cooker and let sit until heated through, about 5 minutes. Strain onion-sauerkraut mixture, discarding liquid, and transfer to bowl. Cut bratwurst into 2-inch pieces. Serve on rolls with onion-sauerkraut mixture and extra mustard.

SMART SHOPPING BRATWURST

At Midwestern barbecues and tailgates, these sweet and herbal sausages are more common than hot dogs. They are made from ground pork and veal lightly seasoned with caraway, coriander, ginger, and nutmeg. We prefer the coarse texture of fresh, uncooked bratwurst to the mealiness of partially cooked versions.

Street Fair Sausages with Peppers and Onions

Serves 4   **Cooking Time** 2 to 3 hours on Low   **Slow Cooker Size** 5½ to 7 Quarts

✔ **WHY THIS RECIPE WORKS:** For a fun and easy weeknight meal, we used the slow cooker to make super-flavorful peppers and onions together with perfectly cooked Italian sausage. First, we jump-started the vegetables in the microwave to ensure that they'd cook through, then we added them to the slow cooker and nestled in raw Italian sausages. To season the vegetables as they cooked, we used a potent mixture of chicken broth, tomato paste, and garlic. As they simmered, the peppers and onions absorbed the flavors of the sausage and braising liquid. Once the sausages were cooked through, all we needed to do was strain the peppers and onions and pile them high on sub rolls with the tender, juicy sausages.

2	**red or green bell peppers, cored and cut into ¾-inch-wide strips**
2	**onions, sliced into ½-inch-thick rings**
2	**tablespoons tomato paste**
1	**tablespoon vegetable oil**
1	**teaspoon minced garlic**
½	**cup chicken broth**
1½	**pounds hot or sweet Italian sausage**
	Salt and pepper
4	**(6-inch) sub rolls**

1. Microwave peppers, onions, tomato paste, oil, and garlic in bowl, stirring occasionally, until vegetables are softened, about 8 minutes; transfer to slow cooker. Stir in broth. Nestle sausage into slow cooker, cover, and cook until sausage is tender, 2 to 3 hours on low.

2. Transfer sausage to cutting board and tent with aluminum foil. Strain vegetable mixture, discarding liquid, and transfer to bowl. Season with salt and pepper to taste. Cut sausage into 2-inch pieces. Serve on rolls with pepper-onion mixture.

QUICK PREP TIP
SLICING ONIONS INTO RINGS
To slice onion into rings, start by trimming ¼ inch from one curved side to create flat surface for steady cutting. Place onion cut side down on board, then slice into ½-inch rings.

Greek-Style Stuffed Bell Peppers

Serves 4   **Cooking Time** 4 to 5 hours on Low or 3 to 4 hours on High
Slow Cooker Size 5½ to 7 Quarts

✔ **WHY THIS RECIPE WORKS:** Traditional versions of stuffed peppers can be problematic, with bland fillings and tough or mushy peppers, so we knew that creating an easy stuffed pepper recipe in the slow cooker would require some tinkering. We also wanted to add everything straight to the slow cooker without spending time precooking the meatloaf mix or the peppers. We just needed to get the bell peppers to soften in the time it took the meat to cook through. The trick was to add a little water to the slow cooker so the peppers gently steamed until they were just crisp-tender. Precooked white rice was a great timesaver and was readily available at the supermarket. To give the filling bold Greek flavors, we added crumbled feta cheese, kalamata olives, and garlic and oregano for aroma. We topped the cooked peppers with a slice of provolone cheese and a sprinkling of scallions. Choose peppers with flat bottoms so that they stay upright in the slow cooker. Meatloaf mix is a prepackaged mix of ground beef, pork, and veal; if it's unavailable, use 8 ounces each of ground pork and 85 percent lean ground beef. Feel free to use leftover rice or precooked rice from the supermarket.

4	**(6-ounce) red, orange, or yellow bell peppers**
1	**pound meatloaf mix**
¾	**cup crumbled feta cheese**
¾	**cup cooked rice**
½	**cup pitted kalamata olives, chopped fine**
3	**scallions, sliced thin**
1	**tablespoon minced garlic**
1	**teaspoon dried oregano**
1	**teaspoon salt**
4	**slices deli provolone cheese**

1. Trim ½ inch off top of each pepper, then remove core and seeds. Finely chop pepper tops, discarding stems. Gently mix chopped peppers, meatloaf mix, feta, rice, olives, two-thirds of scallions, garlic, oregano, and salt together in bowl with hands until thoroughly combined. Pack filling evenly into cored peppers.

2. Pour ⅓ cup water into slow cooker. Place stuffed peppers upright in slow cooker. Cover and cook until peppers are tender, 4 to 5 hours on low.

3. Top each pepper with 1 slice provolone, cover, and continue to cook on high until cheese is melted, about 5 minutes. Using tongs and slotted spoon, transfer peppers to serving dish; discard cooking liquid. Sprinkle with remaining scallions and serve.

QUICK PREP TIP MAKING STUFFED PEPPERS
Arrange stuffed peppers in slow cooker, leaning them against one another and sides of slow-cooker insert, so that they remain upright during cooking.

Italian Meatloaf

Serves 4 to 6   **Cooking Time** 3 to 4 hours on Low or 2 to 3 hours on High
Slow Cooker Size 5½ to 7 Quarts

WHY THIS RECIPE WORKS: Slow-cooker meatloaf is often greasy and unappealing. To fix this, we started with meatloaf mix combined with a panade, which stayed moist and flavorful—but it was also mushy and greasy. To fix the mushy texture, we swapped the bread crumbs in the panade for extra-crunchy panko. We liked the ease of pressing the loaf directly into the slow cooker, but when we tried to pull it out, it fell apart. Our solution was a simple aluminum foil sling. The sling also solved our grease problem: Once we had removed the sling with the meatloaf, it was easy to skim the extra fat from the sauce. For Italian flair, we added jarred marinara sauce and topped the loaf with a layer of provolone cheese. Meatloaf mix is a prepackaged mix of ground beef, pork, and veal; if it's unavailable, use 1 pound each of ground pork and 85 percent lean ground beef. You will need an oval slow cooker for this recipe.

½   **cup panko bread crumbs**
2½   **cups jarred marinara sauce**
2   **pounds meatloaf mix**
½   **cup grated Parmesan cheese**
5   **tablespoons chopped fresh basil**
1   **large egg, lightly beaten**
1   **teaspoon minced garlic**
    Salt and pepper
6   **ounces sliced deli provolone cheese**

1. Fold sheet of aluminum foil into 12 by 9-inch sling. Mash panko and ½ cup marinara sauce to paste in medium bowl with fork. Gently mix in meatloaf mix, Parmesan, ¼ cup basil, egg, garlic, ½ teaspoon salt, and ¼ teaspoon pepper with hands until thoroughly combined. Shape mixture into 9 by 4-inch loaf across center of foil sling.

2. Add remaining 2 cups marinara sauce to slow cooker. Using sling, transfer meatloaf to slow cooker and nestle into sauce. Cover and cook until meatloaf is tender, 3 to 4 hours on low.

3. Lay provolone on top of meatloaf, cover, and cook on high until cheese is melted, about 5 minutes. Using sling, transfer meatloaf to serving dish. Using large spoon, skim excess fat from surface of sauce. Stir in remaining 1 tablespoon basil and season with salt and pepper to taste. Slice meatloaf. Serve with sauce.

QUICK PREP TIP **PLACING MEATLOAF IN SLOW COOKER**
To make it easy to get the meatloaf in and out of the slow cooker, we use a foil sling. To make sling, fold sheet of aluminum foil into 12 by 9-inch rectangle, then shape meatloaf across center of sling into 9-inch-long loaf. Be sure to pack meat mixture well so it doesn't break apart while cooking.

Tex-Mex Meatloaf

Serves 4   **Cooking Time** 3 to 4 hours on Low or 2 to 3 hours on High
Slow Cooker Size 5½ to 7 Quarts

✔ **WHY THIS RECIPE WORKS:** To liven up classic, family-friendly meatloaf, we wanted to add flavorful Tex-Mex ingredients like chiles and taco seasoning. However, simply stirring these additions into our meatloaf mixture led to a loose, dry loaf. To add moisture and help bind the loaf together, we made a panade—but in place of the traditional combination of milk and bread crumbs, we used crispy panko bread crumbs and flavorful canned enchilada sauce. Our unique panade, along with the taco seasoning and some spicy chopped green chiles, gave us a moist, tender Tex-Mex meatloaf that had tasters raving. We wrapped the uncooked meatloaf in a foil sling for easy removal and nestled it in a combination of enchilada sauce and tomato sauce to make a flavorful sauce to serve with the meatloaf. A gooey topping of melted Mexican cheese blend was the finishing touch. Meatloaf mix is a prepackaged mix of ground beef, pork, and veal; if it's unavailable, use 1 pound each of ground pork and 85 percent lean ground beef. You will need an oval slow cooker for this recipe.

½ **cup panko bread crumbs**
1 **(10-ounce) can red enchilada sauce**
2 **pounds meatloaf mix**
½ **cup canned chopped green chiles**
1 **large egg, lightly beaten**
1 **(1-ounce) packet taco seasoning**
1 **(15-ounce) can tomato sauce**
1 **cup shredded Mexican cheese blend**
2 **tablespoons minced fresh cilantro**
   Salt and pepper

1. Fold sheet of aluminum foil into 12 by 9-inch sling. Mash panko and ½ cup enchilada sauce to paste in medium bowl with fork. Gently mix in meatloaf mix, chiles, egg, and taco seasoning with hands until thoroughly combined. Shape mixture into 9 by 4-inch loaf across center of foil sling.

2. Combine remaining enchilada sauce and tomato sauce in slow cooker. Using sling, transfer meatloaf to slow cooker and nestle into sauce. Cover and cook until meatloaf is tender, 3 to 4 hours on low.

3. Sprinkle Mexican cheese blend on top of meatloaf, cover, and cook on high until cheese is melted, about 5 minutes. Using sling, transfer meatloaf to serving dish. Using large spoon, skim excess fat from surface of sauce. Stir in cilantro and season with salt and pepper to taste. Slice meatloaf. Serve with sauce.

SMART SHOPPING ENCHILADA SAUCE
Here in the test kitchen we all agree that nothing beats fresh, homemade enchilada sauce, but we have found that canned sauce works well when time is short. We use both the red and green varieties. Both are thin and mostly smooth in consistency. While the red sauce, made from red chiles, is the more traditional choice, you will also see a green sauce (sometimes labeled "chile verde") made from green chiles. Enchilada sauces are available in both mild and hot varieties, so choose the heat level to suit your taste. Do not substitute thinner taco sauce for enchilada sauce.

Mexican-Style Pulled Pork Tacos

Serves 4 **Cooking Time** 9 to 10 hours on Low or 6 to 7 hours on High
Slow Cooker Size 5½ to 7 Quarts

✔ **WHY THIS RECIPE WORKS:** Weeknight tacos are usually limited to quick-cooking fillings like ground beef, but the slow cooker makes it easy to use cuts like pork butt that take several hours to turn tender. We wanted to make easy pulled pork tacos and pair them with a rich mole sauce. Traditionally mole requires an extensive list of ingredients to develop its complex flavor, but we simplified our version by relying on pantry staples like chili powder, cumin, and chipotle chiles. Canned tomato sauce added acidity, and raisins gave us just the right sweetness. Once the pork was cooked through, we quickly blended the sauce to give it the perfect consistency. A little lime juice and cilantro at the end balanced the flavors and completed the dish. Pork butt roast is often labeled Boston butt in the supermarket. For more information on warming tortillas, see page 112. Serve with sour cream, chopped onion, chopped cilantro, thinly sliced radishes, and/or lime wedges.

1   **(15-ounce) can tomato sauce**
1   **cup raisins**
2   **tablespoons chili powder**
2   **tablespoons ground cumin**
1   **tablespoon minced chipotle chile**
3   **garlic cloves, peeled**
1   **(3-pound) boneless pork butt roast**
    Salt and pepper
½   **cup minced fresh cilantro**
3   **tablespoons lime juice**
12 **(6-inch) corn tortillas, warmed**

1. Combine tomato sauce, raisins, chili powder, cumin, chipotle, and garlic in slow cooker. Slice pork roast crosswise into 4 equal pieces, trim excess fat, and season with salt and pepper. Nestle pork into slow cooker, cover, and cook until pork is tender, 9 to 10 hours on low or 6 to 7 hours on high.

2. Transfer pork to bowl and let cool slightly. Shred into bite-size pieces, discarding excess fat. Using large spoon, skim excess fat from surface of mole sauce.

3. Process sauce in blender until smooth, about 1 minute. Stir in cilantro and lime juice, season with salt and pepper to taste, and adjust sauce consistency with extra hot water as needed. Stir 2 cups sauce into shredded pork. Serve with warm tortillas and remaining sauce.

ON THE SIDE CHUNKY CHIPOTLE GUACAMOLE
Using potato masher, roughly mash 3 halved and pitted ripe avocados with ¼ cup minced fresh cilantro, 2 tablespoons minced red onion, 2 tablespoons lime juice, and 1 to 2 teaspoons minced chipotle chile in bowl. Season with salt and pepper to taste. Serves 4.

Poached Swordfish with Warm Tomato and Olive Relish

Serves 4   **Cooking Time** 1 to 2 hours on Low   **Slow Cooker Size** 5½ to 7 Quarts

✔ **WHY THIS RECIPE WORKS:** Hearty swordfish steaks are a great option for gentle poaching in the slow cooker because the low heat renders the fish exceptionally moist and tender. To keep the bottoms of the steaks from overcooking, we propped the steaks up on lemon slices. Removing the steaks from the slow cooker in one piece proved difficult, but a simple aluminum foil sling made this easier. A Mediterranean-style tomato and olive relish dressed up our swordfish and added big flavor. Use swordfish steaks of similar thickness so that they cook at the same rate. Because delicate fish can easily overcook in the slow cooker, it requires some monitoring (at least the first time you make it). Check the swordfish's temperature after 1 hour of cooking and continue to monitor until it registers 140 degrees. You will need an oval slow cooker for this recipe.

1   **lemon, sliced ¼ inch thick**

2   **tablespoons minced fresh parsley, stems reserved**

4   **(6- to 8-ounce) swordfish steaks, about 1¼ inches thick**
    Salt and pepper

1   **pound cherry tomatoes, halved**

½   **cup pitted salt-cured black olives, rinsed and halved**

1   **tablespoon minced garlic**

¼   **cup extra-virgin olive oil**

1. Fold sheet of aluminum foil into 12 by 9-inch sling and press widthwise into slow cooker. Arrange lemon slices in single layer in bottom of prepared slow cooker. Scatter parsley stems over lemon slices. Pour water into slow cooker until it is even with lemon slices (about ½ cup water). Season steaks with salt and pepper and lay on top of lemon slices. Cover and cook until swordfish flakes apart when gently prodded with paring knife and registers 140 degrees, 1 to 2 hours on low.

2. Microwave tomatoes, olives, and garlic in bowl until tomatoes begin to break down, about 4 minutes. Stir in oil and parsley and season with salt and pepper to taste.

3. Using sling, transfer steaks to baking sheet. Gently lift and tilt steaks with spatula to remove parsley stems and lemon slices. Transfer to plates; discard poaching liquid. Serve with relish.

QUICK PREP TIP REMOVING FISH FROM SLOW COOKER
To make it easy to remove delicate fish from the slow cooker, we use a foil sling. To form sling, fold sheet of aluminum foil into 12 by 9-inch rectangle and press widthwise into slow cooker. Before serving, use edges of sling as handles to lift fish out of slow cooker fully intact.

Poached Salmon with Grapefruit and Basil Relish

Serves 4   **Cooking Time** 1 to 2 hours on Low   **Slow Cooker Size** 5½ to 7 Quarts

✓ **WHY THIS RECIPE WORKS:** Poaching salmon in the slow cooker produces supremely tender, silky results, and when paired with a quick citrus relish, it makes a fresh and easy meal. Propping the fillets up on lemon slices added bright flavor and helped the salmon steam evenly. To solve the problem of getting the salmon out of the slow cooker, we made a simple foil sling, which made it easy to lift the fillets out. Use salmon fillets of similar thickness so that they cook at the same rate or buy a 1½- to 2-pound whole center-cut fillet and cut it into 4 equal pieces. Because delicate fish can easily overcook in the slow cooker, it requires some monitoring (at least the first time you make it). Check the salmon's temperature after 1 hour of cooking and continue to monitor until it registers 135 degrees. You will need an oval slow cooker for this recipe.

1   **lemon, sliced ¼ inch thick**
4   **(6- to 8-ounce) skin-on salmon fillets, about 1½ inches thick**
     Salt and pepper
2   **red grapefruits**
3   **tablespoons chopped fresh basil**
1   **shallot, minced**
2   **tablespoons extra-virgin olive oil**

1. Fold sheet of aluminum foil into 12 by 9-inch sling; press widthwise into slow cooker. Arrange lemon slices in single layer in bottom of prepared slow cooker. Pour water into slow cooker until it is even with lemon slices (about ½ cup water). Season fillets with salt and pepper; place skin-side down on top of lemon slices. Cover and cook until salmon is opaque throughout when checked with tip of paring knife and registers 135 degrees, 1 to 2 hours on low.

2. Cut away peel and pith from grapefruits. Cut grapefruits into 8 wedges, then slice each wedge crosswise into ½-inch-thick pieces. Combine grapefruit, basil, shallot, and oil in bowl and season with salt and pepper to taste.

3. Using sling, transfer fillets to baking sheet. Gently lift and tilt fillets with spatula to remove lemon slices and transfer to plates; discard poaching liquid. Serve with relish.

QUICK PREP TIP
CUTTING GRAPEFRUIT FOR RELISH
Slice off top and bottom of grapefruit, then cut away rind and pith using paring knife. Cut grapefruit into 8 wedges. Working with 2 wedges at a time, slice into ½-inch-thick pieces.

Big Roasts and Whole Birds

Pork Loin with Warm Dijon Potato Salad

Serves 6 to 8   **Cooking Time** 3½ to 4½ hours on Low   **Slow Cooker Size** 5½ to 7 Quarts

✓ WHY THIS RECIPE WORKS: A juicy pork loin and potato dinner is a great idea anytime of the week, but achieving one in the slow cooker is tricky. You need to ensure that the potatoes and meat cook through at the same time, and the lean pork can quickly turn overcooked and dry. We seasoned the pork generously with coriander, fennel, salt, and pepper and let it cook unattended for a few hours. Toward the end we monitored its temperature and took it out of the slow cooker as soon as it reached 140 degrees to ensure that it didn't overcook. To get the potatoes to cook at the same rate, we quartered them and gave them a head start in the microwave. While the pork rested, we turned the tender potatoes into a delicious side dish by tossing them with a simple zesty dressing flavored with minced shallot, Dijon mustard, and parsley. Look for small red potatoes measuring 1 to 2 inches in diameter; do not substitute full-size red potatoes or they will not cook through properly. A wider, shorter pork loin roast (about 9 inches long) will fit in the slow cooker best. Check the temperature of the pork loin after 3½ hours of cooking and continue to monitor until it registers 140 degrees. You will need an oval slow cooker for this recipe.

3	**pounds small red potatoes, quartered**
¼	**cup extra-virgin olive oil**
1	**(4-pound) boneless pork loin roast, trimmed**
1	**teaspoon ground coriander**
1	**teaspoon ground fennel**
	Salt and pepper
2	**shallots, minced**
3	**tablespoons minced fresh parsley**
3	**tablespoons white wine vinegar**
2	**tablespoons Dijon mustard**

1. Microwave potatoes and 1 tablespoon oil in covered bowl, stirring occasionally, until potatoes are almost tender, about 10 minutes; transfer to slow cooker. Season roast with coriander, fennel, salt, and pepper and nestle, fat side up, into slow cooker. Cover and cook until pork is tender and registers 140 degrees, 3½ to 4½ hours on low.

2. Transfer roast to carving board, tent with aluminum foil, and let rest for 15 minutes. Whisk remaining 3 tablespoons oil, shallots, parsley, vinegar, mustard, and ½ teaspoon salt together in large bowl. Using slotted spoon, transfer potatoes to bowl with dressing and toss to combine; discard cooking liquid. Season with salt and pepper to taste. Slice meat into ¼-inch-thick slices. Serve with potato salad.

SMART SHOPPING BUYING PORK LOIN ROASTS

Buying the right pork loin will make a difference in these slow-cooker recipes. Look for a 4-pound pork loin roast that is wide and short (about 9 inches long) and steer clear of those that are long and narrow. Narrow pork loins don't fit as easily into the slow cooker and are prone to overcooking because they cook through more quickly.

Pork Loin with Pears and Cherries

Serves 6 to 8   **Cooking Time** 3½ to 4½ hours on Low   **Slow Cooker Size** 5½ to 7 Quarts

✔ **WHY THIS RECIPE WORKS:** Rich pork and sweet, juicy fruits are a classic combination, so we paired pears and dried cherries with pork loin for an easy slow-cooker supper with lots of appeal. We cut the pears into quarters and microwaved them until almost tender so they would cook to the proper doneness in the same amount of time as the pork. Dried cherries were a convenient, prep-free addition, and they plumped up nicely as they cooked. Seasoning the pork with herbes de Provence gave it savory flavor that balanced the fruit's sweetness. To ensure that the pork was perfectly cooked and juicy, we cooked it gently on low. A little brown sugar and butter to finish created the perfect accompanying sauce. Make sure to use the ripest pears you can find; unripe pears will not cook through properly. A wider, shorter pork loin roast (about 9 inches long) will fit in the slow cooker best. Check the temperature of the pork loin after 3½ hours of cooking and continue to monitor until it registers 140 degrees. You will need an oval slow cooker for this recipe.

3   **pounds pears, peeled, quartered, and cored**
½   **cup dried cherries**
2   **tablespoons packed brown sugar**
1   **(4-pound) boneless pork loin roast, trimmed**
1   **tablespoon herbes de Provence**
Salt and pepper
2   **tablespoons unsalted butter**

1. Microwave pears in covered bowl, stirring occasionally, until almost tender, about 8 minutes; transfer to slow cooker. Stir in cherries and sugar. Season roast with herbes de Provence, salt, and pepper and nestle, fat side up, into slow cooker. Cover and cook until pork is tender and registers 140 degrees, 3½ to 4½ hours on low.

2. Transfer roast to carving board, tent with aluminum foil, and let rest for 15 minutes. Stir butter into pear mixture and season with salt and pepper to taste. Slice meat into ¼-inch-thick slices and serve with pear mixture.

ON THE SIDE TOASTED COUSCOUS

Toast couscous with olive oil (see chart for amounts and serving sizes) in skillet over medium heat, stirring occasionally, until lightly browned, 3 to 5 minutes; transfer to medium bowl. Stir in ½ teaspoon salt and boiling water, cover, and let sit until couscous is tender, about 12 minutes. Fluff with fork and season with salt and pepper to taste.

SERVES	COUSCOUS	OLIVE OIL	BOILING WATER
4	1½ cups	2 tablespoons	2 cups
6	2¼ cups	2 tablespoons	3 cups
8	3 cups	3 tablespoons	4 cups
10	3¾ cups	4 tablespoons	5 cups

Cuban-Style Pork Roast with Mojo Sauce

Serves 4 to 6   **Cooking Time** 8 to 9 hours on Low or 5 to 6 hours on High
Slow Cooker Size 5½ to 7 Quarts

WHY THIS RECIPE WORKS: Boldly spiced slow-cooked meats are classic Caribbean fare, and Cuban slow-roasted pork is one of the best examples. Traditionally. pork is marinated in a flavorful mixture of citrus, garlic, and spices and cooked over a fire. We wanted to bring it indoors with a no-fuss slow-cooker version featuring tender, flavorful meat and a bracing garlic-citrus sauce. Well-marbled pork shoulder was our cut of choice; it turned meltingly tender in the slow cooker. To ensure that it cooked evenly, we tied it to make it a more uniform shape. To keep our prep time short, we skipped the lengthy marinating and simply cooked the roast in an aromatic mixture of orange juice, onion, chipotle, oregano, and cumin. To re-create the tart Cuban *mojo* sauce, we combined olive oil and orange juice with a healthy dose of vinegar, garlic, oregano, and some ground cumin. With its citrusy spiced sauce and rich, tender pork, this dish will liven up any weeknight. Boneless pork butt roast is often labeled Boston butt in the supermarket. Serve with rice.

2	**cups water**
1	**onion, peeled and quartered through root end**
1	**tablespoon minced chipotle chile**
2	**teaspoons dried oregano**
1½	**teaspoons ground cumin**
	Salt and pepper
1	**orange, halved**
1	**(4-pound) boneless pork butt roast, trimmed**
½	**cup extra-virgin olive oil**
¼	**cup white vinegar**
4	**teaspoons minced garlic**

1. Combine water, onion, chipotle, 1 teaspoon oregano, 1 teaspoon cumin, 1 teaspoon salt, and ½ teaspoon pepper in slow cooker. Juice orange into bowl and remove any seeds. Measure out and reserve ¼ cup juice. Add remaining juice to slow cooker, then add spent orange halves.

2. Tie roast around circumference with kitchen twine, season with salt and pepper, and nestle into slow cooker. Cover and cook until pork is tender, 8 to 9 hours on low or 5 to 6 hours on high.

3. Transfer roast to carving board, tent with aluminum foil, and let rest for 15 minutes; discard cooking liquid. Whisk reserved orange juice, oil, vinegar, garlic, 1 teaspoon salt, 1 teaspoon pepper, remaining 1 teaspoon oregano, and remaining ½ teaspoon cumin together in bowl. Remove twine from roast and slice against grain into ½-inch-thick slices. Serve with sauce.

SMART SHOPPING EXTRA-VIRGIN OLIVE OIL
Extra-virgin olive oil is an essential ingredient in many dishes, but the available options can be overwhelming. Many things impact the quality and flavor of olive oil, but the type of olives, timing of harvest (earlier means greener, more peppery; later, more golden and mild), and processing are the most important factors. The best-quality oil comes from olives picked at their peak and processed quickly, without heat or chemicals (which coax more oil from the olives at the expense of flavor). Our favorite oils were made from a blend of olives and, thus, were well rounded. Our favorite is **Columela Extra Virgin Olive Oil** from Spain.

Southwestern Pork Roast

Serves 4 to 6   **Cooking Time** 8 to 9 hours on Low or 5 to 6 hours on High
Slow Cooker Size 5½ to 7 Quarts

✓ **WHY THIS RECIPE WORKS:** To put a Southwestern spin on a slow-cooker pork roast, we started with a well-marbled pork shoulder and seasoned it liberally with chili powder, oregano, salt, and pepper. We also added some of the spices to a mixture of canned tomato sauce and spicy chipotle chile to make a boldly flavored braising liquid. Blooming the spices in oil in the microwave gave them deeper, more complex flavors. As the roast cooked, it lent its juices to the braising liquid, transforming it into a meaty, spicy sauce. We simply skimmed off the excess fat and stirred in some cilantro while the roast rested, then sliced the roast and served it with the bold sauce. Boneless pork butt roast is often labeled Boston butt in the supermarket. Serve with rice.

1½ tablespoons chili powder
1 teaspoon dried oregano
   Salt and pepper
2 cups chopped onions
1 tablespoon vegetable oil
1 (15-ounce) can tomato sauce
2 teaspoons minced chipotle chile
1 (4-pound) boneless pork butt
   roast, trimmed
3 tablespoons minced fresh cilantro

1. Mix chili powder, oregano, 1 teaspoon salt, and 1 teaspoon pepper together in bowl. Microwave onions, oil, and half of spice mixture in separate bowl, stirring occasionally, until onions are softened, about 5 minutes; transfer to slow cooker. Stir in tomato sauce and chipotle.

2. Tie roast around circumference with kitchen twine, season with remaining spice mixture, and nestle into slow cooker. Cover and cook until pork is tender, 8 to 9 hours on low or 5 to 6 hours on high.

3. Transfer roast to carving board, tent with aluminum foil, and let rest for 15 minutes. Using large spoon, skim excess fat from surface of braising liquid. Stir in cilantro and season with salt and pepper to taste. Remove twine from roast and slice against grain into ½-inch-thick slices. Serve with sauce.

QUICK PREP TIP REVIVING TIRED HERBS

We rarely use an entire bunch of herbs at once. Inevitably, a few days later they look less than fresh, and we have to throw them out and start all over. Is there a way to revive tired herbs? With a little research, we found that soaking herbs in water restores the pressure of the cell contents against the cell wall, causing them to become firmer as the dehydrated cells plump up. So, to test the theory, we purposely let several bunches of parsley, cilantro, and mint sit in the refrigerator until they became limp, sorry-looking versions of their former selves, then we tried bringing the herbs back to life by soaking them in tepid and cold water. We found that trimming the stems, then soaking the herbs for 10 minutes in cold water perks them up better than tepid water. These herbs had a fresher look and an improved texture.

Holiday Glazed Ham

Serves 16 to 20   **Cooking Time** 5 to 6 hours on Low   **Slow Cooker Size** 6½ to 7 Quarts

✔ **WHY THIS RECIPE WORKS:** Every time a big holiday dinner rolls around, we find ourselves facing the eternal dilemma of how to pull off an abundance of dishes with just one oven. What if we could free up some oven space by cooking a beautifully bronzed glazed ham in the slow cooker? We lacquered hams with every thick, sticky, sugary coating we could think of, but every glaze slid right off in the moist environment of the slow cooker. What we needed was a glaze that wouldn't need to be cooked. It would need to come together easily and have a consistency thick enough to cling to the ham without needing to be reduced on the stovetop. We tested countless glazes in the microwave with results that ranged from hard and brittle to tough and chewy. Ultimately we found that equal parts dark brown sugar and apple jelly thickened with a tablespoon of cornstarch gave us the ideal consistency. Along with some Dijon mustard and pepper for balancing zest, our glaze had a sweet, fruity flavor that perfectly complemented the ham. Do not substitute spiral-cut ham, as it dries out during slow cooking. You will need an oval slow cooker for this recipe.

1	(6- to 7½-pound) cured bone-in ham
½	cup apple jelly
½	cup packed dark brown sugar
2	tablespoons Dijon mustard
1	tablespoon cornstarch
1	teaspoon pepper

1. Remove skin from exterior of ham and trim fat to ¼-inch thickness. Score remaining fat at 1-inch intervals in crosshatch pattern. Place ham, cut side down, in slow cooker. Add 1 cup water, cover, and cook until fat is rendered and ham registers 100 degrees, 5 to 6 hours on low.

2. Transfer ham to carving board, tent with aluminum foil, and let rest for 20 minutes. Microwave jelly, sugar, mustard, cornstarch, and pepper in bowl, stirring occasionally, until glaze is slightly thickened, about 3 minutes; let cool slightly. Brush ham evenly with glaze and let sit for 5 minutes. Carve and serve.

QUICK PREP TIP
PREPARING GLAZED HAM
Bone-in, uncut hams are the best choice for the slow cooker, but they do require some up-front work. To prepare ham, start by removing tough skin or rind with chef's knife, then carefully trim fat to ¼-inch thickness. Finally, slice 1-inch grid pattern into ham's exterior fat to help glaze adhere.

ALL ABOUT Roasts in the Slow Cooker

The slow cooker is a great vehicle for cooking roasts, especially for the busy cook who has little time to spend monitoring the oven. But simply placing a roast in the slow cooker and walking away isn't likely going to give you the results you are after. Here are a few important tips to ensure your roasts are successful every time.

TYPE OF ROAST	COOKING TIME ON LOW	COOKING TIME ON HIGH
Top Sirloin Beef Roast	2 to 3 hours	—
Boneless Beef Chuck-Eye Roast	9 to 10 hours	6 to 7 hours
Beef Brisket	8 to 9 hours	5 to 6 hours
Pork Tenderloin	1 to 2 hours	—
Boneless Pork Loin	3½ to 4½ hours	—
Boneless Pork Butt Roast	8 to 9 hours	5 to 6 hours
Ham	5 to 6 hours	—
Whole Chicken	4 to 5 hours	—
Turkey Breast	5 to 6 hours	—

Pick the Right Roast

When selecting roasts for the slow cooker, our first choices are those that benefit the most from braising, namely the tougher, fattier roasts like beef chuck, beef brisket, and pork butt. These cuts are ideal for the slow cooker because low and slow cooking turns the meat meltingly tender after hours of cooking (when the collagen in the meat has broken down). Leaner roasts such as pork loin, whole chickens, and bone-in turkey breasts also work well, though they require a bit more attention to cooking time and temperature to turn out properly. Avoid premium cuts like beef tenderloin and rib-eye—they would be a waste of money. Save them for the grill or oven.

PORK BUTT   CHUCK-EYE ROAST   PORK LOIN

Pay Attention to Positioning

In our testing, we learned that getting juicy roasts had a lot to do with how we positioned them in the slow cooker. Nestling two pork tenderloins side by side, alternating the narrow and thicker ends, helped to insulate the lean meat and prevent it from overcooking. Positioning larger roasts like brisket, pork loins, and turkey breasts fat and skin side up allowed more fat to render and baste the meat as it cooked. When it came to whole chickens, we found that the trick was to place them in the slow cooker breast side down. This allowed the fat from the legs and thighs to drip down onto the lean breast meat, and as the chicken released its juices, the breast became partially submerged in the rendered fat and juices, which helped it to retain moisture.

ALL ABOUT Roasts in the Slow Cooker

Secure Pot Roasts with Twine

Our favorite cuts for pot roast are a beef chuck-eye roast and a pork butt roast (also called Boston butt), because they are well marbled and become very tender over the long braising time. In our experience, these roasts often come unevenly cut or oddly shaped, so

to ensure that they cook evenly, we tie them once or twice around the center with kitchen twine to produce a more uniformly shaped roast that will cook through evenly.

Take Temperature of Lean Roasts

While well-marbled roasts can cook all day and still come out moist, leaner roasts like pork loins, whole chickens, and turkey breasts can easily dry out from overcooking. To make sure these roasts remain moist, we cook them on low and monitor their temperature toward the end of cooking and take them out of the slow cooker as soon as they reach the desired temperature.

TYPE OF ROAST	COOKING TEMP
Pork Tenderloin	145 degrees
Pork Loin	140 degrees
Beef Top Sirloin Roast	120–125 degrees
Chicken Breast	160 degrees
Chicken Thighs	175 degrees
Turkey Breast	160 degrees

Maximize Flavor

The moist environment and extended cooking times of the slow cooker are notorious for producing dull, washed out flavors. To prevent our roasts from turning out bland,

we season them liberally with spice rubs and convenient flavor-packed ingredients like barbecue sauce or prepared pesto. We also create concentrated bases for braising with plenty of aromatics and spices. As the roasts cook, they are infused with the bold flavor of the braising liquid.

Make a Sauce

Once our roasts are done, we put the flavorful cooking liquid to work by turning it into a sauce to serve

with the meat. Often all it needs is a quick skim to remove the excess fat from the surface and some salt and pepper for seasoning. We also frequently stir in some acidic citrus juice or vinegar or some chopped fresh herbs to brighten and balance the flavors.

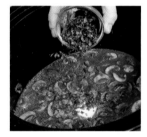

Make it a Meal

What's better than making a no-fuss roast in the slow cooker? Having a side dish to serve along with it. To get a complete meal all in one pot, we add beans, rice, and vegetables including potatoes, carrots, onions, and sweet

potatoes to the slow cooker along with our roasts. To ensure the vegetables cook through in time, we jumpstart them in the microwave before adding them to the slow cooker. Then, while our roast rests, we can quickly mash the sweet potatoes or toss the potatoes in dressing for an easy salad.

Atlanta Brisket

Serves 6   **Cooking Time** 8 to 9 hours on Low or 5 to 6 hours on High
Slow Cooker Size 5½ to 7 Quarts

✔ **WHY THIS RECIPE WORKS:** Atlanta brisket is a braised Southern dish featuring boxed onion soup mix, ketchup, and Atlanta's own Coca-Cola. For a slow-cooker version of this regional classic, we replaced the artificial-tasting soup mix with our own aromatic blend of softened onions, onion powder, garlic, brown sugar, and dried thyme. We stirred this into the slow cooker along with the ketchup and cola. We also included some instant tapioca to help thicken the braising liquid into a sweet yet savory sauce with caramelized complexity. The low, even heat of the slow cooker was perfect for getting meltingly tender brisket. Once the brisket was done, we simply sliced it and served it with the sweet and tangy sauce. You will need an oval slow cooker for this recipe.

1	**pound onions, halved and sliced ½ inch thick**
1	**tablespoon vegetable oil**
2	**teaspoons minced garlic**
1	**teaspoon dried thyme**
1	**(3-pound) beef brisket, flat cut, fat trimmed to ¼ inch**
	Salt and pepper
1	**cup cola**
¾	**cup ketchup**
2	**tablespoons instant tapioca**
4	**teaspoons onion powder**

1. Microwave onions, oil, garlic, and thyme in bowl, stirring occasionally, until onions are softened, about 5 minutes; transfer to slow cooker. Season brisket with salt and pepper and nestle, fat side up, into slow cooker. Whisk cola, ketchup, tapioca, onion powder, 1 teaspoon salt, and 1 teaspoon pepper together in bowl and pour over brisket. Cover and cook until beef is tender, 8 to 9 hours on low or 5 to 6 hours on high.

2. Transfer brisket to carving board, tent with aluminum foil, and let rest for 15 minutes. Using large spoon, skim excess fat from surface of sauce, then season with salt and pepper to taste. Slice meat against grain into ¼-inch-thick slices and transfer to serving dish. Pour 1 cup sauce over meat. Serve with remaining sauce.

ON THE SIDE QUICK COLLARD GREENS
Boil 2½ pounds collard greens, stemmed and leaves halved lengthwise, in large pot of salted boiling water until tender, about 5 minutes. Drain collards, then rinse with cold water; pat dry with paper towels. Cut greens crosswise into ¼-inch-thick slices. Heat 3 tablespoons vegetable oil in 12-inch nonstick skillet over medium-high heat until just smoking. Scatter greens in skillet and cook, stirring often, until just beginning to brown, about 4 minutes. Stir in 2 teaspoons minced garlic and ¼ teaspoon red pepper flakes and cook until greens are spotty brown, about 2 minutes. Season with salt and pepper to taste. Serves 6.

Classic Corned Beef and Cabbage Dinner

Serves 6   **Cooking Time** 9 to 10 hours on Low or 6 to 7 hours on High
Slow Cooker Size 6½ to 7 Quarts

✔ **WHY THIS RECIPE WORKS:** In the States, corned beef and cabbage is rarely eaten outside of St. Patrick's Day—and maybe for good reason. When traditionally boiled, the meat often comes out salty and dry, and the vegetables are usually overcooked and bland. We wanted to use the steady, gentle heat of the slow cooker to get moist, tender corned beef and perfectly cooked vegetables. We made a spiced braising liquid with chicken broth, peppercorns, allspice, and thyme, then gently simmered a corned beef brisket until it was moist, tender, and infused with the spices. Once the brisket was cooked, we put the flavorful cooking liquid to work, using it to microwave the cabbage so that it was perfectly tender, then pouring it over the meat to keep it moist and juicy. Small red potatoes and 3-inch pieces of carrots cooked to the perfect doneness along with the beef for a hearty winter meal. Look for small red potatoes measuring 1 to 2 inches in diameter; if your potatoes are larger, cut them into 1-inch pieces to ensure that they cook through. You will need an oval slow cooker for this recipe.

1   **(3-pound) corned beef brisket, rinsed and fat trimmed to ¼ inch**
2   **cups chicken broth**
2   **cups water**
1   **teaspoon dried thyme**
½   **teaspoon black peppercorns**
¼   **teaspoon whole allspice**
1½   **pounds small red potatoes**
1½   **pounds carrots, peeled, halved lengthwise, and cut into 3-inch lengths**
1   **head green cabbage (2 pounds), cut into 8 wedges**

1. Place corned beef, broth, water, thyme, peppercorns, and allspice in slow cooker. Place potatoes and carrots on top of brisket. Cover and cook until beef is tender, 9 to 10 hours on low or 6 to 7 hours on high.

2. Transfer vegetables to serving dish and cover tightly with aluminum foil. Transfer brisket to carving board, tent with foil, and let rest for 15 minutes. Using large spoon, skim excess fat from surface of cooking liquid.

3. Microwave cabbage and ½ cup cooking liquid in covered bowl until leaves of cabbage are pliable and translucent, about 15 minutes; transfer to serving dish. Slice meat against grain into ¼-inch-thick slices and transfer to serving dish. Moisten corned beef and vegetables with cooking liquid as needed before serving.

QUICK PREP TIP **SERVING BEEF BRISKET**
When serving brisket, it is important to slice it thin (we're talking about ¼ inch) and against the grain in order for the meat to taste tender. If the slices are cut too thick, the meat will have a tougher, chewy texture.

Easy Roast Beef with Mushroom Gravy

Serves 6   **Cooking Time** 2 to 3 hours on Low   **Slow Cooker Size** 5½ to 7 Quarts

✓ **WHY THIS RECIPE WORKS:** Achieving a tender and rosy roast beef with a slow cooker may seem impossible, but it's actually easier than you think. We found that timing was everything—the key to a perfectly medium-rare roast was to monitor the temperature of the roast after a couple of hours and take it out of the slow cooker once it registered between 120 and 125 degrees. In our winning slow cooker (see pages 6–7 for our testing results), the roast was perfectly cooked after three hours. We chose a top sirloin roast for its beefy flavor and reasonable price. After trimming excess fat from the roast, we seasoned it with salt and pepper and placed it in the slow cooker. We skipped browning the roast to keep things simple, then to give the roast plenty of meaty flavor, we made a rich gravy to pair with the beef. For the easiest-ever gravy, we came up with a surprisingly tasty shortcut: condensed French onion soup. This flavor-packed ingredient already contained plenty of aromatics and, along with some savory tomato paste, gave us an instant beefy gravy base. We also tossed in some sliced mushrooms for extra heft. A pat of butter and some fresh parsley to finish gave the gravy richness and color, perfect for serving over thin slices of the rosy roast. Check the temperature of the roast after 2 hours of cooking and continue to monitor until it registers 120 to 125 degrees.

1 **(10.5-ounce) can condensed French onion soup**
2 **tablespoons tomato paste**
8 **ounces sliced cremini mushrooms**
1 **(3-pound) beef top sirloin roast, trimmed**
   Salt and pepper
2 **tablespoons minced fresh parsley**
1 **tablespoon unsalted butter**

1. Whisk soup and tomato paste together in slow cooker; stir in mushrooms. Season roast with salt and pepper and nestle into slow cooker. Cover and cook until beef is tender and registers 120 to 125 degrees (for medium-rare), 2 to 3 hours on low.

2. Transfer roast to carving board, tent with aluminum foil, and let rest for 15 minutes. Using large spoon, skim excess fat from surface of gravy. Whisk in parsley and butter and season with salt and pepper to taste. Slice meat thin against grain. Serve with gravy.

ON THE SIDE POTATOES WITH LEMON AND PARSLEY
In large pot, simmer 1½ pounds small red potatoes, 1 tablespoon salt, and enough water to cover potatoes by 1 inch, covered, stirring once or twice, until potatoes are just tender, 10 to 14 minutes. Drain well. Cut potatoes in half, transfer to bowl, and toss with 3 tablespoons extra-virgin olive oil, 3 tablespoons chopped fresh parsley, and 1½ teaspoons grated lemon zest. Season with salt and pepper to taste. Serves 6.

Classic Pot Roast

Serves 6   **Cooking Time** 9 to 10 hours on Low or 6 to 7 hours on High
Slow Cooker Size 5½ to 7 Quarts

☑ **WHY THIS RECIPE WORKS:** The slow, even, and moist heat of the slow cooker is the perfect environment for creating a delicious, fork-tender pot roast. We wanted a pot roast with classic flavors that was easy to assemble. We started with a chuck-eye roast—our favorite cut for pot roast because it's well marbled with fat and connective tissue—and tied it around the center to help it cook more evenly. Usually pot roast is simmered in broth with a mix of spices or herbs plus chopped onions and garlic. To cut out all that prep work, we turned to condensed French onion soup. This single convenience product, along with some dried porcini mushrooms, created a beefy braising liquid with built-in aromatic flavor. Plus, its condensed state meant that the sauce wouldn't get watered down as the meat released its juices. We cooked the roast until it was perfectly tender and our finished jus had great body and complex flavor—you'd never guess it wasn't made from scratch. Finally, to make a hearty meal, we arranged small, unpeeled potatoes and baby carrots on top of the meat before cooking it. Look for small Yukon Gold potatoes measuring 1 to 2 inches in diameter; if your potatoes are larger, cut them into 1-inch pieces to ensure that they cook through.

1 **(10.5-ounce) can condensed French onion soup**

2 **tablespoons tomato paste**

½ **ounce dried porcini mushrooms, rinsed**

1 **(3-pound) boneless beef chuck-eye roast, trimmed**
  Salt and pepper

2 **pounds small Yukon Gold potatoes**

1 **pound baby carrots**

1. Whisk soup, tomato paste, and mushrooms together in slow cooker. Tie roast around circumference with kitchen twine, season with salt and pepper, and nestle into slow cooker. Place potatoes and carrots on top of roast. Cover and cook until beef is tender, 9 to 10 hours on low or 6 to 7 hours on high.

2. Transfer roast to carving board, tent with aluminum foil, and let rest for 15 minutes. Transfer vegetables to serving dish and cover tightly with foil. Using large spoon, skim excess fat from surface of sauce, then season with salt and pepper to taste. Remove twine from roast and slice against grain into ½-inch-thick slices. Serve with vegetables and sauce.

Whole "Roast" Pesto Chicken

Serves 4   **Cooking Time** 4 to 5 hours on Low   **Slow Cooker Size** 5½ to 7 Quarts

✔ **WHY THIS RECIPE WORKS:** Getting a perfectly cooked, juicy whole chicken out of a slow cooker is actually much easier than it sounds. In our testing, we learned that the trick to getting a juicy chicken was to place the chicken in the slow cooker upside down. This was important for two reasons: First, it put the lean breast meat underneath the fattier legs and thighs, so that as the juices and fat rendered from the thighs, they dripped over the breast meat. Second, as the juices pooled in the bottom of the slow cooker, the breast was submerged, further helping the lean meat to retain moisture. For a big boost of flavor without any fuss, we turned to nutty, cheesy prepared basil pesto, which we spread both over and under the skin of the chicken. Check the temperature of the chicken after 4 hours of cooking and continue to monitor until breast registers 160 degrees and thighs register 175 degrees. You will need an oval slow cooker for this recipe.

1 **(4½- to 5-pound) whole chicken, giblets discarded**
1 **cup prepared basil pesto**
   Salt and pepper

1. Use your fingers to gently loosen skin covering breast and thighs of chicken; place ¼ cup pesto under skin, directly on meat of breast and thighs. Gently press on skin to distribute pesto over meat. Spread entire exterior surface of chicken with ¼ cup pesto and place, breast side down, in slow cooker. Cover and cook until breast registers 160 degrees and thighs register 175 degrees, 4 to 5 hours on low.

2. Transfer chicken to carving board, tent with aluminum foil, and let rest for 15 minutes. Strain cooking liquid into fat separator and let sit for 5 minutes; reserve ½ cup defatted liquid. Combine reserved liquid and remaining ½ cup pesto in bowl and season with salt and pepper to taste. Carve chicken, discarding skin if desired, and serve with sauce.

QUICK PREP TIP PASTE IT ON
Distributing a flavorful paste (or sauce) both over and under the skin of the chicken ensures the best taste. To do this, loosen skin from over thighs and breast and rub half of paste directly over meat. Spread remaining paste over skin of entire chicken.

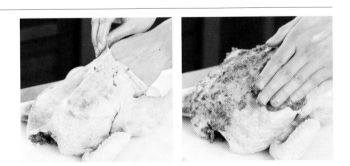

Whole "Roast" Spice-Rubbed Chicken

Serves 4   **Cooking Time** 4 to 5 hours on Low   **Slow Cooker Size** 5½ to 7 Quarts

✓ **WHY THIS RECIPE WORKS:** Inspired by the success of our Whole "Roast" Pesto Chicken (page 165), we wanted to create a version with a fragrant, warm spice rub. To make the spice blend, we combined garam masala, chili powder, garlic, salt, and pepper. But when we simply rubbed the chicken with the spice mixture, we were disappointed with the results. The meat had weak flavor at best, and, even after hours in the slow cooker, the spices had a raw, harsh flavor. We found that the solution was to microwave the spices with a little oil to bloom their flavors before rubbing them onto the chicken. Now our chicken was moist and juicy and had the bold, warmly spiced flavor we were hoping for. Note that garam masala is a boldly flavored spice blend; its potency will vary from brand to brand. Check the temperature of the chicken after 4 hours of cooking and continue to monitor until breast registers 160 degrees and thighs register 175 degrees. You will need an oval slow cooker for this recipe.

2 **tablespoons vegetable oil**

1 **tablespoon chili powder**

1 **tablespoon garam masala**

1 **tablespoon minced garlic**
   Salt and pepper

1 **(4½- to 5-pound) whole chicken, giblets discarded**

1. Microwave oil, chili powder, garam masala, garlic, 2 teaspoons salt, and 2 teaspoons pepper in bowl, stirring occasionally, until fragrant, about 1 minute; let cool slightly.

2. Use your fingers to gently loosen skin covering breast and thighs of chicken; place half of paste under skin, directly on meat of breast and thighs. Gently press on skin to distribute paste over meat. Spread entire exterior surface of chicken with remaining paste and place chicken, breast side down, in slow cooker. Cover and cook until breast registers 160 degrees and thighs register 175 degrees, 4 to 5 hours on low.

3. Transfer chicken to carving board, tent with aluminum foil, and let rest for 15 minutes. Carve chicken, discarding skin if desired. Serve.

ON THE SIDE LEMONY STEAMED BROCCOLI
Microwave 1 pound broccoli florets and ¼ cup water in large covered bowl until broccoli is bright green and tender, about 4 minutes. Drain broccoli, toss with 2 tablespoons melted butter and 1 tablespoon lemon juice, and season with salt and pepper to taste. Serves 4.

Whole Barbecue Chicken with Mashed Sweet Potatoes

Serves 4   **Cooking Time** 4 to 5 hours on Low   **Slow Cooker Size** 5½ to 7 Quarts

✔ **WHY THIS RECIPE WORKS:** Looking for another way to flavor a whole chicken, we turned to barbecue sauce, which we rubbed under the skin and all over the outside of the chicken. As the chicken cooked, the sauce infused the meat with great barbecue flavor and thickened to a nice glazed consistency. And since sweet potatoes are a natural partner to barbecue-flavored chicken, we cooked them along with the chicken. A quick stint in the microwave before going into the slow cooker ensured that they would cook through by the time the chicken was done. Then, while the chicken rested, we mashed the potatoes with some butter and cream for extra richness. Finally, we took advantage of some of the leftover cooking liquid, mixing it with more barbecue sauce to create a simple sauce for serving. Check the temperature of the chicken after 4 hours of cooking and continue to monitor until breast registers 160 degrees and thighs register 175 degrees. You will need an oval slow cooker for this recipe.

2   pounds sweet potatoes, peeled and cut into 1-inch pieces

1   tablespoon vegetable oil

1   (4½- to 5-pound) whole chicken, giblets discarded

1   cup barbecue sauce

4   tablespoons unsalted butter, melted

¼   cup heavy cream, warmed
     Salt and pepper

1. Microwave potatoes and oil in covered bowl, stirring occasionally, until potatoes are almost tender, about 10 minutes; transfer to slow cooker.

2. Use your fingers to gently loosen skin covering breast and thighs of chicken; place ¼ cup barbecue sauce under skin, directly on meat of breast and thighs. Gently press on skin to distribute sauce over meat. Spread entire exterior surface of chicken with ¼ cup barbecue sauce and place, breast side down, on top of potatoes. Cover and cook until breast registers 160 degrees and thighs register 175 degrees, 4 to 5 hours on low.

3. Transfer chicken to carving board and tent with aluminum foil. Using slotted spoon, transfer potatoes to large bowl. Strain cooking liquid into fat separator and let sit for 5 minutes; reserve ½ cup defatted liquid.

4. Add melted butter and cream to potatoes and mash with potato masher until smooth. Season with salt and pepper to taste. Combine reserved liquid and remaining ½ cup barbecue sauce in separate bowl and season with salt and pepper to taste. Carve chicken, discarding skin if desired. Serve with mashed potatoes and barbecue sauce.

Cajun Turkey Breast with Red Beans and Rice

Serves 6 to 8   **Cooking Time** 5 to 6 hours on Low   **Slow Cooker Size** 5½ to 7 Quarts

✓ **WHY THIS RECIPE WORKS:** For a turkey dinner that feeds a crowd—but not an army—bone-in turkey breast is a great option. It didn't require any prep work; we simply added it to the slow cooker and walked away while the low, gentle heat kept the lean meat tender and moist. To spice up the mild-tasting turkey, we had Cajun flavors in mind. While we were at it, we also would create a smoky, spicy side of red beans and rice. To prepare the turkey breast, we simply seasoned it with salt, pepper, and a generous amount of Cajun seasoning. Canned kidney beans were convenient, and they cooked through in the same amount of time as the turkey. We combined the beans with spicy andouille sausage and cooked them underneath the turkey so that the beans absorbed the rich flavors of the rendered juices. While the turkey rested, we stirred cooked wild rice into the beans and sausage. A splash of red wine vinegar and a sprinkling of scallions before serving provided welcome brightness. You can find precooked wild rice in the pasta aisle of the supermarket. If the turkey breast's backbone and wings are still intact, you may need to remove them to fit the breast in the slow cooker. Check the temperature of the turkey breast after 5 hours of cooking and continue to monitor until it registers 160 degrees. You will need an oval slow cooker for this recipe.

2 **(15-ounce) cans dark red kidney beans, rinsed**

8 **ounces andouille sausage, halved lengthwise and sliced ¼ inch thick**

1 **tablespoon minced garlic**

1 **(6- to 7-pound) whole bone-in turkey breast, trimmed**

1 **tablespoon Cajun seasoning Salt and pepper**

4 **cups cooked wild rice**

6 **scallions, sliced thin**

1 **tablespoon red wine vinegar**

1. Combine beans, andouille, and garlic in slow cooker. Season turkey with Cajun seasoning, salt, and pepper and nestle, skin side up, into slow cooker. Cover and cook until turkey is tender and registers 160 degrees, 5 to 6 hours on low.

2. Transfer turkey to carving board, tent with aluminum foil, and let rest for 20 minutes. Stir rice into bean mixture, cover, and cook on high until heated through, about 10 minutes. Stir in scallions and vinegar and season with salt, pepper, and extra vinegar to taste. Carve turkey, discarding skin if desired. Serve with beans and rice.

SMART SHOPPING CANNED KIDNEY BEANS

To see whether the brand of canned kidney beans you buy matters, we put six brands through side-by-side taste tests. Tasting them both straight from the can and in a simple chili recipe, we noticed substantial differences in both texture and flavor among the various brands. While some brands tasted mushy, chalky, and bland, **Goya Dark Red Kidney Beans** were "beautiful, plump red beans" with a "very sweet, strong bean flavor."

Turkey Breast with Cranberry and Pear Sauce

Serves 6 to 8   **Cooking Time** 5 to 6 hours on Low   **Slow Cooker Size** 5½ to 7 Quarts

✔ **WHY THIS RECIPE WORKS:** We often think of turkey as being reserved for big holiday dinners, but cooking just the turkey breast hands-off in the slow cooker makes this recipe weeknight friendly. The bone-in turkey breast is prep free, and the gentle heat of the slow cooker produces moist and tender meat every time. For a classic accompaniment to roast turkey, a batch of cranberry sauce seemed like the perfect choice. To keep it interesting, we included pears, spicy ginger, and cinnamon. By the time the turkey was fully cooked, the pears were tender and the flavors of the spices had melded and deepened. This sauce tasted great, but it lacked the thick, gel-like consistency of traditional cranberry sauce. To give it a thicker consistency, we simply mashed the cranberries and pears together until almost smooth. If using frozen cranberries, do not defrost. If the turkey breast's backbone and wings are still intact, you may need to remove them to fit the breast in the slow cooker. Check the temperature of the turkey breast after 5 hours of cooking and continue to monitor until it registers 160 degrees. You will need an oval slow cooker for this recipe.

12   ounces (3 cups) fresh or frozen cranberries

2   pears, peeled, halved, cored, and cut into 1-inch pieces

1   cup sugar

2   tablespoons grated ginger

½   teaspoon ground cinnamon
  Salt and pepper

1   (6- to 7-pound) whole bone-in turkey breast, trimmed

1. Combine cranberries, pears, sugar, ginger, cinnamon, and ½ teaspoon salt in slow cooker. Season turkey with salt and pepper and nestle, skin side up, into slow cooker. Cover and cook until turkey is tender and registers 160 degrees, 5 to 6 hours on low.

2. Transfer turkey to carving board, tent with aluminum foil, and let rest for 20 minutes. Mash cranberries and pears with potato masher until almost smooth. Season with salt and pepper to taste. Carve turkey, discarding skin if desired. Serve with sauce.

ON THE SIDE **EASY MASHED POTATOES**

Cover 4 pounds russet potatoes, peeled, sliced ¾ inch thick, and rinsed well, with water in Dutch oven. Bring to boil, then reduce to simmer and cook until tender, 18 to 20 minutes. Drain potatoes, wipe pot dry, then return potatoes to pot. Mash potatoes thoroughly with potato masher. Fold in 12 tablespoons melted unsalted butter, then fold in 2 cups hot half-and-half, adding more as needed. Season with salt and pepper to taste. Serves 6 to 8. (This recipe can be halved to serve 4.)

Pasta and Pasta Sauces

Penne alla Vodka

Serves 4 to 6   **Cooking Time** 3 to 4 hours on High   **Slow Cooker Size** 5½ to 7 Quarts

✓ **WHY THIS RECIPE WORKS:** Most recipes where raw pasta is tossed into the slow cooker are a huge letdown, resulting in pasta that's mushy or blown out. We wanted to devise a way to take advantage of this convenient appliance to turn out both a flavorful sauce and tender pasta, for a complete dinner that was light on prep. Numerous tests and many pounds of pasta later, we discovered two keys to tender slow-cooked pasta. First, we "toasted" the raw pasta in the microwave in a bit of olive oil for a few minutes, which guaranteed our pasta didn't become blown out in the slow cooker. Then, we combined the pasta with boiling water to jump-start the cooking process before adding the sauce. Placing a foil collar on one side of the slow cooker ensured that the pasta cooked through evenly. For a bright and tangy vodka sauce to accompany our pasta, we tried combining a variety of canned tomato products with vodka; a good dose of heavy cream ensured it was plenty rich. But when we stirred in more sauce at the end to liven up the dish, we were disappointed to find that it tasted one-dimensional and had a raw tomato flavor. Jarred marinara sauce, which is cooked, worked much better and offered long-simmered depth and complexity. For more information on cooking pasta in the slow cooker and making a foil collar, see page 180.

1	**pound penne**
1	**tablespoon olive oil**
1	**cup boiling water**
2	**(25-ounce) jars marinara sauce (6 cups)**
¼	**cup vodka**
	Salt and pepper
⅛	**teaspoon red pepper flakes**
¾	**cup heavy cream**
¼	**cup chopped fresh basil**

1. Line slow cooker with aluminum foil collar and spray with vegetable oil spray. Microwave penne and oil in bowl at 50 percent power, stirring occasionally, until some pieces look toasted and blistered, 5 to 7 minutes. Transfer hot pasta to prepared slow cooker and immediately stir in boiling water (pasta will sizzle). Stir in 3½ cups marinara sauce, vodka, ½ teaspoon salt, ½ teaspoon pepper, and pepper flakes. Cover and cook until pasta is tender, 3 to 4 hours on high.

2. Remove foil collar. Gently stir in cream and remaining 2½ cups marinara sauce, adjusting sauce consistency with extra hot water as needed. Stir in basil; season with salt and pepper to taste. Serve.

SMART SHOPPING JARRED MARINARA SAUCE

We lean on jarred marinara sauce in slow-cooker pastas and casseroles to help reduce prep work. But with so many options on supermarket shelves, what should you buy? We have a few favorites in the test kitchen. **Victoria Marinara Sauce** is our top-rated premium brand; it has a short ingredient list (just tomatoes, olive oil, fresh onions, fresh basil, fresh garlic, salt, and spices) and, accordingly, boasts a "robust" flavor that tastes like "homemade" and fresh tomatoes. For a runner-up, we also like Classico Marinara with Plum Tomatoes and Olive Oil, which tasters found to have a "great texture" that's "hearty." For a traditional, everyday sauce, we prefer Bertolli Tomato and Basil Sauce for its "good balance of flavors" and "chunky texture."

Penne with Tomato and Almond Pesto

Serves 4 to 6   **Cooking Time** 3 to 4 hours on High   **Slow Cooker Size** 5½ to 7 Quarts

✓ **WHY THIS RECIPE WORKS:** For a flavorful but uncomplicated penne dish, we set our sights on a robust pesto that would come together quickly in the food processor and retain its bold flavor and color after a stint in the slow cooker. Taking our inspiration from a Sicilian pesto that trades the basil and pine nuts for tomatoes and almonds, we opted for cherry tomatoes, which made this dish a year-round option, and tossed them into our food processor with garlic and toasted slivered almonds. Red pepper flakes offered a subtle heat, and grated Parmesan cheese contributed more nutty flavor. After briefly toasting the pasta in the microwave with oil to prevent it from becoming mushy in the slow cooker, we combined it with hot water and our pesto and hit the start button. For a punch of flavor and brightness, we stirred in more pesto and fresh basil when the pasta was done. For more information on cooking pasta in the slow cooker and making a foil collar, see page 180.

1½	pounds cherry or grape tomatoes
1	cup grated Parmesan cheese
½	cup slivered almonds, toasted
2	teaspoons minced garlic
	Salt and pepper
	Pinch red pepper flakes
⅔	cup plus 1 tablespoon extra-virgin olive oil
1	pound penne
2½	cups boiling water
¼	cup chopped fresh basil

1. Process tomatoes, Parmesan, almonds, garlic, 1 teaspoon salt, and pepper flakes in food processor until smooth, 30 to 60 seconds, scraping down sides of bowl as needed. With processor running, slowly add ⅔ cup oil until incorporated. Season with salt and pepper to taste. Measure out and reserve 2 cups pesto.

2. Line slow cooker with aluminum foil collar and spray with vegetable oil spray. Microwave penne and remaining 1 tablespoon oil in bowl at 50 percent power, stirring occasionally, until some pieces look toasted and blistered, 5 to 7 minutes. Transfer hot pasta to prepared slow cooker and immediately stir in boiling water (pasta will sizzle). Stir in remaining pesto, cover, and cook until pasta is tender, 3 to 4 hours on high.

3. Remove foil collar. Gently stir in reserved pesto and basil, adjusting sauce consistency with extra hot water as needed. Season with salt and pepper to taste and serve.

SMART SHOPPING PENNE

Curious if there was any difference among the various brands of penne you find at the supermarket—from fancy imported brands to inexpensive domestic brands—we pitted eight brands against each other in a taste-off. Though fancier brands from Italy boasted traditional techniques and ingredients (such as slow kneading, mixing cold mountain spring water with hard durum semolina, and extruding the dough through traditional bronze cast dies for a coarse texture), we found they didn't necessarily translate into better-tasting pasta. In the end, tasters gave a domestic brand, **Mueller's Penne Rigate**, top honors for its "hearty," "wheaty" flavor.

Easy Meaty Ziti

Serves 4   **Cooking Time** 2 to 3 hours on High   **Slow Cooker Size** 5½ to 7 Quarts

✓ **WHY THIS RECIPE WORKS:** Our Easy Meaty Ziti has all the flavor and depth of a sauce that's been on the stovetop all day—but none of the work. And because the ziti cooks right in the sauce—we simply toasted it in the microwave with a little oil to ensure that every forkful was perfectly tender—you don't even need to bring a pot of water to boil. We tried a variety of canned tomato products for the sauce, but only jarred marinara delivered long-simmered depth of flavor. Meatloaf mix ensured that our sauce tasted meaty and hearty, and cooking it briefly in the microwave helped to render its fat, which we drained off to avoid a greasy sauce. For herbal notes, we added a little Italian seasoning. Stirring in a little more marinara sauce, plus some hot water, at the end of cooking guaranteed a saucy dish with fresh flavor. Victoria Marinara Sauce is the test kitchen's favorite brand; see page 174 for more information. Meatloaf mix is a prepackaged mix of ground beef, pork, and veal; if it's unavailable, use 8 ounces each of ground pork and 85 percent lean ground beef. For more information on cooking pasta in the slow cooker and making a foil collar, see page 180.

1	pound meatloaf mix
½	teaspoon Italian seasoning
1	(25-ounce) jar marinara sauce (3 cups)
2	tablespoons tomato paste
	Salt and pepper
8	ounces (2½ cups) ziti
2	teaspoons olive oil
1½	cups boiling water

1. Microwave meatloaf mix and Italian seasoning in bowl, stirring occasionally, until meat is no longer pink, about 5 minutes. Break up any large pieces of meat with spoon, then drain off fat; return to now-empty bowl. Stir in 2 cups marinara sauce, tomato paste, 1 teaspoon salt, and ½ teaspoon pepper.

2. Line slow cooker with aluminum foil collar and spray with vegetable oil spray. Microwave ziti and oil in bowl at 50 percent power, stirring occasionally, until some pieces look toasted and blistered, 3 to 5 minutes. Transfer hot pasta to prepared slow cooker and immediately stir in boiling water (pasta will sizzle). Stir in meat and sauce mixture, cover, and cook until pasta is tender, 2 to 3 hours on high.

3. Remove foil collar. Gently stir in remaining 1 cup marinara sauce, adjusting sauce consistency with extra hot water as needed. Season with salt and pepper to taste and serve.

ON THE SIDE **GARLIC BREAD**
Toast 10 unpeeled garlic cloves in small skillet over medium heat, shaking pan occasionally, until fragrant, about 8 minutes. Let garlic cool, then peel and mince. Using fork, mash garlic in bowl with 2 tablespoons unsalted butter, 2 tablespoons grated Parmesan cheese, and ½ teaspoon salt. Cut 1 (10-inch) loaf of Italian bread in half lengthwise, spread both pieces with butter mixture, then season with salt and pepper. Lay bread, buttered side up, on baking sheet. Bake in 500-degree oven until surface of bread is golden brown and toasted, 8 to 10 minutes. Slice and serve warm. Serves 4 to 6. (This recipe can be doubled.)

Penne with Chicken, Sun-Dried Tomatoes, and Spinach

Serves 4   **Cooking Time** 2 to 3 hours on High   **Slow Cooker Size** 5½ to 7 Quarts

✓ **WHY THIS RECIPE WORKS:** With its enticing combination of moist chicken, fresh spinach, and sweet sun-dried tomatoes, all enrobed in a rich, creamy sauce and paired with tender penne, this dish offers surprising complexity and flavor with a minimum of effort. For the chicken, we opted for tenderloins, which required no prep and simply needed to be stirred into the sauce and pasta in the slow cooker at the outset of cooking. Adding chicken broth, rather than water, to the slow cooker to help cook the pasta ramped up the savory notes of the dish. As for the cream sauce, homemade sauces took too long to make and separated in the slow cooker, but store-bought Alfredo sauce kept things easy and provided plenty of rich flavor; plus, it didn't taste raw when we added some at the end to freshen the flavor of our dish. Moisture released from the chicken as it cooked infused the sauce with more savory depth and ensured that it was the right consistency. For the spinach, we simply stirred in a few handfuls at the end so it would warm through and wilt. A little Parmesan cheese, sprinkled over the top, added more savory, salty tang. If you can't find chicken tenderloins, you can substitute 1 pound boneless, skinless chicken breasts, trimmed and cut crosswise into ½-inch-thick slices. For more information on cooking pasta in the slow cooker and making a foil collar, see page 180.

2½ **cups chicken broth**

8 **ounces (2½ cups) penne**

2 **teaspoons olive oil**

1 **(15-ounce) jar Alfredo sauce**

½ **cup oil-packed sun-dried tomatoes, chopped coarse**
   Salt and pepper

1 **pound chicken tenderloins**

4 **ounces (4 cups) baby spinach**

½ **cup grated Parmesan cheese**

1. Line slow cooker with aluminum foil collar; spray with vegetable oil spray. Microwave broth in bowl until steaming, about 2 minutes. In separate bowl, microwave penne and oil at 50 percent power, stirring occasionally, until some pieces look toasted and blistered, 3 to 5 minutes. Transfer hot pasta to prepared slow cooker and immediately stir in hot broth (pasta will sizzle). Stir in ½ cup Alfredo sauce, tomatoes, ½ teaspoon pepper, and ¼ teaspoon salt. Season chicken with salt and pepper; nestle into pasta. Cover and cook until pasta is tender, 2 to 3 hours on high.

2. Remove foil collar. Gently stir in remaining Alfredo sauce, adjusting sauce consistency with hot water as needed. Stir in spinach and let sit until spinach is wilted, about 5 minutes. Season with salt and pepper to taste. Sprinkle with Parmesan and serve.

SMART SHOPPING SUN-DRIED TOMATOES
Here in the test kitchen, we prefer oil-packed sun-dried tomatoes to their leather-like counterparts. Because the packing oil can impart a musty, herbal flavor to the tomatoes, we recommend rinsing them before using them in any recipe. We've found that washing away excess herbs and spices improves their taste.

ALL ABOUT Cooking Pasta in the Slow Cooker

Cooking pasta right in the sauce in the slow cooker is an easy way to get a great-tasting dinner on the table—if you can avoid the common pitfalls of mushy, flabby pasta and dull, washed-out sauces. After lots of trial and error, we came up with foolproof recipes that turned out both well-cooked (not overcooked) pastas and full-flavored sauces from the slow cooker, for complete dinners that didn't require the use of the stovetop or dragging out an extra pot. While not every pasta dish follows the same hard-and-fast rules, there are a few general guidelines we discovered that will guarantee perfect pasta, plus a flavorful sauce, from the slow cooker every time.

Shape Matters

We find that tubular pasta, like penne and ziti, and small pasta, such as macaroni and small shells, work the best in the slow cooker—they are easy to combine with the other ingredients, maintain their shape, and consistently cook to the proper doneness. Do not use strand pasta, such as spaghetti or linguine, because the strands clump together into a sticky mess when cooked.

Start with Cooked Sauces

For pasta dinners that were full-flavored but not heavy on prep, we started with supermarket staples, like jarred marinara and Alfredo sauces. These convenience products provided a flavor-packed foundation with depth and complexity. Because these sauces are already cooked, we could stir some in at the end of cooking to help brighten the flavors of our dishes and add freshness; when we tried this with uncooked tomato or cream sauces, the flavor was harsh-tasting and one-dimensional.

Cook on High

None of our pasta dishes could withstand an all-day stay on the low setting—they ended up mushy and bland. Cooking the pasta on high for a shorter period of time (our recipes take anywhere from 1½ hours to 4 hours) ensured properly cooked, richly flavored pasta.

Toast the Pasta in the Microwave

The main structural elements of pasta are starch and protein. When pasta is cooked in boiling water, the moisture causes the starch to swell up; simultaneously, the heat causes the protein to set, constraining the expansion of the starch and resulting in pasta with the proper texture. In the slow cooker, however, the liquid heats up slowly, so the starch has more time to swell before being checked by the protein, resulting in soggy, mushy pasta. Toasting our raw pasta with oil in the microwave before adding it to the slow cooker helped to set the protein and prevented the pasta from becoming bloated. We found that microwaving the pasta at 50 percent power, and stirring it occasionally, gently toasted the pasta; note that only a portion will look toasted and blistered. However, if you have a weaker microwave you may need to toast your pasta for a longer period than we've specified in the recipe. Also, if your microwave does not have a power level button, you can toast the pasta on high power for half the amount of time given in the recipe, stirring the pasta more frequently.

Make a Foil Collar

Most slow cookers have a hotter side (typically the back side, opposite the side with the controls) that can cause pastas and other dense dishes, such as casseroles, to burn. To solve this problem, we line the slow-cooker insert with an aluminum foil collar. To make an aluminum foil collar, fold sheets of heavy-duty foil until you have a six-layered foil rectangle that measures roughly 16 inches long by 4 inches wide for a large slow cooker or 12 by 4 inches for a small slow cooker. (Depending on the width of the foil, you will need either two or three sheets of foil.) Then press the collar into the back side of the slow-cooker insert; the food will help hold the collar in place during cooking, and the collar will prevent the food from cooking unevenly.

Pasta Puttanesca with Shrimp

Serves 4   **Cooking Time** 2 to 3 hours on High   **Slow Cooker Size** 5½ to 7 Quarts

✓ **WHY THIS RECIPE WORKS:** Puttanesca sauce features bright, bold flavors that can become dulled with hours of cooking. For ours, we stirred in the most potent ingredients—the olives and capers—toward the end of cooking. Adding the shrimp then ensured that it wasn't exposed to the heat too long. Jarred marinara, anchovies, and red pepper flakes gave us a deeply flavored sauce. If you prefer a less spicy dish, use the smaller amount of red pepper flakes. For more information on cooking pasta in the slow cooker and making a foil collar, see page 180. Victoria Marinara Sauce is the test kitchen's favorite brand; see page 180 for more information.

8	ounces (2½ cups) penne
2	teaspoons olive oil
1½	cups boiling water
1	(25-ounce) jar marinara sauce (3 cups)
2	anchovy fillets, rinsed and minced
⅛–¼	teaspoon red pepper flakes
	Salt and pepper
1	pound extra-large shrimp (21 to 25 per pound), peeled, deveined, and tails removed
¼	cup pitted kalamata olives, chopped coarse
2	tablespoons capers, rinsed
2	tablespoons minced fresh parsley

1. Line slow cooker with aluminum foil collar and spray with vegetable oil spray. Microwave penne and oil in bowl at 50 percent power, stirring occasionally, until some pieces look toasted and blistered, 3 to 5 minutes. Transfer hot pasta to prepared slow cooker; immediately stir in boiling water (pasta will sizzle). Stir in 2 cups marinara sauce, anchovies, pepper flakes, ½ teaspoon salt, and ½ teaspoon pepper. Cover; cook until pasta is tender, 2 to 3 hours on high.

2. Remove foil collar. Gently stir in remaining 1 cup marinara sauce, adjusting sauce consistency with extra hot water as needed. Stir in shrimp, olives, and capers, cover, and cook on high until shrimp are opaque throughout, about 20 minutes. Stir in parsley and season with salt and pepper to taste. Serve.

SMART SHOPPING SHRIMP SIZES

Shrimp are sold by size (small, medium, large, and so on) as well as by the number needed to make 1 pound, usually given in a range. Choosing shrimp by the numerical rating is more accurate than choosing them by the size label, which varies from store to store. Here's how the two sizing systems generally compare.

SIZE	COUNT PER POUND
Colossal	under 12
Extra-Jumbo	under 15
Jumbo	16 to 20
Extra-Large	21 to 25
Large	26 to 30
Medium-Large	31 to 40
Medium	41 to 50
Small	51 to 60

Tortellini with Creamy Wild Mushroom Sauce

Serves 4   **Cooking Time** 1½ to 2½ hours on High   **Slow Cooker Size** 5½ to 7 Quarts

☑ **WHY THIS RECIPE WORKS:** To make the most of ultraconvenient store-bought stuffed tortellini, we dressed it up with a rich, velvety mushroom sauce. Alfredo sauce provided a creamy base, and a little thyme contributed an herbal backbone. For deep, earthy flavor and heartiness, we included two types of mushrooms: Dried porcini added meaty, savory notes, and sliced cremini offered bold flavor and some texture. Microwaving the cremini helped jump-start their cooking and also worked to draw forth excess moisture that would have watered down the sauce. Grated Parmesan ensured that the sauce clung nicely to our tortellini, and minced parsley balanced the richness of the dish. For the tortellini, we found the dried variety worked best and didn't need any prep or toasting—we simply added them to the slow cooker with the sauce and mushrooms; in about two hours, they were perfectly tender. Do not substitute fresh or frozen tortellini, which will overcook. For more information on cooking pasta in the slow cooker and making a foil collar, see page 180.

1	**pound sliced cremini mushrooms**
1	**tablespoon olive oil**
2	**teaspoons dried thyme**
2½	**cups chicken broth**
1	**(15-ounce) jar Alfredo sauce**
12	**ounces dried cheese tortellini**
½	**ounce dried porcini mushrooms, rinsed and minced**
	Salt and pepper
1	**cup grated Parmesan cheese**
2	**tablespoons minced fresh parsley**

1. Line slow cooker with aluminum foil collar and spray with vegetable oil spray. Microwave cremini mushrooms, oil, and thyme in bowl until softened, about 5 minutes; drain mushrooms and transfer to prepared slow cooker. Stir in broth, 1 cup Alfredo sauce, tortellini, porcini mushrooms, ½ teaspoon salt, and ½ teaspoon pepper. Cover and cook until pasta is tender, 1½ to 2½ hours on high.

2. Remove foil collar. Gently stir in Parmesan and remaining Alfredo sauce, adjusting sauce consistency with hot water as needed. Stir in parsley and season with salt and pepper to taste. Serve.

SMART SHOPPING TORTELLINI

Handmade tortellini are rich-tasting, but they make a time-consuming kitchen project. Store-bought tortellini are a great runner-up, offering both good flavor and tender texture in a fraction of the time. To find the best kind, we recently sampled seven supermarket brands of cheese tortellini, including two refrigerated, two dried, and three frozen. Our winner, surprisingly, was a dried brand, **Barilla Tortellini Three Cheese**. It was praised for a filling that tasters called "creamy," "pungent," and "tangy," thanks to its bold mixture of ricotta, Emmentaler, and Grana Padano cheeses. Another factor in Barilla's win was the texture of the pasta: The delicate wrappers of these petite tortellini were strong enough to contain the filling during cooking, but not overly gummy or prone to blowouts like other brands.

Macaroni and Cheese with Ham and Peas

Serves 4   **Cooking Time** 2 to 3 hours on High   **Slow Cooker Size** 5½ to 7 Quarts

✔ **WHY THIS RECIPE WORKS:** Slow-cooker macaroni and cheese is notoriously finicky—the pasta is usually overcooked and flabby, and the cream-based sauce breaks and curdles during the long cooking time, resulting in a grainy, separated sauce. Fortunately, we had already established a method for turning out nicely done pasta in the slow cooker. After toasting our macaroni with a bit of oil, we combined it with boiling water to jump-start its cooking. As for the sauce, we found that the duo of evaporated milk and condensed cheddar cheese soup, because of their stabilizers, created a creamy base that didn't break. Shredded cheddar ramped up the flavor, but it brought back some of the graininess. Adding Monterey Jack, which has a creamier texture when melted, produced a rich-tasting sauce with a smooth consistency; a bit of dry mustard boosted the cheesy flavor. For more substance and color, we stirred in small pieces of ham and frozen peas at the end of cooking; they needed just a few minutes to warm through. Be sure to use mild cheddar here; sharp cheddar will become grainy during cooking. Either elbow macaroni or small shells can be used here; note that the cooking time will be the same. For more information on cooking pasta in the slow cooker and making a foil collar, see page 180. For a crisp, buttery topping, sprinkle individual servings with our Toasted Bread-Crumb Topping.

8 ounces (2 cups) elbow macaroni or small shells

2 teaspoons olive oil

1½ cups boiling water

1 (12-ounce) can evaporated milk

1 (11-ounce) can condensed cheddar cheese soup

1 cup shredded mild cheddar cheese

1 cup shredded Monterey Jack cheese

½ teaspoon dry mustard

Salt and pepper

8 ounces ham steak, chopped

½ cup frozen peas

1. Line slow cooker with aluminum foil collar and spray with vegetable oil spray. Microwave macaroni and oil in bowl at 50 percent power, stirring occasionally, until some pieces look toasted and blistered, 3 to 5 minutes. Transfer hot pasta to prepared slow cooker and immediately stir in boiling water (pasta will sizzle). Stir in evaporated milk, condensed soup, cheddar, Monterey Jack, mustard, ½ teaspoon salt, and ½ teaspoon pepper. Cover and cook until pasta is tender, 2 to 3 hours on high.

2. Remove foil collar. Gently stir pasta to recombine, adjusting sauce consistency with extra hot water as needed. Stir in ham and peas and let sit until heated through, about 5 minutes. Season with salt and pepper to taste. Serve.

QUICK PREP TIP TOASTED BREAD-CRUMB TOPPING
Pulse 2 slices hearty white sandwich bread, torn into pieces, in food processor to coarse crumbs, about 10 pulses. Melt 2 tablespoons butter in 12-inch skillet over medium heat. Add bread crumbs and toast, stirring often, until golden brown, 5 to 7 minutes. Transfer bread crumbs to bowl and season with salt and pepper to taste. Makes about 1 cup.

Pepperoni Macaroni and Cheese

Serves 4   **Cooking Time** 2 to 3 hours on High   **Slow Cooker Size** 5½ to 7 Quarts

WHY THIS RECIPE WORKS: For another take on this comfort-food classic, we swapped out the ham and peas in favor of pepperoni. Cutting pepperoni slices into quarters guaranteed spicy, meaty bites throughout. The combination of evaporated milk and condensed cheddar cheese soup gave us a rich, creamy sauce that held up to a couple of hours in the slow cooker, and cheddar and Monterey Jack delivered the ideal flavor and texture. Tomato paste ensured that our mac and cheese had a robust yet well-rounded tomato flavor, and minced garlic reinforced the spice of the pepperoni. Be sure to use mild cheddar here; sharp cheddar will become grainy while cooking. Either elbow macaroni or small shells can be used here; note that the cooking time will be the same. For more information on cooking pasta in the slow cooker and making a foil collar, see page 180. For a crisp, buttery topping, sprinkle individual servings with our Toasted Bread-Crumb Topping (page 184).

8	ounces (2 cups) elbow macaroni or small shells
2	teaspoons olive oil
1½	cups boiling water
1	(12-ounce) can evaporated milk
1	(11-ounce) can condensed cheddar cheese soup
1	cup shredded mild cheddar cheese
1	cup shredded Monterey Jack cheese
4	ounces sliced pepperoni, quartered
2	tablespoons tomato paste
1	tablespoon minced garlic
½	teaspoon dry mustard
	Salt and pepper

1. Line slow cooker with aluminum foil collar and spray with vegetable oil spray. Microwave macaroni and oil in bowl at 50 percent power, stirring occasionally, until some pieces look toasted and blistered, 3 to 5 minutes. Transfer hot pasta to prepared slow cooker and immediately stir in boiling water (pasta will sizzle). Stir in evaporated milk, condensed soup, cheddar, Monterey Jack, pepperoni, tomato paste, garlic, mustard, and ½ teaspoon pepper. Cover and cook until pasta is tender, 2 to 3 hours on high.

2. Remove foil collar. Gently stir pasta to recombine, adjusting sauce consistency with extra hot water as needed. Season with salt and pepper to taste and serve.

SMART SHOPPING MACARONI

With so many brands of elbow macaroni on the market, which one should you buy? Are they all the same? To find out, we rounded up eight contenders and tasted them simply dressed with vegetable oil and in a macaroni and cheese recipe. What we found is that an Italian brand (which makes pasta for the American market domestically) won our tasting by a large margin. Our tasters praised **Barilla Elbows** for their "wheaty," "buttery" flavor and "firm texture," and they especially liked that these elbows have small ridges and a slight twist that "holds sauce well."

Macaroni and Cheese with Broccoli and Parmesan

Serves 4   **Cooking Time** 2 to 3 hours on High   **Slow Cooker Size** 5½ to 7 Quarts

✔ **WHY THIS RECIPE WORKS:** This recipe gives kid-friendly mac and cheese a decidedly grown-up feel. Rather than reach for cheddar and Monterey Jack, we opted for savory, nutty Parmesan. However, cooking the Parmesan with the pasta wasn't an option: the cheese turned gummy and the sauce was broken and separated by the time the pasta was done. Stirring in the cheese at the end ensured that our sauce was ultracreamy. Plus, the Parmesan's robust flavor wasn't lost during cooking. To round out our dinner, we added broccoli, which made a great match for the rich, cheesy dish. To preserve its bright green color and ensure that it didn't become mushy in the slow cooker, we simply microwaved it with a little water until tender, then stirred it into the pasta before serving. Either elbow macaroni or small shells can be used here; note that the cooking time will be the same. For more information on cooking pasta in the slow cooker and making a foil collar, see page 180. For a crisp, buttery topping, sprinkle individual servings with our Toasted Bread-Crumb Topping (page 184).

8	ounces (2 cups) elbow macaroni or small shells
2	teaspoons olive oil
1¾	cups boiling water
1	(12-ounce) can evaporated milk
1	(11-ounce) can condensed cheddar cheese soup
½	teaspoon dry mustard
	Salt and pepper
12	ounces broccoli florets, cut into 1-inch pieces
8	ounces grated Parmesan cheese (4 cups)

1. Line slow cooker with aluminum foil collar and spray with vegetable oil spray. Microwave macaroni and oil in bowl at 50 percent power, stirring occasionally, until some pieces look toasted and blistered, 3 to 5 minutes. Transfer hot pasta to prepared slow cooker and immediately stir in boiling water (pasta will sizzle). Stir in evaporated milk, condensed soup, mustard, ½ teaspoon salt, and ½ teaspoon pepper. Cover and cook until pasta is tender, 2 to 3 hours on high.

2. Microwave broccoli and ¼ cup water in covered bowl until bright green and tender, about 4 minutes; drain broccoli. Remove foil collar. Gently stir Parmesan into pasta, adjusting sauce consistency with extra hot water as needed. Stir in broccoli and season with salt and pepper to taste. Serve.

QUICK PREP TIP PREPPING BROCCOLI FLORETS
Bagged precut broccoli florets are a huge timesaver, but they usually need to be trimmed down into evenly sized pieces before cooking. The best way to do this is to place each floret upside down on the cutting board and slice down through the stem. This way you'll have fewer small crumbly pieces.

Spicy Meatballs and Marinara

Makes 8 meatballs and 5 cups sauce; enough for 1 pound pasta
Cooking Time 4 to 5 hours on Low   **Slow Cooker Size** 5½ to 7 Quarts

WHY THIS RECIPE WORKS: To up the ante on this satisfying Italian classic, we decided to infuse our dish with some heat and spice. A couple cans of tomato puree plus some tomato paste, garlic, and oregano provided a sauce with depth and the right consistency; a bit of sugar balanced the acidity of the tomatoes. For the meatballs, convenient meatloaf mix offered hearty flavor, and a panade (a mixture of bread crumbs and milk) kept them moist. Chopped pepperoncini and red pepper flakes delivered a solid punch of heat. To prevent our sauce from being greasy, we found it necessary to microwave the meatballs before transferring them to the slow cooker; this worked to render excess fat and also helped to firm up the meatballs so they didn't fall apart in the slow cooker. Meatloaf mix is a prepackaged mix of ground beef, pork, and veal; if it's unavailable, use 8 ounces each of ground pork and 85 percent lean ground beef.

1	**pound meatloaf mix**
½	**cup panko bread crumbs**
¼	**cup whole milk**
¼	**cup grated Parmesan cheese**
¼	**cup sliced pepperoncini, chopped fine**
2	**tablespoons minced garlic**
2	**teaspoons dried oregano**
¾	**teaspoon red pepper flakes**
	Salt and pepper
2	**(28-ounce) cans tomato puree**
2	**tablespoons tomato paste**
1	**teaspoon sugar**

1. Using hands, mix meatloaf mix, panko, milk, Parmesan, pepperoncini, 1 tablespoon garlic, 1 teaspoon oregano, ½ teaspoon pepper flakes, ½ teaspoon salt, and ½ teaspoon pepper together in bowl until uniform. Pinch off and roll mixture into 2-inch meatballs (about 8 meatballs total) and arrange on large plate. Microwave meatballs until fat renders and meatballs are firm, about 5 minutes.

2. Combine tomato puree, tomato paste, sugar, ½ teaspoon salt, ½ teaspoon pepper, remaining 1 tablespoon garlic, and remaining 1 teaspoon oregano in slow cooker. Transfer microwaved meatballs to slow cooker, discarding rendered fat. Cover and cook until meatballs are tender, 4 to 5 hours on low.

3. Using large spoon, skim excess fat from surface of sauce. Season with salt, pepper, and extra sugar to taste and serve.

QUICK PREP TIP GRATING HARD CHEESE
When grating Parmesan and other hard cheeses, we use a rasp-style grater because it produces lighter, fluffier shreds of cheese that melt seamlessly into pasta dishes and sauces.

Turkey Pesto Meatballs and Marinara

Makes 8 meatballs and 5 cups sauce; enough for 1 pound pasta
Cooking Time 4 to 5 hours on Low   **Slow Cooker Size** 5½ to 7 Quarts

✔ **WHY THIS RECIPE WORKS:** Turkey meatballs make a great alternative to the traditional beef and pork meatballs—if you can find a way to infuse them with rich flavor and keep them moist. One ultraconvenient product helped us on both fronts. Store-bought pesto offered big garlic and herb flavors—no knife needed—and contributed much-needed richness that kept our meatballs moist. Panko bread crumbs helped to bind the mixture, and grated Parmesan delivered deep, savory flavor. Microwaving the meatballs guaranteed that they didn't fall apart in the slow cooker. To brighten the flavor of our slow-cooked marinara sauce (we relied on tomato puree and tomato paste for depth of flavor and the right consistency), we stirred in more pesto just before serving. Be sure to use ground turkey, not ground turkey breast (also labeled 99 percent fat free), in this recipe. You can make your own pesto or use your favorite store-bought brand from the refrigerated section of the supermarket—they have a fresher flavor than the jarred pesto sold in the grocery aisles.

1   **pound ground turkey**
1   **cup prepared basil pesto**
½   **cup panko bread crumbs**
¼   **cup grated Parmesan cheese**
     Salt and pepper
2   **(28-ounce) cans tomato puree**
2   **tablespoons tomato paste**
2   **tablespoons soy sauce**
1   **teaspoon sugar**

1. Using hands, mix ground turkey, ½ cup pesto, panko, Parmesan, and ½ teaspoon pepper together in bowl until uniform. Pinch off and roll mixture into 2-inch meatballs (about 8 meatballs total) and arrange on large plate. Microwave meatballs until fat renders and meatballs are firm, about 5 minutes.

2. Combine tomato puree, tomato paste, soy sauce, sugar, ½ teaspoon salt, and ½ teaspoon pepper in slow cooker. Transfer microwaved meatballs to slow cooker, discarding rendered fat. Cover and cook until meatballs are tender, 4 to 5 hours on low.

3. Using large spoon, skim excess fat from surface of sauce. Before serving, stir in remaining ½ cup pesto and season with salt, pepper, and extra sugar to taste.

QUICK PREP TIP SMALL-BATCH PESTO
Process 4 cups fresh basil leaves, ⅔ cup extra-virgin olive oil, 3 tablespoons toasted pine nuts, and 1 minced garlic clove in food processor until smooth, 30 to 60 seconds, scraping down sides of bowl as needed. Transfer pesto to bowl, stir in ½ cup grated Parmesan cheese, and season with salt and pepper to taste. Makes about 1 cup.

Chicken Cacciatore Sauce

Makes 6 cups; enough for 1 pound pasta
Cooking Time 4 to 5 hours on Low   **Slow Cooker Size** 5½ to 7 Quarts

WHY THIS RECIPE WORKS: To adapt this classic chicken stew, featuring mushrooms, tomatoes, and garlic, into a hearty pasta sauce made in the slow cooker, we started by selecting the right cut of meat. Boneless, skinless chicken thighs provided a rich flavor and were easy to break down into bite-size pieces by the end of the cooking time. Onion and garlic were a given for the aromatic notes they provided, and a large can of tomato puree gave our sauce the right consistency and bright, tomatoey flavor. We found that using two types of mushrooms—sliced white mushrooms and dried porcini—ensured that our easy sauce offered both tender bites of mushroom and intense, earthy flavor. Woodsy herbs provide complexity in the traditional dish, but we found a shortcut in herbes de Provence, a blend that typically combines basil, fennel seeds, marjoram, rosemary, sage, and thyme. Finally, a sprinkling of minced parsley, stirred in just before serving, contributed a hit of fresh flavor to our Chicken Cacciatore Sauce.

8	**ounces sliced white mushrooms**
1	**cup chopped onion**
2	**tablespoons tomato paste**
1	**tablespoon olive oil**
1	**tablespoon minced garlic**
½	**teaspoon herbes de Provence**
1	**(28-ounce) can tomato puree**
¼	**ounce dried porcini mushrooms, rinsed and minced**
	Salt and pepper
1½	**pounds boneless, skinless chicken thighs, trimmed**
¼	**cup chopped fresh parsley**

1. Microwave white mushrooms, onion, tomato paste, oil, garlic, and herbes de Provence in bowl, stirring occasionally, until vegetables are softened, about 5 minutes; drain vegetable mixture and transfer to slow cooker. Stir in tomato puree, porcini mushrooms, 1 teaspoon salt, and ½ teaspoon pepper. Season chicken with salt and pepper and nestle into slow cooker. Cover and cook until chicken is tender, 4 to 5 hours on low.

2. Using large spoon, skim excess fat from surface of sauce. Break chicken into about 1-inch pieces with tongs. Before serving, stir in parsley and season with salt and pepper to taste.

SMART SHOPPING PORCINI MUSHROOMS
Like fresh fruits and vegetables, the quality of dried porcini mushrooms can vary dramatically from package to package and brand to brand. Always inspect the mushrooms before you buy. Avoid those with small holes, which indicate that the mushroom was perhaps home to pinworms. Instead, look for large, smooth porcini, free of worm holes, dust, and grit.

Beef Ragu with Warm Spices

Makes 5 cups; enough for 1 pound pasta
Cooking Time 8 to 9 hours on Low or 5 to 6 hours on High   **Slow Cooker Size** 5½ to 7 Quarts

WHY THIS RECIPE WORKS: Making a true, long-simmered Italian meat sauce requires tending the stovetop for hours—so we decided to move ours to the slow cooker. Boneless beef short ribs turned meltingly tender after several hours of low, slow cooking and were easy enough to break apart into fork-friendly pieces right in the slow cooker once they were done. Onion and garlic provided essential aromatic notes, and a generous amount of tomato paste—2 tablespoons—added depth of flavor. To infuse our sauce with warm spice notes, we included cinnamon and cloves, blooming them in the microwave with the aromatics. Tomato puree ensured that our sauce had the right consistency. Though untraditional in pasta sauce, a big dose of soy sauce enhanced the meaty flavor of our ragu. After cooking, we stirred in some chopped parsley for a fresh finish. No one would ever guess this rich-tasting sauce was so easy to make.

1	cup chopped onion
2	tablespoons tomato paste
1	tablespoon olive oil
2	teaspoons minced garlic
⅛	teaspoon ground cinnamon
	Pinch ground cloves
1	(28-ounce) can tomato puree
2	tablespoons soy sauce
	Salt and pepper
1½	pounds boneless beef short ribs
¼	cup minced fresh parsley

1. Microwave onion, tomato paste, oil, garlic, cinnamon, and cloves in bowl, stirring occasionally, until onion is softened, about 5 minutes; transfer to slow cooker. Stir in tomato puree, soy sauce, 1 teaspoon salt, and ½ teaspoon pepper. Trim fat from top and bottom of short ribs, season with salt and pepper, and nestle into slow cooker. Cover and cook until beef is tender, 8 to 9 hours on low or 5 to 6 hours on high.

2. Using large spoon, skim excess fat from surface of sauce. Break beef into about 1-inch pieces with tongs. Before serving, stir in parsley and season with salt and pepper to taste.

SMART SHOPPING TOMATO PUREE
Tomato puree, like tomato sauce, is cooked and strained to remove the tomato seeds, making it much smoother and thicker than other canned tomato products. But tomato puree has a slightly thicker consistency than tomato sauce, which is why we use it in our slow-cooker sauces—it helps us achieve the consistency of a stovetop sauce without the benefit of the reduction that comes with a long simmer in an uncovered pot or skillet. Our favorite brand is **Hunt's Tomato Puree**, which offers a nice, thick consistency and tomatoey flavor.

Shredded Pork Ragu

Makes 5 cups; enough for 1 pound pasta
Cooking Time 6 to 7 hours on Low or 4 to 5 hours on High   **Slow Cooker Size** 5½ to 7 Quarts

✔ **WHY THIS RECIPE WORKS:** Iterations of this dish found in the Italian countryside simply combine a can of tomatoes with a stray piece of pork and an onion before the pot is left to simmer for hours, resulting in a sauce that's flavorful but not fussy. In our quest for an effortless yet full-flavored pork ragu that we could let simmer away in our slow cooker, we began by searching for the best cut of meat. Though pork shoulder offered richness and depth of flavor, it required some knife work. Instead, we turned to another fatty but prep-free cut: boneless country-style pork ribs. The ribs turned ultratender after a long stay in the slow cooker and gave our sauce a truly meaty, rich flavor. Boosting the pork's meaty flavor with tomato paste and soy sauce ensured that our ragu offered serious depth and complexity, and tomato puree guaranteed that it was plenty thick and coated our pasta nicely. Microwaving the tomato paste with our aromatics—onion, garlic, and a bit of oregano and red pepper flakes—worked to intensify its flavor. Finishing with parsley brightened up this hearty dish.

1	**cup chopped onion**
2	**tablespoons tomato paste**
1	**tablespoon minced garlic**
1	**tablespoon olive oil**
1	**teaspoon dried oregano**
⅛	**teaspoon red pepper flakes**
1	**(28-ounce) can tomato puree**
2	**tablespoons soy sauce**
	Salt and pepper
1½	**pounds boneless country-style pork ribs, trimmed**
¼	**cup minced fresh parsley**

1. Microwave onion, tomato paste, garlic, oil, oregano, and pepper flakes in bowl, stirring occasionally, until onion is softened, about 5 minutes; transfer to slow cooker. Stir in tomato puree, soy sauce, ½ teaspoon salt, and ½ teaspoon pepper. Season pork with salt and pepper and nestle into slow cooker. Cover and cook until pork is tender, 6 to 7 hours on low or 4 to 5 hours on high.

2. Using large spoon, skim excess fat from surface of sauce. Break pork into about 1-inch pieces with tongs. Before serving, stir in parsley and season with salt and pepper to taste.

ON THE SIDE ARUGULA SALAD WITH BALSAMIC-MUSTARD VINAIGRETTE
Whisk 2 tablespoons balsamic vinegar, 1½ teaspoons Dijon mustard, ½ teaspoon minced shallot, ⅛ teaspoon salt, and pinch pepper together in large bowl. Whisking constantly, drizzle in 2 tablespoons extra-virgin olive oil. Add 6 ounces (6 cups) baby arugula and toss to combine. Serves 4.

Weeknight Chicken Ragu

Makes 6 cups; enough for 1 pound pasta
Cooking Time 2 to 3 hours on Low   **Slow Cooker Size** 5½ to 7 Quarts

✓ **WHY THIS RECIPE WORKS:** This easy ragu is ready for the slow cooker in mere minutes and needs just a couple of hours of simmering for the perfect effortless weeknight dinner. For a hearty texture and rich flavor, we started with ground chicken; microwaving it briefly prevented it from becoming grainy during cooking. Using two tomato products—puree and paste—ensured that our ragu was plenty saucy and offered complex tomato flavor. Onion and garlic added a flavorful foundation, and Italian seasoning provided the requisite flavors of oregano, thyme, and basil. For more savory depth and to enhance the meaty qualities of our sauce, we included soy sauce. To complete our weeknight-friendly ragu, we added chopped basil at the end of cooking. Be sure to use ground chicken, not ground chicken breast (also labeled 99 percent fat free).

1½	**pounds ground chicken**
1	**cup chopped onion**
2	**tablespoons tomato paste**
1	**tablespoon minced garlic**
1	**teaspoon Italian seasoning**
1	**(28-ounce) can tomato puree**
2	**tablespoons soy sauce**
	Salt and pepper
¼	**cup chopped fresh basil**

1. Microwave ground chicken, onion, tomato paste, garlic, and Italian seasoning in bowl, stirring occasionally, until chicken is no longer pink, about 5 minutes. Break up any large pieces of chicken with spoon, then drain off fat; transfer to slow cooker. Stir in tomato puree, soy sauce, 1 teaspoon salt, and ½ teaspoon pepper. Cover and cook until chicken is tender, 2 to 3 hours on low.

2. Using large spoon, skim excess fat from surface of sauce. Before serving, stir in basil and season with salt and pepper to taste.

QUICK PREP TIP **RESERVING PASTA COOKING WATER**
When cooking pasta, before draining it, be sure to reserve about ½ cup of the cooking water. This flavorful water can be used to help loosen a thick sauce.

Rustic Kale, Fennel, and Sun-Dried Tomato Sauce

Makes 4 cups; enough for 1 pound pasta
Cooking Time 5 to 6 hours on Low or 3 to 4 hours on High   **Slow Cooker Size** 5½ to 7 Quarts

✔ **WHY THIS RECIPE WORKS:** Pasta and braised kale is a popular pairing for a reason—the earthy, meaty notes of the tender greens add depth and flavor to the mild-tasting pasta for a simple yet incredibly satisfying dish. To prepare our kale for the slow cooker, we sliced it into thin strips, then tossed it in with chopped onion, minced garlic, and red pepper flakes. This combination tasted good, but swapping the onion for fennel promised a more filling and more flavorful dish. We used chicken broth, rather than water, for the cooking liquid; it imparted salty, savory notes to our sauce. To add some much-needed brightness, we included chopped sun-dried tomatoes. A big drizzle of extra-virgin olive oil, plus some grated Parmesan, enriched this fairly lean sauce, and toasted pine nuts offered a welcome crunch. So their flavors wouldn't become dulled in the slow cooker, we added them just before serving. Be sure to use high-quality extra-virgin olive oil here; the test kitchen's favorite brand is Columela.

1 **pound kale, stemmed and sliced into 1-inch-wide strips**
2 **fennel bulbs, cored and sliced ¼ inch thick**
2 **cups chicken broth**
1 **cup oil-packed sun-dried tomatoes, rinsed, patted dry, and chopped coarse**
2 **tablespoons minced garlic**
¼ **teaspoon red pepper flakes**
  Salt and pepper
½ **cup grated Parmesan cheese**
½ **cup extra-virgin olive oil**
¼ **cup pine nuts, toasted**

1. Combine kale, fennel, broth, tomatoes, garlic, pepper flakes, 1 teaspoon salt, and ½ teaspoon pepper in slow cooker. Cover and cook until kale is tender, 5 to 6 hours on low or 3 to 4 hours on high.

2. Before serving, stir in Parmesan, oil, and pine nuts and season with salt and pepper to taste.

SMART SHOPPING PINE NUTS

Also called *piñons* (Spanish) or *pignoli* (Italian), these diminutive nutlike seeds are harvested from pine-cones. There are two main types of pine nuts: the delicately flavored, torpedo-shaped Mediterranean pine nuts and the more assertive corn kernel–shaped Chinese pine nuts (shown). The less-expensive Chinese variety is more widely available, but both can be used interchangeably. Pine nuts have a mild taste and a slightly waxy texture. Pine nuts need to be stored with care to prevent rancidity. They are best transferred to an airtight container as soon as their original packaging is opened. They will keep in the refrigerator for up to three months or in the freezer for up to nine months.

Escarole and White Bean Sauce

Makes 5 cups; enough for 1 pound pasta
Cooking Time 9 to 10 hours on Low or 6 to 7 hours on High   **Slow Cooker Size** 5½ to 7 Quarts

✔ **WHY THIS RECIPE WORKS:** The moist cooking environment of the slow cooker turns beans perfectly creamy and tender, so we set about using the slow cooker to create a sauce that paid homage to the classic dish of beans, greens, and pasta. Cannellini beans offered an earthy flavor and ultracreamy texture after simmering in chicken broth for several hours. Borrowing a trick used in many stew recipes, we mashed some of the beans to help thicken the sauce. For the greens, we opted for escarole, which we chopped and added to the slow cooker for the last 20 minutes of cooking so it would wilt but retain its color. Diced tomatoes and dried thyme, cooked with the beans, contributed brightness and woodsy notes, and a Parmesan cheese rind (another trick used in stews and sauces) offered complexity and bolstered the flavor of our sauce—and made use of an often-overlooked byproduct of pasta night. For an easy garnish, we microwaved a few slices of chopped bacon, then sprinkled the crisped pieces over the finished sauce for some crunch and salty, savory bites.

1	**cup chopped onion**
5	**tablespoons extra-virgin olive oil**
1	**teaspoon dried thyme**
8	**ounces dried cannellini beans, picked over and rinsed**
1	**(14.5-ounce) can diced tomatoes, drained**
5	**cups chicken broth**
1	**Parmesan cheese rind (optional)**
	Salt and pepper
½	**head escarole, chopped coarse**
4	**slices bacon, chopped**

1. Microwave onion, 1 tablespoon oil, and thyme in bowl, stirring occasionally, until onion is softened, about 5 minutes; transfer to slow cooker. Stir in beans, tomatoes, broth, Parmesan rind, if using, 1 teaspoon salt, and ½ teaspoon pepper. Cover and cook until beans are tender, 9 to 10 hours on low or 6 to 7 hours on high.

2. Discard Parmesan rind. Transfer 1 cup of bean-tomato mixture to bowl and mash with potato masher until mostly smooth. Stir escarole and mashed bean mixture into slow cooker, cover, and cook on high until escarole is tender, 20 to 30 minutes.

3. Line plate with double layer of coffee filters. Spread bacon in even layer over filters and microwave until crisp, about 5 minutes. Before serving, stir in crisp bacon and remaining ¼ cup oil and season with salt and pepper to taste.

SMART SHOPPING ESCAROLE
Escarole is a leafy green that looks much like green leaf lettuce. Its bitter flavor makes it a great choice for salads. But unlike lettuce, escarole stands up well to cooking, which makes it a great addition to this simple pasta sauce. Make sure to slice the escarole before washing it well. Use a salad spinner to wash it, as the fine, feathery leaves tend to hold a lot of soil.

All-Season Tomato Sauce

Makes 6 cups; enough for 1 pound of pasta
Cooking Time 5 to 6 hours on Low or 3 to 4 hours on High   **Slow Cooker Size** 5½ to 7 Quarts

✓ **WHY THIS RECIPE WORKS:** Nothing is more classic than a simple tomato sauce, but the truth is that to make a simple sauce with really big flavor, you need perfectly ripe, in-season tomatoes—and you have to not mind monitoring the stovetop for a couple of hours. For a full-flavored tomato sauce that was hands-off and could be made year-round, we started with cherry tomatoes, which offer bright, sweet flavor no matter the season, plus they didn't need any prep at all—we just tossed them into the slow cooker with some vegetable broth. For our aromatics, onion, garlic, and oregano provided a flavorful backbone, and tomato paste offered depth and complexity. To achieve just the right consistency, we mashed the tomatoes, but our sauce was still slightly thin. Because the slow cooker doesn't allow for any evaporation, we needed to include a thickener. For our next test, we stirred in a couple of tablespoons of instant tapioca. Finally, we had a rustic, chunky sauce that clung nicely to our pasta. With a drizzle of olive oil for richness and chopped basil for freshness, this simple tomato sauce delivered all the robust, bright flavors we expected—and we didn't have to wait until the height of summer to make it.

1	cup chopped onion
¼	cup extra-virgin olive oil
2	tablespoons minced garlic
¼	cup tomato paste
1	teaspoon dried oregano
2½	pounds cherry or grape tomatoes
½	cup vegetable broth
2	tablespoons instant tapioca
	Salt and pepper
¼	cup chopped fresh basil

1. Microwave onion, 1 tablespoon oil, garlic, tomato paste, and oregano in bowl, stirring occasionally, until onion is softened, about 5 minutes; transfer to slow cooker. Stir in tomatoes, broth, tapioca, ½ teaspoon salt, and ½ teaspoon pepper. Cover and cook until tomatoes are very soft and beginning to disintegrate, 5 to 6 hours on low or 3 to 4 hours on high.

2. Using potato masher, mash tomatoes until mostly smooth. Before serving, stir in basil and remaining 3 tablespoons oil and season with salt and pepper to taste.

SMART SHOPPING TOMATO PASTE

Tomato paste is naturally full of glutamates, which stimulate tastebuds just as salt and sugar do, and it brings out subtle flavors and savory notes, even in recipes in which tomato flavor isn't at the forefront. In our slow-cooker recipes, we made maximum use of tomato paste since the long cooking time tends to dull flavors. To find the best tomato paste, we gathered 10 top-selling brands and sampled each one uncooked, cooked plain, and in marinara sauce. **Goya Tomato Paste** earned top marks in both the uncooked and cooked tastings, and it came in second in our marinara test. Tasters praised it for being "rich, bold, and complex" and found it offered a "bright, robust tomato flavor."

Casseroles

Farmhouse Chicken Casserole

Serves 4 to 6   **Cooking Time** 4 to 5 hours on Low   **Slow Cooker Size** 5½ to 7 Quarts

✔ **WHY THIS RECIPE WORKS:** This satisfying, rustic casserole combines moist chicken and tender potatoes and carrots in a velvety sauce, topped off with a layer of crunchy croutons. To keep our prep work to a minimum, we chose boneless, skinless chicken thighs, which remained moist and tender during the long cooking time. Once tender, we shredded the chicken into bite-size pieces, then gently stirred them back into the slow cooker. To jump-start the cooking of our carrots and potatoes, we microwaved them briefly until they began to soften. For more color and a hint of sweetness, we added frozen peas, too. Boursin cheese, added when we set the chicken aside to cool, gave us the makings of an ultracreamy and flavor-packed sauce; a couple of tablespoons of tapioca, added to the slow cooker with the chicken, ensured that the sauce was thick and clingy. Croutons, sprinkled over the top of the finished casserole, provided a big crunch. We like the convenience of using store-bought croutons here; however, you can prepare and use our Rustic Croutons if desired. Don't shred the chicken too finely in step 2; it will break up more as it is stirred back into the casserole.

1   **pound red potatoes, cut into ½-inch pieces**

3   **carrots, peeled, halved lengthwise, and sliced ½ inch thick**

1   **tablespoon vegetable oil**

¼   **cup chicken broth**

2   **tablespoons instant tapioca**

2   **pounds boneless, skinless chicken thighs, trimmed**
    Salt and pepper

1   **(5.2-ounce) package Boursin Garlic and Fine Herbs cheese, crumbled**

½   **cup frozen peas**

3   **cups croutons**

1. Microwave potatoes, carrots, and oil in bowl, stirring occasionally, until vegetables are softened, about 5 minutes; transfer to slow cooker. Stir in broth and tapioca. Season chicken with salt and pepper and nestle into slow cooker. Cover and cook until chicken is tender, 4 to 5 hours on low.

2. Transfer chicken to cutting board, let cool slightly, then shred into bite-size pieces. Stir Boursin into slow cooker until cheese is melted and mixture is thickened slightly. Gently stir in shredded chicken and peas and season with salt and pepper to taste. (Adjust filling consistency with extra hot broth as needed.) Sprinkle with croutons and let sit until casserole is heated through, about 5 minutes. Serve.

QUICK PREP TIP RUSTIC CROUTONS
Tear 1 (18-inch) baguette into ¾-inch pieces. Toss bread with 2 tablespoons vegetable oil and season with ¼ teaspoon salt and ¼ teaspoon pepper. Spread bread in rimmed baking sheet and bake in 475-degree oven until golden brown, about 10 minutes. Let croutons cool to room temperature before using. Makes 3 cups.

Cheesy Chicken and Frito Casserole

Serves 4 to 6   **Cooking Time** 4 to 5 hours on Low   **Slow Cooker Size** 5½ to 7 Quarts

✔ **WHY THIS RECIPE WORKS:** To bring some excitement to the weeknight dinner table, we wanted to create a family-friendly casserole that offered all the bold, bright flavors of Tex-Mex cuisine. We started with boneless chicken thighs, which needed no prep. Black beans and corn added substance, and Ro-tel tomatoes provided spicy, piquant flavor. A couple of teaspoons of cumin contributed warm spice notes and earthiness, and minced cilantro offered bright, citrusy notes. When the chicken was done cooking, we stirred in some shredded Mexican cheese, which melted into a rich-tasting sauce. For a crunchy topping that went with our Tex-Mex theme, we sprinkled the casserole with crumbled tortilla chips, but they tasted stale. Fritos, on the other hand, delivered both big corn flavor and plenty of crunch. Stirring more Frito crumbs into the casserole helped to thicken the sauce, as did a small amount of tapioca. Don't shred the chicken too finely in step 2; it will break up more as it is stirred back into the casserole.

2	**(10-ounce) cans Ro-tel Diced Tomatoes & Green Chilies, drained**
1	**(15-ounce) can black beans, rinsed**
2	**tablespoons instant tapioca**
2	**teaspoons ground cumin**
2	**pounds boneless, skinless chicken thighs, trimmed**
	Salt and pepper
4	**cups Fritos corn chips, crushed into coarse crumbs**
1½	**cups shredded Mexican cheese blend**
½	**cup frozen corn, thawed**
¼	**cup minced fresh cilantro**

1. Combine tomatoes, beans, tapioca, and cumin in slow cooker. Season chicken with salt and pepper and nestle into slow cooker. Cover and cook until chicken is tender, 4 to 5 hours on low.

2. Transfer chicken to cutting board, let cool slightly, then shred into bite-size pieces. Stir 1 cup Fritos, 1 cup Mexican cheese blend, corn, and cilantro into slow cooker until cheese is melted and mixture is thickened slightly. Gently stir in shredded chicken and season with salt and pepper to taste. (Adjust filling consistency with hot water as needed.)

3. Sprinkle with remaining ½ cup cheese and remaining 3 cups Fritos, cover, and cook on high until casserole is heated through and cheese is melted, about 5 minutes. Serve.

SMART SHOPPING CANNED BLACK BEANS
Most canned black beans have three main ingredients: beans, water, and salt. Still, we found when we sampled six national brands that taste can vary wildly. Our tasters had a strong preference for well-seasoned beans, but texture was important, too. The "clean," "mild," and "slightly earthy" flavor of **Bush's Best Black Beans**, along with their "firm," "almost al dente" texture made them our winner.

Shepherd's Pie with Chicken

Serves 4 to 6   **Cooking Time** 2 to 3 hours on Low   **Slow Cooker Size** 5½ to 7 Quarts

✓ **WHY THIS RECIPE WORKS:** To put a new spin on the classic shepherd's pie, we swapped out the usual ground beef for ground chicken. Microwaving the chicken for a few minutes before transferring it to the slow cooker ensured that it didn't turn grainy, and cooking our casserole on low prevented the chicken from drying out. Carrots, mushrooms, and peas worked well for the vegetables. Including Worcestershire sauce and tomato paste in the filling helped to amp up the meaty, savory notes of the chicken. Mashed potatoes were a given for the topping, and starting with the prepared variety kept our recipe easy. Adding shredded cheddar to our potatoes ramped up their flavor so they didn't taste store-bought. Be sure to use ground chicken, not ground chicken breast (also labeled 99 percent fat free). We like the convenience of using prepared mashed potatoes from the supermarket (often found in the prepared food and/or refrigerated section); however, you can prepare and use our Homemade Mashed Potato Topping, if desired. The mashed potatoes should be warm and have a loose but not soupy texture; otherwise they will be difficult to spread over the chicken filling.

2   **pounds ground chicken**

8   **ounces sliced white mushrooms**

2   **carrots, peeled, halved lengthwise, and sliced ½ inch thick**

3   **tablespoons tomato paste**

½   **teaspoon dried thyme**
     Salt and pepper

2   **tablespoons Worcestershire sauce**

2   **tablespoons instant tapioca**

1   **cup frozen peas**

½   **cup heavy cream**

3   **cups prepared mashed potatoes, warmed**

½   **cup shredded cheddar cheese**

1. Microwave ground chicken in bowl, stirring occasionally, until chicken is no longer pink, about 5 minutes. Transfer chicken to slow cooker, breaking up any large pieces. Microwave mushrooms, carrots, tomato paste, thyme, and ½ teaspoon salt in bowl, stirring occasionally, until vegetables are softened, about 5 minutes; drain vegetables and transfer to slow cooker. Stir in Worcestershire and tapioca. Cover and cook until chicken is tender, 2 to 3 hours on low.

2. Stir in peas and cream and season with salt and pepper to taste. (Adjust filling consistency with hot water as needed.) Combine potatoes and cheddar, then spoon mixture over chicken filling and smooth into even layer using spatula. Cover and cook on high until potatoes are heated through, 20 to 30 minutes. Serve.

QUICK PREP TIP HOMEMADE MASHED POTATO TOPPING

Cover 1½ pounds russet potatoes, peeled, sliced ¾ inch thick, and rinsed well, with water in Dutch oven. Bring to boil, then reduce to simmer and cook until tender, 18 to 20 minutes. Drain potatoes, wipe pot dry, then return potatoes to pot. Mash potatoes thoroughly with potato masher. Fold in 3 tablespoons melted unsalted butter, then fold in ¾ cup hot half-and-half. (Add additional hot half-and-half as needed until potatoes have loose but not soupy texture.) Season with salt and pepper to taste. Makes 3 cups.

Thanksgiving Turkey Pot Pie

Serves 4 to 6   **Cooking Time** 4 to 5 hours on Low   **Slow Cooker Size** 5½ to 7 Quarts

✔ **WHY THIS RECIPE WORKS:** This Thanksgiving-inspired meal makes it easy to enjoy the flavors of the holidays year-round. To cut down on prep and save time, we reached for convenient boneless, skinless turkey thighs; once they were tender, we shredded them into bite-size pieces. Thinly sliced carrots added a vegetal element and some sweetness. Stirring a splash of heavy cream into the braising liquid gave us an instant "gravy" that coated the turkey and carrots nicely. For the topping, we thought stuffing seemed perfect. Instead of making our own from scratch, we went with a store-bought mix, which included a number of herbs and spices and allowed us to cut back on our ingredient list. In a nod to the traditional Thanksgiving dinner, we added dried cranberries; their sweet, tart notes contrasted nicely with the savory stuffing. After moistening the mix with water, we crumbled it on top of the filling, covered the slow cooker, and let it heat through. If you cannot find boneless turkey thighs, you can substitute boneless chicken thighs. Be sure to use a boxed stuffing mix, such as Stove Top Stuffing Mix, rather than any of the bags of loose crumbs that are sold as stuffing mix; you can use any flavor here.

2	**carrots, peeled and sliced ½ inch thick**
1	**tablespoon vegetable oil**
1	**teaspoon dried sage**
¼	**cup chicken broth**
2	**tablespoons instant tapioca**
2	**pounds boneless, skinless turkey thighs, trimmed**
	Salt and pepper
1	**(6-ounce) box stuffing mix**
1½	**cups boiling water**
½	**cup dried cranberries**
¼	**cup heavy cream**

1. Microwave carrots, oil, and sage in bowl, stirring occasionally, until carrots are softened, about 5 minutes; transfer to slow cooker. Stir in broth and tapioca. Season turkey with salt and pepper and nestle into slow cooker. Cover and cook until turkey is tender, 4 to 5 hours on low.

2. Transfer turkey to cutting board, let cool slightly, then shred into bite-size pieces. Combine stuffing mix, boiling water, and cranberries in bowl and let sit, stirring occasionally, until stuffing is completely softened, about 5 minutes.

3. Gently stir shredded turkey and cream into slow cooker and season with salt and pepper to taste. (Adjust filling consistency with extra hot broth as needed.) Spoon stuffing mixture over turkey filling and smooth into even layer. Cover and cook on high until stuffing is heated through, 20 to 30 minutes. Serve.

ON THE SIDE CRANBERRY SAUCE
Bring 1 cup sugar, ¾ cup water, and ¼ teaspoon salt to boil in medium saucepan over medium heat, stirring occasionally to help dissolve sugar. Stir in 12 ounces fresh or frozen cranberries and simmer until slightly thickened and berries begin to pop, 10 to 12 minutes. Cool to room temperature before serving, about 1 hour. Makes 2 cups.

Italian Pork and Polenta Bake

Serves 4 to 6   **Cooking Time** 6 to 7 hours on Low or 4 to 5 hours on High
Slow Cooker Size 5½ to 7 Quarts

✔ **WHY THIS RECIPE WORKS:** For a rich and hearty Italian-style casserole we combined two classics: pork ragu and polenta. While pork shoulder is the most common choice for slow-cooked pork, using it required cutting up the meat. Instead we chose boneless country-style pork ribs, which contained plenty of intramuscular fat to keep the meat moist during the extended cooking time and required no extra knife work. A combination of white and porcini mushrooms ramped up the meaty flavor of the sauce, and tapioca ensured that it was glossy and silky. Precooked polenta, sliced thin and sprinkled with Parmesan, made for a golden, flavor-packed crown.

8	ounces sliced white mushrooms
1	cup chopped onion
2	tablespoons tomato paste
1	tablespoon olive oil
1	tablespoon minced garlic
¼	teaspoon red pepper flakes
¼	ounce dried porcini mushrooms, rinsed and minced
2	tablespoons instant tapioca
	Salt and pepper
2	pounds boneless country-style pork ribs, trimmed
1	(18-ounce) tube precooked polenta, sliced ¼ inch thick
1	cup grated Parmesan cheese

1. Microwave white mushrooms, onion, tomato paste, oil, garlic, and pepper flakes in bowl, stirring occasionally, until vegetables are softened, about 5 minutes; drain vegetables and transfer to slow cooker. Stir in porcini mushrooms, tapioca, 1 teaspoon salt, and ½ teaspoon pepper. Season pork with salt and pepper and nestle into slow cooker. Cover and cook until pork is tender, 6 to 7 hours on low or 4 to 5 hours on high.

2. Transfer pork to cutting board, let cool slightly, then shred into bite-size pieces. Gently stir shredded pork into slow cooker and season with salt and pepper to taste. (Adjust filling consistency with hot water as needed.) Shingle polenta on top of pork filling and sprinkle with Parmesan. Cover and cook on high until polenta is heated through and cheese is melted, 20 to 30 minutes. Serve.

QUICK PREP TIP **STORING MUSHROOMS**

Curious as to the best way to store mushrooms once you get them home from the market, we pitted several storing methods against each other over a five-day period to see what worked and what didn't. Among the things we tried were leaving them in their original box and covering them with plastic wrap or a damp paper towel, wrapping them in aluminum foil, storing them in a paper bag, storing them in a paper bag cut with air holes, storing them in an airtight zipper-lock bag, and simply leaving them uncovered. The winning method turned out to be either the original packaging (if purchased in a tray wrapped in plastic), or a simple paper bag (if purchased loose). The other methods were flat-out losers and turned the mushrooms either slimy or dried out in just a couple of days.

Monterey Chicken and Rice

Serves 4 to 6   **Cooking Time** 4 to 5 hours on Low   **Slow Cooker Size** 5½ to 7 Quarts

✔ **WHY THIS RECIPE WORKS:** To up the ante on the standard chicken and rice, we added bacon, barbecue sauce, tomatoes, and pepper Jack cheese for a lively, full-flavored dinner. Cooking the chicken and rice together gave us moist meat, but the rice was underdone. Both instant rice and leftover precooked white rice turned mushy. Luckily, we had success when we tried store-bought precooked white rice, which remained tender and didn't become blown out. Chunks of avocado and crisped bacon, cooked briefly in the microwave, added richness and salty, savory bites. Store-bought precooked rice is important to the success of this dish; it consistently remains intact and retains the proper doneness. Do not use freshly made or leftover rice, as it will turn mushy and blown out in the slow cooker. Don't shred the chicken too finely in step 2; it will break up more as it is stirred back into the casserole.

1	**red onion, halved and sliced ¼ inch thick**
1	**tablespoon vegetable oil**
1	**tablespoon chili powder**
4	**cups cooked rice**
½	**cup barbecue sauce**
1	**tablespoon Dijon mustard**
2	**pounds boneless, skinless chicken thighs, trimmed**
	Salt and pepper
2	**tomatoes, cored and chopped**
1½	**cups shredded pepper Jack cheese**
1	**avocado, halved, pitted, and cut into ½-inch pieces**
4	**slices bacon, chopped**

1. Microwave onion, oil, and chili powder in bowl, stirring occasionally, until onion is softened, about 5 minutes; transfer to slow cooker. Stir in rice, barbecue sauce, and mustard. Season chicken with salt and pepper and nestle into slow cooker. Cover and cook until chicken is tender, 4 to 5 hours on low.

2. Transfer chicken to cutting board, let cool slightly, then shred into bite-size pieces. Gently stir shredded chicken, tomatoes, and 1 cup pepper Jack into slow cooker and season with salt and pepper to taste. Sprinkle with avocado and remaining ½ cup pepper Jack, cover, and cook on high until casserole is heated through and cheese is melted, about 5 minutes.

3. Meanwhile, line plate with double layer of coffee filters. Spread bacon in even layer over filters and microwave until crisp, about 5 minutes. Sprinkle casserole with crisp bacon. Serve.

SMART SHOPPING PRECOOKED RICE

We find the ease and convenience of precooked rice, which is parboiled, to be real assets when we're trying to save time in the kitchen—plus, there's no need to worry about gummy, burnt, or overcooked rice ruining the dish. After testing five national brands to find the best option, we found one brand that stood apart with "nicely separate" grains and a "toasted, buttery" flavor. The favorite, **Minute Ready to Serve White Rice**, even fooled a few tasters who thought it tasted like freshly made rice. Note that each package yields 2 cups of rice.

Lemony Chicken and Rice with Spinach and Feta

Serves 4 to 6   **Cooking Time** 4 to 5 hours on Low   **Slow Cooker Size** 5½ to 7 Quarts

✔ **WHY THIS RECIPE WORKS:** For another chicken and rice dinner that was big on flavor but light on prep, we looked to the Mediterranean for inspiration and included feta for its briny tang, lemon for brightness, and baby spinach for freshness and color. Precooked rice, purchased at the supermarket, worked best and kept our recipe super-easy; starting with uncooked rice gave us underdone grains, and using leftover white rice resulted in mushy, blown-out grains. Once the chicken and rice were done, we stirred in a generous amount of crumbled feta and a few handfuls of baby spinach; some half-and-half ensured that our dish was rich and creamy. Using both lemon zest and juice delivered bright and citrusy, but not tart, flavor. So that the lemon would retain its bold, bright notes, we didn't add it until the end. Store-bought precooked rice is important to the success of this dish; it consistently remains intact and retains the proper doneness. Do not use freshly made or leftover rice, as it will turn mushy and blown out in the slow cooker. Don't shred the chicken too finely in step 2; it will break up more as it is stirred back into the casserole. See page 209 for more information on our top-rated precooked rice.

1	cup chopped onion
1	tablespoon vegetable oil
1	tablespoon minced garlic
½	teaspoon dried oregano
4	cups cooked rice
2	pounds boneless, skinless chicken thighs, trimmed
	Salt and pepper
4	ounces (4 cups) baby spinach
1½	cups crumbled feta cheese
½	cup half-and-half
1	teaspoon grated lemon zest plus 2 tablespoons juice

1. Microwave onion, oil, garlic, and oregano in bowl, stirring occasionally, until onion is softened, about 5 minutes; transfer to slow cooker. Stir in rice. Season chicken with salt and pepper and nestle into slow cooker. Cover and cook until chicken is tender, 4 to 5 hours on low.

2. Transfer chicken to cutting board, let cool slightly, then shred into bite-size pieces. Gently stir shredded chicken, spinach, 1 cup feta, and half-and-half into slow cooker and let sit until spinach is wilted and casserole is heated through, about 5 minutes. Stir in lemon zest and juice and season with salt and pepper to taste. Sprinkle with remaining ½ cup feta. Serve.

SMART SHOPPING FETA CHEESE

In 2005, the European Union ruled that only cheese produced in Greece from at least 70 percent sheep's milk can rightfully bear the label "feta." Here in the United States, where these stipulations don't apply, imitators abound. We tasted five brands, both imports and domestic. Tasters preferred the "barnyard" taste of the sheep's- and goat's-milk imports, giving **Mt. Vikos Traditional Feta**, which hails from the mother country, the top spot. Keep feta submerged in the brine in which it was packed. When stored properly, feta can keep for up to three months, though it will become considerably saltier and more pungent over time.

Easy Mexican Lasagna

Serves 4 to 6   **Cooking Time** 2 to 3 hours on Low   **Slow Cooker Size** 5½ to 7 Quarts

✓ **WHY THIS RECIPE WORKS:** Homemade enchiladas are tedious and time-consuming to make, which is a shame because the robust, spicy flavors and varying textures are incredibly satisfying. For an easier take on this popular Mexican dish, we started with canned enchilada sauce and boosted its flavor with chopped jalapeños. Shredded Monterey Jack gave the sauce some much-needed richness. For the meat, we opted for ground beef, which contributed big, hearty flavor, but it had a tendency to turn gritty after hours of slow cooking. We found that microwaving it briefly firmed it up so we could break it into coarse crumbles that didn't turn grainy. Instead of rolling up the filling in tortillas, we simply layered it between the tortillas, then covered them with more sauce and cheese. So that everything cooked through evenly, we lined our slow cooker with aluminum foil. With a bit of minced fresh cilantro, we had the perfect finish to our cheesy—and easy—homage to beef enchiladas. For more information on making a foil collar, see page 180. Serve with sour cream and salsa.

2 pounds 85 percent lean ground beef

2 (10-ounce) cans red enchilada sauce

2 cups shredded Monterey Jack cheese

¼ cup jarred jalapeños, chopped

½ cup minced fresh cilantro

12 (6-inch) corn tortillas

1. Microwave ground beef in large bowl, stirring occasionally, until beef is no longer pink, about 10 minutes. Break up any large pieces of beef with spoon, then drain off fat; return to now-empty bowl. Stir in 1 cup enchilada sauce, 1 cup Monterey Jack, jalapeños, and ¼ cup cilantro.

2. Line slow cooker with aluminum foil collar and spray with vegetable oil spray. Spread ¼ cup enchilada sauce in prepared slow cooker. Arrange 3 corn tortillas in single layer in bottom of slow cooker, tearing tortillas as needed to fit. Top with one-third of beef mixture and 3 more corn tortillas; repeat layering 2 more times. Spread remaining enchilada sauce over tortillas and sprinkle with remaining 1 cup Monterey Jack. Cover and cook until casserole is heated through, 2 to 3 hours on low.

3. Remove foil collar. Sprinkle with remaining ¼ cup cilantro. Serve.

QUICK PREP TIP STORING CORN TORTILLAS

Corn tortillas are smaller and richer in flavor than their flour cousins, and they are often sold in packages of 24 or more. Since we rarely go through that many tortillas at once, we find it best to store extra tortillas in our freezer for later use. To freeze corn tortillas, gently peel individual tortillas from the stack and place them between pieces of wax or parchment paper, then freeze up to 12 tortillas in a zipper-lock freezer bag. When you're ready to use them, defrost stacks of four to six tortillas in the microwave at 50 percent power until thawed, 10 to 20 seconds per stack.

American Chop Suey

Serves 4   **Cooking Time** 2 to 3 hours on High   **Slow Cooker Size** 5½ to 7 Quarts

✔ **WHY THIS RECIPE WORKS:** This diner favorite pairs tender elbow macaroni with a meaty tomato sauce flavored with bell pepper and celery. But most of the time, the pasta is blown out and the flavors are washed out. For a full-flavored chop suey with tender pasta—all prepared in the slow cooker—we toasted our pasta with oil in the microwave before combining it with hot water to jump-start its cooking. For the sauce, 85 percent lean ground beef worked well, and microwaving it briefly helped to render excess fat and ensured that the beef didn't turn grainy over the long cooking time. A large can of tomato sauce provided brightness and gave our meat sauce just the right consistency. To bump up its flavor, we included bell pepper, celery, garlic, and red pepper flakes; a small amount of Worcestershire amped up the savory notes of the sauce. Finally, to ensure a dish with bright, fresh flavors, we stirred in more tomato sauce just before serving. For more information on cooking pasta in the slow cooker and making a foil collar, see page 180.

1 **pound 85 percent lean ground beef**

1 **green bell pepper, cored and chopped**

2 **celery ribs, minced**

1 **tablespoon minced garlic**

¼ **teaspoon red pepper flakes**

1 **(29-ounce) can tomato sauce**

1 **tablespoon Worcestershire sauce Salt and pepper**

8 **ounces (2 cups) elbow macaroni**

2 **teaspoons vegetable oil**

½ **cup boiling water**

½ **cup grated Parmesan cheese**

1. Microwave ground beef, bell pepper, celery, garlic, and pepper flakes in bowl, stirring occasionally, until beef is no longer pink, about 5 minutes. Break up any large pieces of beef with spoon, then drain off fat; return to now-empty bowl. Stir in 2½ cups tomato sauce, Worcestershire, ½ teaspoon salt, and ½ teaspoon pepper.

2. Line slow cooker with aluminum foil collar and spray with vegetable oil spray. Microwave macaroni and oil in separate bowl at 50 percent power, stirring occasionally, until some pieces look toasted and blistered, 3 to 5 minutes. Transfer hot pasta to prepared slow cooker and immediately stir in boiling water (pasta will sizzle). Stir in meat and sauce mixture, cover, and cook until pasta is tender, 2 to 3 hours on high.

3. Remove foil collar. Gently stir in remaining tomato sauce, adjusting sauce consistency with extra hot water as needed. Season with salt and pepper to taste. Sprinkle with Parmesan. Serve.

ON THE SIDE SESAME ROLLS
Cut 1 pound pizza dough into 4 equal pieces and roll into balls. Arrange on well-oiled baking sheet, brush lightly with beaten egg, and sprinkle with 2 teaspoons sesame seeds and salt. Bake in 350-degree oven until golden, about 25 to 30 minutes. Let cool for 5 minutes before serving. Makes 4 large rolls.

Cheeseburger Pasta Bake

Serves 4   **Cooking Time** 2 to 3 hours on High   **Slow Cooker Size** 5½ to 7 Quarts

✔ **WHY THIS RECIPE WORKS:** For another practically prep-free pasta casserole, we added ground beef, pickles, American cheese, and chopped onion to macaroni for a dish with all the bright, tangy, meaty flavors of our favorite burger. Tomato sauce, with its smooth texture and long-cooked flavor, provided the perfect base for our sauce, which we seasoned with Worcestershire sauce and dry mustard for more savory, meaty notes. Slices of American cheese made the perfect topping. To preserve the cheese's flavor and texture, we added it at the very end, then covered the slow cooker and turned it to high for just a few minutes so the cheese would melt into a gooey layer. For more information on cooking pasta in the slow cooker and making a foil collar, see page 180.

1   **pound 85 percent lean ground beef**

1   **(29-ounce) can tomato sauce**

½   **cup chopped dill pickles**

2   **teaspoons Worcestershire sauce**

2   **teaspoons dry mustard**
     Salt and pepper

8   **ounces (2 cups) elbow macaroni**

2   **teaspoons vegetable oil**

½   **cup boiling water**

6   **ounces sliced deli American cheese**

1. Microwave ground beef in bowl, stirring occasionally, until beef is no longer pink, about 5 minutes. Break up any large pieces of beef with spoon, then drain off fat; return to now-empty bowl. Stir in 2½ cups tomato sauce, pickles, Worcestershire, mustard, ½ teaspoon salt, and ½ teaspoon pepper.

2. Line slow cooker with aluminum foil collar and spray with vegetable oil spray. Microwave macaroni and oil in separate bowl at 50 percent power, stirring occasionally, until some pieces look toasted and blistered, 3 to 5 minutes. Transfer hot pasta to prepared slow cooker and immediately stir in boiling water (pasta will sizzle). Stir in meat and sauce mixture, cover, and cook until pasta is tender, 2 to 3 hours on high.

3. Remove foil collar. Gently stir in remaining tomato sauce, adjusting sauce consistency with extra hot water as needed. Season with salt and pepper to taste. Lay American cheese on top of pasta, cover, and cook on high until cheese is melted, about 5 minutes. Serve.

ON THE SIDE ROASTED BROCCOLI

Adjust oven rack to lowest position and heat oven to 500 degrees. Place aluminum foil–lined baking sheet in oven. Cut 1 pound broccoli at juncture of crown and stalk. Peel stalk and cut into ½-inch-thick planks about 3 inches long. Place crown upside down and cut in half through central stalk, then cut each half into 3 or 4 wedges for 3- to 4-inch-diameter crown, or into 6 wedges for 4- to 5-inch-diameter crown. Toss with 3 tablespoons extra-virgin olive oil and ½ teaspoon sugar and season with salt and pepper. Place on baking sheet and roast until tender, 14 to 16 minutes. Serves 4.

Baked Penne with Chicken Sausage and Red Pepper Pesto

Serves 4   **Cooking Time** 2 to 3 hours on High   **Slow Cooker Size** 5½ to 7 Quarts

WHY THIS RECIPE WORKS: Smoky and sweet, roasted red peppers star in a potently flavored pesto in this surprisingly simple casserole. To start, we processed jarred roasted red peppers with olive oil, garlic, and thyme. Then, we combined the pesto with penne (toasted briefly in the microwave) in the slow cooker, adding Italian chicken sausage for heartiness. For freshness and color, we stirred in more pesto and a few cups of baby spinach once the casserole had finished cooking. Finally, for a gooey, tangy topping, we placed a few slices of provolone over the pasta and let it melt. For more information on cooking pasta in the slow cooker and making a foil collar, see page 180.

3	cups jarred roasted red peppers, patted dry
¼	cup plus 2 teaspoons extra-virgin olive oil
2	garlic cloves, peeled
½	teaspoon dried thyme
	Salt and pepper
8	ounces (2½ cups) penne
1	cup boiling water
1	pound hot or sweet Italian chicken sausage, casings removed
4	ounces (4 cups) baby spinach
6	ounces sliced deli provolone cheese

1. Process peppers, ¼ cup oil, garlic, thyme, ½ teaspoon salt, and ½ teaspoon pepper in food processor until smooth, 30 to 60 seconds, scraping down sides of bowl as needed. Measure out and reserve ½ cup pesto.

2. Line slow cooker with aluminum foil collar and spray with vegetable oil spray. Microwave penne and remaining 2 teaspoons oil in bowl at 50 percent power, stirring occasionally, until some pieces look toasted and blistered, 3 to 5 minutes. Transfer hot pasta to prepared slow cooker and immediately stir in boiling water (pasta will sizzle). Pinch off sausage into tablespoon-size pieces and drop over pasta. Stir in remaining pesto, cover, and cook until pasta is tender, 2 to 3 hours on high.

3. Remove foil collar. Gently stir in reserved ½ cup pesto, adjusting sauce consistency with extra hot water as needed. Season with salt and pepper to taste. Stir in spinach, then lay provolone on top of pasta. Cover and cook on high until spinach is wilted and cheese is melted, about 5 minutes. Serve.

SMART SHOPPING **ROASTED RED PEPPERS**

We tasted eight brands of roasted red peppers, both straight out of the jars and in roasted red pepper soup, to find the best one. Overall, tasters preferred firmer, smokier, sweeter-tasting peppers packed in simple brines made of salt and water. Peppers packed in brines that contained garlic, vinegar, olive oil, and grape must—characteristic of most of the European brands—rated second. Our winner? Tasters preferred the domestically produced **Dunbars Sweet Roasted Peppers**, which lists only red bell peppers, water, salt, and citric acid in its ingredient list.

Spinach Manicotti

Serves 4   **Cooking Time** 3 to 4 hours on High   **Slow Cooker Size** 5½ to 7 Quarts

WHY THIS RECIPE WORKS: The key to slow-cooked manicotti with perfectly tender noodles was adding the right amount of liquid to the slow cooker. If we used too much, the manicotti tubes were bloated; too little, and they didn't cook through evenly. A 25-ounce jar of marinara sauce and 1½ cups of water proved just the right amounts. For a rich-tasting filling, we started with Alfredo sauce and shredded Italian cheese blend; ricotta guaranteed that it was creamy, and frozen spinach ensured that we got our greens in. Panko worked well to bind the creamy, flavorful mixture so it stayed put when piped into the shells. Be sure to let the manicotti cool for the full 20 minutes; they are fragile and will be easier to lift out of the slow cooker when cooled slightly. For more information on cooking pasta in the slow cooker and making a foil collar, see page 180. You will need an oval slow cooker for this recipe.

8	**manicotti shells**
	Vegetable oil spray
1	**(25-ounce) jar marinara sauce (3 cups)**
1½	**cups water**
1½	**cups shredded Italian cheese blend**
8	**ounces (1 cup) whole-milk ricotta cheese**
6	**ounces frozen chopped spinach, thawed and squeezed dry**
¾	**cup jarred Alfredo sauce**
¼	**cup panko bread crumbs**
½	**teaspoon salt**
2	**tablespoons chopped basil**

1. Spray exterior of manicotti shells with vegetable oil spray and microwave on large plate at 50 percent power, turning occasionally, until some pieces look toasted and blistered in spots, 3 to 5 minutes; let cool slightly. Combine marinara sauce and water in bowl.

2. In separate bowl, combine 1 cup Italian cheese blend, ricotta, spinach, Alfredo sauce, panko, and salt. Transfer ricotta mixture to pastry bag or large zipper-lock bag. (If using zipper-lock bag, cut ¾ inch off one bottom corner.) Pipe filling evenly into cooled manicotti shells from both ends, working outward from center.

3. Line slow cooker with aluminum foil collar and spray with vegetable oil spray. Spread half of sauce mixture in prepared slow cooker and nestle filled manicotti into sauce. Spoon remaining sauce mixture over manicotti, cover, and cook until pasta is tender, 3 to 4 hours on high.

4. Sprinkle with remaining ½ cup Italian cheese blend. Let casserole cool for 20 minutes, sprinkle with basil, and serve.

SMART SHOPPING RICOTTA CHEESE
Originally crafted from the whey byproduct of Romano cheese making (its name means "recooked"), ricotta cheese is used in many baked pasta dishes. Nowadays, ricotta is made from milk, not whey. We like **Calabro Ricotta Cheese**, which is made of milk, a starter, and salt. (Note that Calabro makes both part-skim and whole-milk ricotta.) If you can't find this brand, look for one without gums or stabilizers.

Vegetarian Dinners

Miso Soup with Ramen and Tofu

Serves 6   **Cooking Time** 4 to 5 hours on Low or 3 to 4 hours on High
Slow Cooker Size 5½ to 7 Quarts

✔ **WHY THIS RECIPE WORKS:** A great miso soup requires a great broth—and hunting down obscure ingredients. To get a broth with the same complexity and earthy, briny flavor without a special shopping trip, we created a flavor-packed base with shiitake mushrooms, ginger, soy sauce, and sesame oil. We tried different types of miso, but tasters preferred the white variety. Water worked well for the liquid base; vegetable broth overshadowed the delicate flavors of the miso and aromatics. For the tofu, we selected the extra-firm variety, as it held its shape best during cooking. Supermarket ramen noodles (minus the seasoning packets) ensured that our miso soup was filling and were tender in a matter of minutes. Baby spinach and radish slices offered freshness and balance. Be sure not to overcook the ramen noodles or else they will become mushy.

12 ounces shiitake mushrooms, stemmed and sliced thin

 1 (2-inch) piece ginger, sliced into ¼-inch-thick rounds

 2 tablespoons toasted sesame oil

 2 tablespoons minced garlic

 8 cups water

 ½ cup white miso

14 ounces extra-firm tofu, cut into ½-inch pieces

 2 tablespoons soy sauce

 2 (3-ounce) packages ramen noodles, seasoning discarded

 6 ounces (6 cups) baby spinach

 5 radishes, trimmed, halved, and sliced thin

    Salt and pepper

1. Microwave mushrooms, ginger, 1 tablespoon oil, and garlic in bowl, stirring occasionally, until mushrooms are softened, about 5 minutes. Whisk 1 cup water and miso together in slow cooker until miso is fully dissolved. Stir in remaining 7 cups water, mushroom mixture, tofu, and soy sauce. Cover and cook until flavors meld and mushrooms are tender, 4 to 5 hours on low or 3 to 4 hours on high.

2. Discard ginger. Stir in ramen noodles, cover, and cook on high until tender, 4 to 8 minutes. Stir in spinach, 1 handful at a time, and let sit until wilted, about 5 minutes. Stir in radishes and remaining 1 tablespoon oil. Season with extra soy sauce, salt, and pepper to taste and serve.

SMART SHOPPING MISO
Made from a fermented mixture of soybeans and rice, barley, or rye, miso is incredibly versatile, suitable for use in soups, braises, dressings, and sauces. This salty, deep-flavored paste ranges in strength and color from mild pale yellow (referred to as white) to stronger-flavored red or brownish black, depending on the fermentation method and ingredients.

Spanish Lentil Stew

Serves 6   **Cooking Time** 6 to 7 hours on Low or 4 to 5 hours on High
Slow Cooker Size 5½ to 7 Quarts

✔ **WHY THIS RECIPE WORKS:** Lentil stew is one of the easiest dishes to make in the slow cooker, yet all too often, it turns into a hodgepodge of lentils, canned tomatoes, and whatever assorted vegetables are lingering in the crisper drawer. To elevate our lentil stew from ordinary to extraordinary, we included a hefty amount of smoked paprika for a definitively Spanish bent. A bit of cumin reinforced the sweet, earthy notes of the paprika. For a flavorful foundation, we cooked the spices and aromatics in the microwave to bloom their flavors. Sweet potatoes and chopped kale paired nicely with the smoky paprika and added heartiness. For brightness, we kept the tomatoes but opted for the fresh variety and stirred them in at the end to warm through. Finishing each bowl with a drizzle of olive oil offered richness. We prefer French green lentils, or *lentilles du Puy*, for this recipe, but it will work with any type of lentil except red or yellow. The lentils and sweet potatoes become very tender in this stew; be sure to stir it gently to prevent them from breaking down too much.

1   **cup chopped onion**

2   **tablespoons smoked paprika**

1   **tablespoon extra-virgin olive oil**

1   **tablespoon minced garlic**

1   **teaspoon ground cumin**

8   **cups vegetable broth**

1   **cup lentils, picked over and rinsed**

1   **pound sweet potatoes, peeled and cut into ¾-inch pieces**
    Salt and pepper

8   **ounces kale, stemmed and sliced into ½-inch-wide strips**

2   **tomatoes, cored and cut into ½-inch pieces**

1. Microwave onion, paprika, oil, garlic, and cumin in bowl, stirring occasionally, until onion is softened, about 5 minutes; transfer to slow cooker. Stir in broth, lentils, potatoes, 1 teaspoon salt, and ½ teaspoon pepper. Cover and cook until lentils are tender, 6 to 7 hours on low or 4 to 5 hours on high.

2. Gently stir in kale, cover, and cook on high until tender, 20 to 30 minutes. (Adjust stew consistency with extra hot broth as needed.) Stir in tomatoes and season with salt and pepper to taste. Drizzle individual portions with extra oil and serve.

ON THE SIDE SCALLION-CHEDDAR MUFFINS
Whisk 3 cups all-purpose flour, 1 tablespoon baking powder, 1 teaspoon salt, and ⅛ teaspoon pepper together in large bowl. Stir in 1 cup shredded cheddar cheese and 2 thinly sliced scallions. In separate bowl, whisk together 1¼ cups whole milk, ¾ cup sour cream, 3 tablespoons melted unsalted butter, and 1 lightly beaten large egg. Gently fold milk mixture into flour mixture (batter will be very thick). Portion batter into greased 12-cup muffin tin and sprinkle with ½ cup grated Parmesan cheese. Bake in 350-degree oven until golden brown, 25 to 30 minutes. Let cool for 15 minutes before serving. Makes 12.

Wheat Berry and Wild Mushroom Stew

Serves 6   **Cooking Time** 10 to 11 hours on Low or 7 to 8 hours on High
Slow Cooker Size 5½ to 7 Quarts

✔ **WHY THIS RECIPE WORKS:** For a vegetarian stew that was so flavorful and substantial even carnivores would be satisfied, we started with sweet, nutty wheat berries and added mushrooms for earthy, meaty depth. The wheat berries were hearty enough to withstand the long cooking time of the slow cooker, yet still maintain their chewy texture. Including two types of mushrooms—sliced cremini and dried porcini—ensured that our stew had tender bites of mushroom and intense, earthy flavor. To reinforce the woodsy notes of the mushrooms, we included dried thyme. Vegetable broth worked well for the cooking liquid and provided a subtly sweet backbone. To give it a boost, we stirred in some Madeira; adding more of the fortified wine at the end of cooking contributed brightness to our hearty stew. Baby spinach provided some color and freshness. Finally, for a hint of richness, we stirred in a couple of pats of butter. The wheat berries will retain a chewy texture once fully cooked. You can substitute dry sherry for the Madeira if desired.

2	**pounds sliced cremini mushrooms**
1	**tablespoon vegetable oil**
1	**tablespoon minced garlic**
½	**teaspoon dried thyme**
6	**cups vegetable broth**
1½	**cups wheat berries**
½	**cup dry Madeira**
½	**ounce dried porcini mushrooms, rinsed and minced**
	Salt and pepper
6	**ounces (6 cups) baby spinach**
2	**tablespoons unsalted butter**

1. Microwave cremini mushrooms, oil, garlic, and thyme in bowl, stirringly occasionally, until mushrooms are softened, about 5 minutes; transfer to slow cooker. Stir in broth, wheat berries, 6 tablespoons Madeira, porcini mushrooms, and ½ teaspoon salt. Cover and cook until wheat berries are tender, 10 to 11 hours on low or 7 to 8 hours on high.

2. Stir in spinach, 1 handful at a time, and let sit until wilted, about 5 minutes. (Adjust stew consistency with extra hot broth as needed.) Stir in butter and remaining 2 tablespoons Madeira and season with salt and pepper to taste. Serve.

SMART SHOPPING WHEAT BERRIES
Wheat berries, often erroneously referred to as "whole wheat," are whole, unprocessed kernels of wheat. Since none of the grain has been removed, wheat berries are an excellent source of fiber, protein, and iron and other minerals. Compared to more refined forms of wheat (cracked wheat, bulgur, and flour), wheat berries require a long cooking time, which makes them a good fit for the slow cooker.

Quinoa and Vegetable Stew

Serves 6   **Cooking Time** 4 to 5 hours on Low or 3 to 4 hours on High
Slow Cooker Size 5½ to 7 Quarts

✓ **WHY THIS RECIPE WORKS:** In countries such as Peru, along the Andean highlands, quinoa plays a starring role in many dishes, such as a hearty stew that also includes potatoes and corn. We set about making our own version of this dish using the slow cooker, where the flavors could meld over time for a richer-tasting dish. Red potatoes were a given, and microwaving them with onion and garlic provided a flavorful base for our stew. Diced tomatoes offered brightness and acidity. Along with the corn—we opted for the frozen variety for convenience and consistent flavor year-round—we included peas for more color and sweetness. To keep our quinoa from overcooking, we stirred it in near the end of the cooking time. Tasters liked the flavor of our Peruvian-inspired stew but found it on the thin side. Luckily, we found an easy way to thicken it: We simply mashed a portion of the cooked potatoes and tomatoes and stirred them back in when we added the quinoa. Serve with diced avocado, *queso fresco*, and/or lime wedges.

1   **pound red potatoes, cut into ½-inch pieces**
1   **cup chopped onion**
1   **tablespoon vegetable oil**
1   **tablespoon minced garlic**
1   **tablespoon chili powder**
6   **cups vegetable broth**
1   **(14.5-ounce) can diced tomatoes, drained**
    Salt and pepper
1   **cup quinoa, rinsed**
1   **cup frozen peas**
1   **cup frozen corn**
2   **tablespoons minced fresh cilantro**

1. Microwave potatoes, onion, oil, garlic, and chili powder in bowl, stirring occasionally, until vegetables are softened, about 5 minutes; transfer to slow cooker. Stir in broth, tomatoes, and ½ teaspoon salt. Cover and cook until flavors meld and potatoes are tender, 4 to 5 hours on low or 3 to 4 hours on high.

2. Transfer 2 cups potato-tomato mixture to bowl and mash with potato masher until mostly smooth. Stir quinoa and mashed potato-tomato mixture into stew, cover, and cook on high until quinoa is tender, 20 to 30 minutes. Stir in peas and corn and let sit until heated through, about 5 minutes. (Adjust stew consistency with extra hot broth as needed.) Stir in cilantro and season with salt and pepper to taste. Serve.

SMART SHOPPING QUINOA

Quinoa originated in the Andes Mountains of South America, and while it is generally treated as a grain, it is actually the seed of the goosefoot plant. Sometimes referred to as a "supergrain," quinoa is high in protein and possesses all of the amino acids in the balanced amounts that our bodies require.

Beyond its nutritional prowess, we love quinoa for its addictive crunch and nutty taste. Unless labeled as "prewashed," quinoa should always be rinsed before cooking to remove its protective layer (called saponin), which is unpleasantly bitter.

Hearty White Bean and Kale Stew

Serves 6   **Cooking Time** 9 to 10 hours on Low or 6 to 7 hours on High
Slow Cooker Size 5½ to 7 Quarts

✓ **WHY THIS RECIPE WORKS:** In this homage to Tuscan cuisine, we combined creamy, tender cannellini beans with earthy kale and rosemary and salty, nutty Parmesan for a rustic stew with deep flavor. Though most recipes call for soaking the beans overnight, we found this step was unnecessary; we simply added them straight to the slow cooker, where the gentle simmering heat helped them cook through evenly. Onions, garlic, and red pepper flakes offered robust background notes, and vegetable broth, cut with a small amount of water, provided a flavorful cooking liquid. When the beans were creamy, we added the kale and a sprig of rosemary; in about 20 minutes, the kale was tender and the rosemary had infused the stew with its woodsy, sweet notes. To finish, we added grated Parmesan cheese for a salty, savory tang and body and a squeeze of lemon juice for brightness. Serve with Garlic Toasts (page 16).

2	cups chopped onions
1	tablespoon extra-virgin olive oil
1	tablespoon minced garlic
¼	teaspoon red pepper flakes
1	pound dried cannellini beans, picked over and rinsed
8	cups vegetable broth
1	cup water
	Salt and pepper
12	ounces kale, stemmed and sliced into ½-inch-wide strips
1	sprig fresh rosemary
½	cup grated Parmesan cheese
1	teaspoon lemon juice

1. Microwave onions, oil, garlic, and pepper flakes in bowl, stirring occasionally, until onions are softened, about 5 minutes; transfer to slow cooker. Stir in beans, broth, water, and ½ teaspoon salt. Cover and cook until beans are tender, 9 to 10 hours on low or 6 to 7 hours on high.

2. Stir in kale and rosemary, cover, and cook on high until kale is tender, 20 to 30 minutes. Discard rosemary. (Adjust stew consistency with extra hot broth as needed.) Stir in Parmesan and lemon juice and season with salt and pepper to taste. Drizzle individual portions with extra oil and serve with extra Parmesan.

SMART SHOPPING PARMESAN CHEESE
Genuine Italian Parmigiano-Reggiano cheese offers a buttery, nutty taste and crystalline crunch. Produced for the past 800 years in northern Italy using traditional methods, this hard cow's-milk cheese has a distinctive flavor, but it comes at a steep price. Our top-rated brand, chosen from a lineup of supermarket cheeses, is **Boar's Head Parmigiano-Reggiano**; this Italian import costs about $18 per pound, and our tasters say it offers a "good crunch" and "nice tangy, nutty" flavor. For a more affordable option, they also liked BelGioioso Parmesan, which costs about half the price.

Indian-Style Vegetable Curry with Tofu

Serves 6   **Cooking Time** 4 to 5 hours on Low or 3 to 4 hours on High
Slow Cooker Size 5½ to 7 Quarts

✓ **WHY THIS RECIPE WORKS:** Curries are especially well suited to the slow cooker. When the ingredients have the opportunity to cook for hours, the flavors meld and the result is a bold-tasting dish with complexity. And though many curries rely on chicken or shrimp for their centerpiece, swapping in tofu ensured an equally satisfying curry—plus, the tofu didn't require any extra prep. For a flavor-packed dish, we included a full table-spoon of curry powder and a whopping 2 tablespoons of grated fresh ginger. Blooming the curry and half of the ginger in the microwave (we added the rest later for a zingy punch) helped to intensify their flavors. For more savory depth, we included tomato paste; cubed red potatoes contributed heartiness. Precut frozen green beans added bulk and needed zero prep. For a rich, velvety sauce, we stirred in 2 cups of coconut milk; heating it and adding it toward the end of cooking prevented it from cooling down our curry and preserved its flavor. Finally, minced cilantro offered a touch of color and freshness. You can use firm tofu here if desired, but do not substitute silken, soft, or medium-firm tofu; these varieties will break down during cooking. Serve over rice.

1	**pound red potatoes, cut into ½-inch pieces**
2	**tablespoons grated ginger**
1	**tablespoon vegetable oil**
1	**tablespoon curry powder**
1	**tablespoon tomato paste**
4	**cups vegetable broth**
14	**ounces extra-firm tofu, cut into ½-inch pieces**
2	**tablespoons instant tapioca Salt and pepper**
2	**cups canned coconut milk**
2	**cups frozen cut green beans**
¼	**cup minced fresh cilantro**

1. Microwave potatoes, 1 tablespoon ginger, oil, curry powder, and tomato paste in bowl, stirring occasionally, until potatoes are softened, about 5 minutes; transfer to slow cooker. Stir in broth, tofu, tapioca, and 1 teaspoon salt. Cover and cook until flavors meld and potatoes are tender, 4 to 5 hours on low or 3 to 4 hours on high.

2. Microwave coconut milk in bowl until hot, about 2 minutes; stir into curry. Stir in green beans and remaining 1 tablespoon ginger and let sit until heated through, about 5 minutes. (Adjust curry consistency with extra hot broth as needed.) Stir in cilantro and season with salt and pepper to taste. Serve.

SMART SHOPPING BUYING TOFU
Tofu is made from the curds of soy milk. Although freshly made tofu is common across the Pacific, in the United States tofu is typically sold in refrigerated blocks packed in water. Tofu is available in a variety of textures, including silken, soft, medium-firm, firm, and extra-firm. We prefer to use extra-firm in our slow-cooker dishes because it holds its shape well when cooked for an extended period of time. Tofu is perishable and should be kept well chilled. If you want to keep an opened package of tofu fresh for several days, cover the tofu with fresh water in an airtight container and store it in the refrigerator, changing the water daily. Any hint of sourness means the tofu is past its prime (we prefer to use it within a few days of opening).

Hearty Vegetarian Chili

Serves 6 to 8   **Cooking Time** 9 to 10 hours on Low or 6 to 7 hours on High
Slow Cooker Size 5½ to 7 Quarts

✔ **WHY THIS RECIPE WORKS:** Vegetarian chilis often rely on a mix of beans and vegetables for heartiness, but neither one really adds meaty depth. We wanted a hearty chili that was as rich, savory, and deeply satisfying as any meat chili out there. We started with dried navy beans, which turned tender and creamy with the long simmer; a good amount of chili powder and cumin delivered a subtle heat and warm spice notes. To up the heartiness of our dish, we tried adding a variety of ingredients, such as rice, nuts, and seeds, but only bulgur provided the textural dimension our chili had been missing, plus it was light on prep. After a quick rinse and a few minutes in the microwave, it needed just 10 minutes in the slow cooker to fully soften and absorb the rich flavors. Finally, we ramped up the intensity and depth of our chili with soy sauce, dried shiitakes, and tomato paste. Serve with your favorite chili garnishes.

2	**cups chopped onions**
3	**tablespoons chili powder**
¼	**cup tomato paste**
2	**tablespoons vegetable oil**
1	**tablespoon ground cumin**
4	**teaspoons dried oregano**
1	**pound (2½ cups) dried navy beans, picked over and rinsed**
11	**cups water**
3	**tablespoons soy sauce**
½	**ounce dried shiitake mushrooms, rinsed and minced**
	Salt and pepper
⅔	**cup medium-grind bulgur, rinsed**

1. Microwave onions, chili powder, tomato paste, oil, cumin, and oregano in bowl, stirring occasionally, until onions are softened, about 5 minutes; transfer to slow cooker. Stir in beans, 9 cups water, soy sauce, mushrooms, and 1 teaspoon salt. Cover and cook until beans are tender, 9 to 10 hours on low or 6 to 7 hours on high.

2. Microwave bulgur, remaining 2 cups water, and ¼ teaspoon salt in covered bowl until bulgur is softened, about 5 minutes; drain bulgur and stir into chili. Cover and cook on high until bulgur is tender, 5 to 10 minutes. Season with salt and pepper to taste. Serve.

SMART SHOPPING BULGUR
Bulgur is made from parboiled or steamed wheat kernels/berries that are then dried, partially stripped of their outer bran layer, and coarsely ground. The result of this process is a relatively fast-cooking, highly nutritious grain that can be used in a variety of applications. Don't confuse bulgur with cracked wheat, which is not parcooked. Most recipes using bulgur call for medium grind, which we rinse to remove any detritus and simply soak in water or another liquid until tender. Medium-grind bulgur is the most widely available size; these grains are about the size of sesame seeds or kosher salt.

Red Beans and Rice with Okra and Tomatoes

Serves 4 to 6   **Cooking Time** 9 to 10 hours on Low or 6 to 7 hours on High
Slow Cooker Size 5½ to 7 Quarts

✓ **WHY THIS RECIPE WORKS:** Rather than monitor the stovetop for an hour or two so we could enjoy this Cajun classic, we moved it to the slow cooker, where the moist environment and gentle heat could turn our red beans tender and creamy without a lot of effort. Though the beans cooked through perfectly with no advance prep (we were able to skip the soaking step called for in many recipes), the rice presented a bit of a challenge. Raw rice didn't cook through evenly, and instant rice was blown out and mushy by the time the beans were done. Precooked rice, stirred in toward the end of cooking, held its shape and absorbed the rich flavors of the beans and broth. Using Cajun seasoning meant we didn't need to include a laundry list of spices, and frozen okra, added at the end with some fresh tomatoes, reinforced the Cajun identity of our dish. Feel free to use either leftover rice or store-bought precooked rice; see page 115 for more information.

- **2   tablespoons Cajun seasoning**
- **1   tablespoon vegetable oil**
- **1   tablespoon minced garlic**
- **4   cups vegetable broth**
- **8   ounces dried small red beans, picked over and rinsed**
- **1   green bell pepper, cored and cut into ½-inch pieces**
    Salt and pepper
- **2   cups frozen cut okra**
- **2   cups cooked rice**
- **2   tomatoes, cored and cut into ½-inch pieces**
- **4   scallions, sliced thin**

1. Microwave Cajun seasoning, oil, and garlic in bowl, stirring occasionally, until fragrant, about 1 minute; transfer to slow cooker. Stir in broth, beans, bell pepper, and ½ teaspoon salt. Cover and cook until beans are tender, 9 to 10 hours on low or 6 to 7 hours on high.

2. Stir in okra and rice and let sit until heated through, about 10 minutes. Stir in tomatoes and scallions and season with salt and pepper to taste. Serve.

QUICK PREP TIP DICING TOMATOES
Tomatoes' shape and texture can make them hard to cut. For the most success when dicing a tomato, begin by coring the tomato, then use a chef's knife or a serrated knife to cut it into round slices. Cut the slices into strips, then cut the strips into a dice. This works with both seeded and unseeded tomatoes.

Warm Mediterranean Lentil Salad

Serves 4   **Cooking Time** 3 to 4 hours on Low or 2 to 3 hours on High
Slow Cooker Size 5½ to 7 Quarts

✔ **WHY THIS RECIPE WORKS:** Lentil salad can make an impressive and easy main course, but all too often the lentils overcook and break down. We discovered that cooking the lentils as gently as possible for a shorter period of time helped keep their delicate skins intact. Also, adding a little salt and vinegar to the cooking liquid (we used vegetable broth) gave us lentils that were firm yet creamy. For an aromatic backbone, we included herbes de Provence. Canned chickpeas added more substance. For freshness, we stirred in cherry tomatoes; crumbled feta and chopped kalamatas delivered tangy, briny bites. A boldly flavored vinaigrette brought everything together. We prefer French green lentils, or *lentilles du Puy*, for this recipe, but it will work with any type of lentil except red or yellow. For a heartier salad, you can serve this dish over mixed greens.

1¾ **cups vegetable broth**

1 **(14-ounce) can chickpeas, rinsed**

1 **cup lentils, picked over and rinsed**

1 **teaspoon herbes de Provence**

¼ **cup white wine vinegar**
    Salt and pepper

½ **cup chopped fresh mint**

¼ **cup extra-virgin olive oil**

1 **teaspoon minced garlic**

12 **ounces cherry tomatoes, quartered**

¼ **cup pitted kalamata olives, chopped**

½ **cup crumbled feta cheese**

1. Combine broth, chickpeas, lentils, herbes de Provence, 1 tablespoon vinegar, and ½ teaspoon salt in slow cooker. Cover and cook until lentils are tender, 3 to 4 hours on low or 2 to 3 hours on high.

2. Whisk mint, oil, garlic, and remaining 3 tablespoons vinegar together in bowl; gently stir into lentils. Stir in tomatoes and olives and season with salt and pepper to taste. Sprinkle with feta and serve.

SMART SHOPPING LENTILS
Lentils come in various sizes and colors, and the differences in flavor and texture are surprisingly distinct. Lentilles du Puy are smaller than the more common brown and green varieties and take their name from the city of Puy in central France. They are dark olive green in color and boast a "rich, earthy flavor" and "firm yet tender texture." Brown lentils are larger and have a uniform brown color and a "light and earthy flavor"; green lentils are similar in size to the brown but are greenish brown in color and have a very "mild flavor." Red lentils are very small, have an orange-red hue, and disintegrate completely when cooked; yellow lentils are also small, brightly colored, and break down completely when cooked. Red and yellow lentils are frequently used in Indian and Middle Eastern cuisines.

Butternut Squash Risotto

Serves 6   **Cooking Time** 2 to 3 hours on High   **Slow Cooker Size** 5½ to 7 Quarts

✔ **WHY THIS RECIPE WORKS:** Risotto usually demands a cook's attention from start to finish, which is why this hands-off slow-cooker version is so appealing. Instead of sautéing our rice until translucent, we microwaved it with butter and chopped onion, then stirred in white wine and allowed the grains to absorb it. Adding all the broth at once led to blown-out grains and a mushy risotto, so we stirred in 4 cups of hot broth at the outset, then gently stirred in more at the end to guarantee an ultracreamy texture. Butternut squash and peas offered sweetness and color, and butter, Parmesan, and fresh sage ramped up the richness and flavor of our effortless risotto. Arborio rice, which is high in starch, gives risotto its characteristic creaminess; do not substitute other types of rice. To save prep time, we prefer to use precut, peeled butternut squash halves from the supermarket; be sure to avoid the precut chunks, which can be dry and stringy.

6	**cups vegetable broth**
2	**cups Arborio rice**
1	**cup chopped onion**
3	**tablespoons unsalted butter**
½	**cup dry white wine**
2	**pounds peeled and seeded butternut squash, cut into ½-inch pieces**
	Salt and pepper
1	**cup frozen peas**
1	**cup grated Parmesan cheese**
1	**tablespoon minced fresh sage**

1. Microwave 4 cups broth in bowl until steaming, about 5 minutes. In separate bowl, microwave rice, onion, and 1 tablespoon butter, stirring occasionally, until ends of rice kernels are transparent, about 5 minutes. Transfer hot rice to slow cooker, immediately stir in wine, and let sit until wine is almost completely absorbed, about 2 minutes. Stir in hot broth, squash, and ½ teaspoon salt. Cover and cook until rice is tender, 2 to 3 hours on high.

2. Microwave remaining 2 cups broth in bowl until steaming, about 2 minutes. Slowly stream hot broth into rice, stirring gently, until liquid is absorbed and risotto is creamy, about 1 minute. Gently stir in peas and let sit until heated through, about 5 minutes. Stir in Parmesan, sage, and remaining 2 tablespoons butter. (Adjust risotto consistency with extra hot broth as needed.) Season with salt and pepper to taste and serve.

SMART SHOPPING ARBORIO RICE
To find the best brand of Arborio rice, we cooked up batches of Parmesan risotto with two domestically grown brands of Arborio rice and four Italian imports; all brands are widely available in supermarkets. To our surprise, the winning rice hailed not from the boot but from the Lone Star State. Texas-grown **RiceSelect Arborio Rice** was prized over all others with "creamy, smooth" grains and a "good bite."

Tamale Pie

Serves 4 to 6   **Cooking Time** 4 to 5 hours on Low or 3 to 4 hours on High
Slow Cooker Size 5½ to 7 Quarts

✓ **WHY THIS RECIPE WORKS:** Popular Tex-Mex fare, tamale pie is typically composed of a saucy meat and vegetable filling, capped off with a hearty cornmeal topping. We wanted to ditch the meat but keep the big flavor. For the topping, we simplified things by using instant polenta and making it in the microwave; Monterey Jack and scallions provided a flavor boost. For the filling, we combined kidney beans, diced tomatoes, and tempeh with tomato sauce for body and taco seasoning for flavor, then spread the polenta over the mixture in the slow cooker. A few hours later, our easy tamale pie was perfectly done and incredibly satisfying. Be sure to use dried, instant polenta here; do not substitute traditional polenta or precooked polenta in a tube. Tempeh comes in a variety of styles and flavors; any style will work here, but be sure to select plain, not flavored, tempeh.

2¼	cups water
¾	cup instant polenta
	Salt and pepper
1	cup shredded Monterey Jack cheese
4	scallions, sliced thin
2	tablespoons unsalted butter
1	(1-ounce) packet taco seasoning mix
1	(15-ounce) can kidney beans, rinsed
1	(15-ounce) can diced tomatoes
2	poblano chiles, stemmed, seeded, and chopped
1	(15-ounce) can tomato sauce
8	ounces tempeh, cut into ½-inch pieces

1. Combine water, polenta, and 1 teaspoon salt in bowl, cover, and microwave until most of water is absorbed, 6 to 8 minutes. Stir polenta thoroughly, then continue to microwave, uncovered, until polenta is creamy and fully cooked, 1 to 3 minutes longer. Stir in Monterey Jack, scallions, and 1 tablespoon butter and season with salt and pepper to taste. Cover to keep warm.

2. Microwave taco seasoning and remaining 1 tablespoon butter in separate bowl, stirring occasionally, until fragrant, about 1 minute; transfer to slow cooker. Stir in beans, tomatoes and their juice, poblanos, tomato sauce, and tempeh. Spoon cooked polenta over filling and smooth into even layer using spatula. Cover and cook until flavors meld and tempeh is tender, 4 to 5 hours on low or 3 to 4 hours on high. Serve.

SMART SHOPPING TEMPEH
While tofu has hit the mainstream, its soy-based cousin, tempeh, might not be as familiar. Tempeh is made by fermenting cooked soybeans and forming the mixture into a firm, dense cake. (Some versions of tempeh also contain beans, grains, and flavorings.) Because it's better than tofu at holding its shape when cooked, it serves as a good meat substitute and is a mainstay of many vegetarian diets. Although it has a strong, almost nutty flavor, it tends to absorb the flavors of any foods or sauces to which it is added, making it a versatile choice for many dishes.

Smoky Roasted Red Pepper Strata

Serves 8   **Cooking Time** 3 to 4 hours on Low   **Slow Cooker Size** 5½ to 7 Quarts

✔ **WHY THIS RECIPE WORKS:** This hearty strata makes a satisfying brunch or casual supper for a crowd. We found that the key to producing a strata with a great texture—one in which the bread didn't turn to mush as it absorbed the eggy custard—was using stale baguette pieces. Rather than simply stir the filling ingredients together, we layered them with the bread before pouring the custard over the top; this ensured big flavor in every bite. We liked Monterey Jack for its mild, cheesy flavor. Roasted red peppers offered sweetness, and scallions ensured a slightly pungent bite. Adding chipotle chiles to the custard lent smokiness and a subtle heat. To prevent uneven cooking or browning on one side, we placed a foil collar in the slow cooker before assembling the strata. For more information on making a foil collar, see page 180. Don't let this strata cook longer than 4 hours or it will become dried out and rubbery.

1	**(18-inch) stale baguette, cut into 1-inch pieces**
2	**cups shredded Monterey Jack cheese**
1	**cup jarred roasted red peppers, patted dry and chopped**
6	**scallions, sliced thin**
12	**large eggs**
2½	**cups whole milk**
2	**tablespoons minced chipotle chile**
½	**teaspoon salt**
¼	**teaspoon pepper**

1. Line slow cooker with aluminum foil collar and spray with vegetable oil spray. Spread half of bread in prepared slow cooker and sprinkle with 1 cup Monterey Jack, half of roasted red peppers, and one-third of scallions. Spread remaining bread in slow cooker and top with remaining 1 cup Monterey Jack, remaining roasted red peppers, and half of remaining scallions. Whisk eggs, milk, chipotle, salt, and pepper together in bowl, then pour mixture evenly over bread. Press gently on bread to submerge. Cover and cook until center of strata is set, 3 to 4 hours on low.

2. Let strata cool for 20 minutes. Sprinkle with remaining scallions and serve.

QUICK PREP TIP QUICK STALED BREAD
Using naturally staled, day-old bread in our Smoky Roasted Red Pepper Strata and bread puddings (pages 300–301) allows us to assemble these dishes quickly. However, if you don't have this on hand, you can also dry out fresh bread pieces by baking them in a rimmed baking sheet in a 225-degree oven for about 35 minutes.

Stuffed Bell Peppers with Spicy Corn and Black Beans

Serves 4   **Cooking Time** 4 to 5 hours on Low or 3 to 4 hours on High
Slow Cooker Size 5½ to 7 Quarts

✔ **WHY THIS RECIPE WORKS:** Creating an easy stuffed pepper recipe in the slow cooker required some tinkering since, in our experience, even traditional versions can suffer from bland fillings and mushy peppers. For a flavor-packed filling, we microwaved our aromatics, then stirred in canned black beans, corn, shredded Monterey Jack, and cooked rice for heartiness. A surprise ingredient—jarred salsa—helped bind the filling and infused it with more flavor. We discovered that just a little bit of water, added to the base of the slow cooker, steamed our stuffed bell peppers to the perfect crisp-tender texture. To finish, we topped the stuffed peppers with more cheese and minced cilantro. Choose peppers with flat bottoms so that they stay upright in the slow cooker. Feel free to use leftover rice or store-bought precooked rice; see page 115 for more information.

4	**(6-ounce) red, orange, or yellow bell peppers**
1	**cup chopped onion**
1	**tablespoon olive oil**
1	**tablespoon minced garlic**
1½	**cups shredded Monterey Jack cheese**
1	**(15-ounce) can black beans, rinsed**
1	**cup cooked rice**
1	**cup frozen corn**
1	**cup jarred tomato salsa**
2	**tablespoons minced fresh cilantro**
½	**teaspoon salt**
¼	**teaspoon pepper**

1. Trim ½ inch off top of each pepper, then remove core and seeds. Finely chop pepper tops, discarding stems. Microwave pepper tops, onion, oil, and garlic in large bowl, stirring occasionally, until vegetables are softened, about 5 minutes. Stir in 1 cup Monterey Jack, beans, rice, corn, salsa, 1 tablespoon cilantro, salt, and pepper. Pack filling evenly into cored peppers.

2. Pour ⅓ cup water into slow cooker. Place stuffed peppers upright in slow cooker. Cover and cook until peppers are tender, 4 to 5 hours on low or 3 to 4 hours on high.

3. Sprinkle peppers evenly with remaining ½ cup Monterey Jack, cover, and cook until cheese is melted, about 5 minutes. Using tongs and slotted spoon, transfer peppers to serving dish; discard cooking liquid. Sprinkle with remaining 1 tablespoon cilantro and serve.

SMART SHOPPING JARRED SALSA
Using jarred salsa in our stuffed peppers added complex vegetal flavor, without extra work, and helped to bind the filling; because it is cooked, it is more saucy and thicker than homemade salsa. We recently tested a number of jarred salsas, looking for a brand that delivered bold spice and real heat, balanced by sweet tomato flavor and bright acidity. In the end, **Chi-Chi's Medium Thick and Chunky Salsa** came out on top. Tasters preferred this salsa for its bright, vibrant flavor, which they found to be "spicy, fresh, and tomatoey."

Individual Ricotta, Spinach, and Egg Casseroles

Serves 4   **Cooking Time** 2 to 3 hours on Low   **Slow Cooker Size** 5½ to 7 Quarts

✓ **WHY THIS RECIPE WORKS:** Perfect for a late breakfast or light supper, these individual egg casseroles are ready for the slow cooker in mere minutes with little effort. Whole-milk ricotta and shredded fontina ensured a dish that was plenty rich, and frozen spinach balanced the richness and needed no chopping—we simply thawed it and squeezed out the excess moisture so it wouldn't water down our eggs. Assembly was easy: We started by microwaving our aromatics (garlic and onion), then stirred in the spinach, ricotta, fontina, and eggs and portioned the mixture into four ramekins. Thin slices of tomato, placed on top, provided bright flavor and color, and a water bath guaranteed that our eggs cooked through gently and evenly. You will need an oval slow cooker and four 6-ounce round ramekins for this recipe.

1	cup chopped onion
1	tablespoon olive oil
1	tablespoon minced garlic
10	ounces (1¼ cups) whole-milk ricotta cheese
8	ounces frozen chopped spinach, thawed and squeezed dry
1	cup shredded fontina cheese
4	large eggs, lightly beaten
¼	teaspoon salt
¼	teaspoon pepper
2	plum tomatoes, cored and sliced crosswise ¼ inch thick

1. Spray four 6-ounce ramekins with vegetable oil spray. Microwave onion, oil, and garlic in large bowl, stirring occasionally, until onion is softened, about 5 minutes. Stir in ricotta, spinach, fontina, eggs, salt, and pepper until well combined. Divide mixture evenly among prepared ramekins and shingle tomatoes over top.

2. Fill slow cooker with ½ inch water (about 2 cups water) and set ramekins in slow cooker. Cover and cook until filling is set, 2 to 3 hours on low. Using tongs and sturdy spatula, remove ramekins from slow cooker and let cool for 15 minutes before serving.

QUICK PREP TIP SQUEEZING FROZEN SPINACH
To rid thawed spinach of excess water before adding it to casseroles or other recipes, simply wrap it in cheesecloth and squeeze it firmly.

Cooking for Two

Black Bean Soup

Serves 2   **Cooking Time** 6 to 7 hours on Low or 4 to 5 hours on High
Slow Cooker Size 3½ to 7 Quarts

WHY THIS RECIPE WORKS: Black bean soup should be thick, hearty, and full of flavor. Unfortunately, most black bean soups from a slow cooker come out watery and bland. Keeping in mind that this was a scaled-down soup for two, we vowed to up the flavor while ensuring that it was a snap to pull together. Though we often call for salt-soaking beans to encourage their skins to remain intact during cooking, we found we could bypass that step here; a few burst beans would only contribute to the thick, rich texture we were after. A few slices of bacon added to the slow cooker infused our soup with smoky, savory depth; a good amount of chili powder provided some heat. Coating the inside of the slow cooker with vegetable oil spray before adding the ingredients prevented our scaled-down dish from sticking and burning. For more body and thickness, we mashed some of the cooked beans and stirred them back into the finished soup. Serve with minced red onion, sour cream, and hot sauce.

1	**cup chopped onion**
1	**tablespoon vegetable oil**
1	**tablespoon minced garlic**
2	**teaspoons chili powder**
1½	**cups chicken broth**
1	**cup water**
¾	**cup dried black beans, picked over and rinsed**
3	**slices bacon**
1	**celery rib, cut into ½-inch pieces**
1	**carrot, peeled and cut into ½-inch pieces**
	Salt and pepper
1	**tablespoon minced fresh cilantro**

1. Lightly spray inside of slow cooker with vegetable oil spray. Microwave onion, oil, garlic, and chili powder in bowl, stirring occasionally, until onion is softened, about 5 minutes; transfer to prepared slow cooker. Stir in broth, water, beans, bacon, celery, carrot, ½ teaspoon salt, and ½ teaspoon pepper. Cover and cook until beans are tender, 6 to 7 hours on low or 4 to 5 hours on high.

2. Discard bacon. Transfer ½ cup of bean mixture to bowl and mash with potato masher until mostly smooth. Stir mashed bean mixture into soup and let sit until heated through, about 5 minutes. (Adjust soup consistency with extra hot broth as needed.) Stir in cilantro and season with salt and pepper to taste. Serve.

SMART SHOPPING DRIED BLACK BEANS

Though canned beans are incredibly convenient, for dishes in which the beans truly take center stage, we prefer the flavor and texture provided by dried beans. To find the best dried black beans, we sampled three brands cooked plain and in a recipe for black beans and rice. Surprisingly, the single mail-order variety, a pricey heirloom bean, became mushy, but the beans from the two national supermarket brands were perfectly creamy. Our favorite was **Goya Dried Black Beans**, which offered "nutty," "buttery" bean flavor and a reliably uniform texture.

Red Lentil Stew

Serves 2   **Cooking Time** 3 to 4 hours on Low or 2 to 3 hours on High
Slow Cooker Size 3½ to 7 Quarts

✓ WHY THIS RECIPE WORKS: For a satisfying, flavorful lentil stew for two, we looked to Indian cuisine for inspiration. Deeply flavored, exotically spiced *dal* are comforting, hearty lentil dishes that have a thick consistency when cooked. For our scaled-down version, we started with red lentils, which are small and cooked down nicely in the slow cooker. Fork-friendly bites of carrot, chopped tomatoes, and sweet peas added color and substance. To capture the complex flavors of Indian cuisine without reaching for several spice jars, we opted for garam masala, a spice blend that contains dried chiles, cinnamon, cardamom, coriander, and other spices. Coconut milk ensured that our stew was rich and creamy. So that the flavor of the coconut milk wouldn't become muted with the long cooking time, and the peas and tomatoes wouldn't disintegrate, we added them at the end and cooked our stew for 5 minutes to absorb the flavors and give the vegetables a chance to soften. You cannot substitute other varieties of lentils for the red lentils here; red lentils produce a very different texture. Do not substitute light coconut milk here. Serve over rice.

1	tablespoon vegetable oil
2	teaspoons minced garlic
1½	teaspoons garam masala
	Pinch red pepper flakes
1¼	cups water
2	carrots, peeled and cut into ¼-inch pieces
½	cup red lentils, picked over and rinsed
	Salt and pepper
2	tomatoes, cored and cut into ½-inch pieces
¾	cup canned coconut milk
⅓	cup frozen peas
1	tablespoon minced fresh cilantro

1. Lightly spray inside of slow cooker with vegetable oil spray. Microwave oil, garlic, garam masala, and pepper flakes in bowl, stirring occasionally, until fragrant, about 1 minute; transfer to prepared slow cooker. Stir in water, carrots, lentils, ½ teaspoon salt, and ½ teaspoon pepper. Cover and cook until lentils are very tender and broken down, 3 to 4 hours on low or 2 to 3 hours on high.

2. Stir in tomatoes, coconut milk, and peas, cover, and cook on high until heated through, about 5 minutes. (Adjust stew consistency with extra hot water as needed.) Stir in cilantro and season with salt and pepper to taste. Serve.

ON THE SIDE GARLIC FLATBREADS
Microwave 2 tablespoons unsalted butter and 2 teaspoons minced garlic in bowl until melted and fragrant, about 30 seconds. Place two (8-inch) store-bought naan breads on rimmed baking sheet, brush with garlic butter, and season with salt and pepper. Bake in 400-degree oven until hot and crisp, 5 to 8 minutes. Serves 2.

Moroccan Chicken Stew

Serves 2   **Cooking Time** 3 to 4 hours on Low   **Slow Cooker Size** 3½ to 7 Quarts

✔ WHY THIS RECIPE WORKS: Most slow-cooker chicken stews deliver ho-hum flavor and dry, tasteless meat. We wanted a rich-tasting stew with tender bites of chicken and decided to incorporate the bright, lively flavors of Moroccan cuisine for an exciting dinner for two. To keep our prep work to a minimum, we chose boneless, skinless chicken thighs, which remained moist and tender during cooking and could be simply seasoned and stirred into the stew right out of the package; once they were tender, we shredded them into bite-size pieces. Chicken broth and white wine kept our chicken moist and infused it with big flavor. For savory depth, we included a good amount of tomato paste. A bit of tapioca ensured that the sauce thickened nicely. Narrowing down the spice list to just the essentials—paprika and garam masala—gave us a dish that tasted like a true tagine but didn't require seeking out obscure ingredients. Creamy chickpeas and dried apricots rounded out our stew and gave it an authentic touch. Serve over couscous or rice.

2   tablespoons tomato paste
1   tablespoon vegetable oil
1   tablespoon paprika
1   teaspoon garam masala
1½ cups chicken broth
1   (14-ounce) can chickpeas, rinsed
¼   cup dry white wine
1   tablespoon instant tapioca
1   pound boneless, skinless chicken thighs, trimmed
    Salt and pepper
3   tablespoons chopped dried apricots

1. Lightly spray inside of slow cooker with vegetable oil spray. Microwave tomato paste, oil, paprika, and garam masala in bowl, stirring occasionally, until fragrant, about 1 minute; transfer to prepared slow cooker. Stir in broth, chickpeas, wine, and tapioca. Season chicken with salt and pepper and nestle into slow cooker. Cover and cook until chicken is tender, 3 to 4 hours on low.

2. Using large spoon, skim excess fat from surface of stew. Break chicken into about 1-inch pieces with tongs. Stir in apricots and let sit until heated through, about 5 minutes. (Adjust stew consistency with extra hot broth as needed.) Season with salt and pepper to taste and serve.

SMART SHOPPING WHITE WINE FOR COOKING
When a recipe calls for dry white wine, it's tempting to grab whatever open bottle is in the fridge. We have found that only Sauvignon Blanc consistently boils down to a "clean" yet sufficiently acidic flavor that meshes nicely with a variety of ingredients in savory recipes. Vermouth can be an acceptable substitute in certain recipes. Never buy supermarket cooking wine, which has added sodium and a vinegary flavor.

Hearty Beef Stew

Serves 2   **Cooking Time** 6 to 7 hours on Low or 4 to 5 hours on High
Slow Cooker Size 3½ to 7 Quarts

✔ **WHY THIS RECIPE WORKS:** For such a humble dish, beef stew requires a lot of effort—you have to prep and brown the meat, then chop loads of veggies. And when you're making just two servings, this can be especially annoying. We wanted a small-batch stew with maximum flavor but minimum effort. To start, we swapped the traditional chuck roast for convenient steak tips, which we simply cut into small pieces and added to the slow cooker; once cooked, they were incredibly tender and flavorful. For the vegetables, we stuck with the traditional lineup of potatoes, carrots, and peas. We selected small red potatoes, which needed no prep and could be added to the slow cooker whole; frozen peas needed just a few minutes in the slow cooker to heat through before serving. Since we were bypassing the step of browning the meat, we bolstered the beefy, savory notes of our broth with tomato paste and soy sauce, which ensured that our easy stew offered deep flavor.

1	tablespoon vegetable oil
1	tablespoon tomato paste
2	teaspoons minced garlic
¼	teaspoon dried thyme
2	cups beef broth
8	ounces small red potatoes
2	carrots, peeled and sliced ½ inch thick
1	tablespoon instant tapioca
1	tablespoon soy sauce
	Salt and pepper
1	pound sirloin steak tips, trimmed
⅔	cup frozen peas

1. Lightly spray inside of slow cooker with vegetable oil spray. Microwave oil, tomato paste, garlic, and thyme in bowl, stirring occasionally, until fragrant, about 1 minute; transfer to prepared slow cooker. Stir in broth, potatoes, carrots, tapioca, soy sauce, ½ teaspoon salt, and ½ teaspoon pepper. Cut beef into 1½-inch pieces, season with pepper, and stir into slow cooker. Cover and cook until beef is tender, 6 to 7 hours on low or 4 to 5 hours on high.

2. Using large spoon, skim excess fat from surface of stew. Stir in peas and let sit until heated through, about 5 minutes. (Adjust stew consistency with extra hot broth as needed.) Season with salt and pepper to taste and serve.

QUICK PREP TIP **SPRAYING YOUR SLOW COOKER**
When cooking a smaller amount of food in the slow cooker, as with our scaled-down recipes for two, more evaporation can occur, leading some dishes to stick to the sides of the slow-cooker insert and burn. To avoid this, be sure to spray the sides of the slow-cooker insert with vegetable oil spray before adding any food. This not only prevents your dishes from burning but also makes serving and cleanup easier.

New Mexican Red Pork Chili

Serves 2   **Cooking Time** 5 to 6 hours on Low or 3 to 4 hours on High
Slow Cooker Size 3½ to 7 Quarts

✔ **WHY THIS RECIPE WORKS:** In this dish, pork butt is braised in a richly flavored red chile sauce, for a chili that's spicy yet sweet, and smoky yet bright. For a for-two version, we opted for country-style pork ribs, which became meltingly tender and were easy to purchase in smaller quantities. Chicken broth, chili powder, tomato paste, and garlic provided a flavorful backbone. Rather than grind our own dried chiles, we added coffee, which offered the same robust, bittersweet notes. Lime juice and zest brightened our hearty dish. Try to buy country-style pork ribs with lots of fat and dark meat; stay away from ribs that look overly lean with pale meat, as they will taste very dry after the extended cooking time. You can substitute ¾ teaspoon of instant espresso powder dissolved in ¼ cup of boiling water for the brewed coffee if desired. Serve with your favorite chili garnishes.

3	**tablespoons tomato paste**
2	**tablespoons chili powder**
1	**tablespoon vegetable oil**
1	**tablespoon minced garlic**
¾	**cup chicken broth**
¼	**cup brewed coffee**
1	**tablespoon instant tapioca**
2	**teaspoons packed brown sugar**
1	**pound boneless country-style pork ribs, trimmed**
	Salt and pepper
2	**tablespoons minced fresh cilantro**
½	**teaspoon grated lime zest plus 1½ teaspoons juice**

1. Lightly spray inside of slow cooker with vegetable oil spray. Microwave tomato paste, chili powder, oil, and garlic in bowl, stirring occasionally, until fragrant, about 1 minute; transfer to prepared slow cooker. Stir in broth, coffee, tapioca, and sugar. Season pork with salt and pepper and nestle into slow cooker. Cover and cook until pork is tender, 5 to 6 hours on low or 3 to 4 hours on high.

2. Using large spoon, skim excess fat from surface of chili. Break pork into about 1-inch pieces with tongs. (Adjust chili consistency with extra hot broth as needed.) Stir in cilantro and lime zest and juice and season with salt and pepper to taste. Serve.

QUICK PREP TIP EASIER ZESTING
When zesting citrus, we prefer to use a rasp-style grater, which has razor-sharp teeth and a design that's easy to maneuver over round or irregular shapes. For zest, place the rasp grater upside down with the fruit on the bottom and the inverted grater on the top. This way, you can see exactly how much zest you have and it won't scatter across your work surface.

Weeknight Beef Chili

Serves 2   **Cooking Time** 5 to 6 hours on Low or 3 to 4 hours on High
Slow Cooker Size 3½ to 7 Quarts

✔ **WHY THIS RECIPE WORKS:** Most slow-cooker recipes for beef chili make enough to serve a crowd. We wanted to scale down our chili, but it still had to offer all the rich, long-simmered flavor and thick, substantial texture we were craving—and it had to be light on prep. The trio of tomato sauce, diced tomatoes, and tomato paste ensured that our chili tasted bright yet complex and was the right consistency after a few hours of simmering. For big flavor, even after a stint in the slow cooker, we incorporated generous amounts of chili powder, garlic, and cumin; minced chipotles added smoky undertones and heat. We also reached for a test kitchen favorite, soy sauce, to boost the meaty, savory notes. For the meat, we went with ground beef, but it turned gritty after hours of slow cooking. The solution was to microwave it briefly so it became firm enough to break into coarse crumbles that didn't turn grainy in the slow cooker. Serve with your favorite chili garnishes.

1	pound 85 percent lean ground beef
2	tablespoons chili powder
2	tablespoons tomato paste
1	tablespoon minced garlic
1½	teaspoons ground cumin
1	(15-ounce) can kidney beans, rinsed
1	(15-ounce) can tomato sauce
1	(14.5-ounce) can diced tomatoes
1½	tablespoons soy sauce
1½	teaspoons packed brown sugar
1	teaspoon minced chipotle chile
	Salt and pepper

1. Lightly spray inside of slow cooker with vegetable oil spray. Microwave beef, chili powder, tomato paste, garlic, and cumin in bowl, stirring occasionally, until beef is no longer pink, about 5 minutes. Transfer mixture to prepared slow cooker, breaking up any large pieces of beef. Stir in beans, tomato sauce, tomatoes and their juice, soy sauce, sugar, chipotle, ½ teaspoon salt, and ½ teaspoon pepper. Cover and cook until beef is tender, 5 to 6 hours on low or 3 to 4 hours on high.

2. Using large spoon, skim excess fat from surface of chili. Break up any remaining large pieces of beef with spoon. Season with salt and pepper to taste and serve.

SMART SHOPPING DICED TOMATOES

Unlike most types of canned produce, which pale in comparison to their fresh counterparts, a great can of diced tomatoes offers flavor almost every bit as intense as that of ripe, in-season fruit. We gathered 16 brands and tasted them plain and in tomato sauce to find the best brand. To our surprise, nearly half fell short. Factors such as geography and additives played into whether or not a sample rated highly in our tasting. Our top-ranked tomatoes were grown in California, source of most of the world's tomatoes, where the dry, hot growing season develops sweet, complex flavor. Tasters also favored those with more salt. In the end, we found our winner in **Hunt's Diced Tomatoes**, which was praised for its "fresh," "bright" flavor.

Lemony Chicken and Potatoes

Serves 2   **Cooking Time** 2 to 3 hours on Low   **Slow Cooker Size** 3½ to 7 Quarts

✓ **WHY THIS RECIPE WORKS:** Moving the classic duo of chicken and potatoes to the slow cooker gave us an easy yet satisfying dinner for two. We started with a pair of bone-in chicken breasts, which stayed moist during the long cooking time thanks to the insulation from the bones. Chicken broth provided a flavorful braising liquid, and a bit of tapioca ensured that it thickened nicely. To give our spuds a head start on cooking, we microwaved them briefly. A pat of butter and some minced garlic added richness and depth. Once the chicken was done, we set it aside and steeped a rosemary sprig in the slow cooker to infuse our potatoes with earthy, woodsy notes. A spritz of lemon juice and some lemon zest brightened this simple supper for two. Be sure to use a small sprig of rosemary or else its flavor will be overpowering.

12	ounces red potatoes, cut into 1-inch pieces
2	tablespoons unsalted butter
2	teaspoons minced garlic
¼	cup chicken broth
1	teaspoon instant tapioca
	Salt and pepper
2	(12-ounce) bone-in split chicken breasts, trimmed
1	small sprig fresh rosemary
½	teaspoon grated lemon zest plus 1 teaspoon juice

1. Lightly spray inside of slow cooker with vegetable oil spray. Microwave potatoes, 1 tablespoon butter, and garlic in bowl, stirring occasionally, until potatoes are softened, about 5 minutes; transfer to prepared slow cooker. Stir in broth, tapioca, ¼ teaspoon salt, and ½ teaspoon pepper. Season chicken with salt and pepper and nestle into slow cooker. Cover and cook until chicken is tender, 2 to 3 hours on low.

2. Transfer chicken to serving dish, remove skin, and tent with aluminum foil. Stir rosemary into potatoes and cook on high until fragrant, about 10 minutes. Discard rosemary. Stir in lemon zest and juice and remaining 1 tablespoon butter and season with salt and pepper to taste. Serve.

QUICK PREP TIP STORING LEMONS

We tested three methods for storing lemons, both at room temperature and in the refrigerator: in an uncovered container, in a sealed zipper-lock bag, and in a sealed zipper-lock bag with ¼ cup of water added. All the lemons stored at room temperature hardened after a week. The refrigerated samples fared much better: The uncovered lemons (which we kept in the crisper drawer) began to lose a small amount of moisture after the first week and 5 percent of their weight in the following weeks; the lemons stored in zipper-lock bags, both with and without water, didn't begin to dehydrate until four weeks had passed. As it turned out, the water wasn't offering any preservation benefits, but the zipper-lock bag did seal in some moisture. For the juiciest, longest-lasting lemons, the best approach is to seal them in a zipper-lock bag and refrigerate them.

Chicken Provençal

Serves 2   **Cooking Time** 3 to 4 hours on Low   **Slow Cooker Size** 3½ to 7 Quarts

✔ **WHY THIS RECIPE WORKS:** A French classic, chicken Provençal traditionally calls on low, slow heat to produce chicken that's fall-off-the-bone tender and a garlicky, tomatoey sauce that's thick and rich-tasting. We thought this dish was the ideal candidate for the slow cooker and would make an elegant dinner for two. Trading the usual whole bird for bone-in chicken thighs was an obvious first move to scale down our dish; we preferred thighs over breasts for the way they held their own against the robustly flavored sauce. Removing the skin prior to cooking kept the sauce from becoming greasy, and a spoonful of tomato paste amped up the rich, savory notes of the dish. Canned whole tomatoes, processed until smooth, gave us the makings of a bright-tasting, nicely clingy sauce. The potent blend of garlic, oregano, white wine, and niçoise olives rounded out our homage to classic French fare. We like serving this dish with polenta, but rice and crusty bread also make good accompaniments.

1	**cup chopped onion**
4	**teaspoons minced garlic**
1	**tablespoon olive oil**
1	**tablespoon tomato paste**
⅛	**teaspoon dried oregano**
1	**(14.5-ounce) can whole peeled tomatoes**
3	**tablespoons dry white wine**
4	**(5- to 7-ounce) bone-in chicken thighs, skin removed**
	Salt and pepper
2	**tablespoons pitted niçoise or kalamata olives, chopped coarse**
2	**tablespoons minced fresh parsley**

1. Lightly spray inside of slow cooker with vegetable oil spray. Microwave onion, garlic, oil, tomato paste, and oregano in bowl, stirring occasionally, until onion is softened, about 5 minutes; transfer to prepared slow cooker.

2. Pulse tomatoes and their juice in food processor until almost smooth, about 10 pulses. Stir tomatoes and wine into slow cooker. Season chicken with salt and pepper and nestle into slow cooker. Cover and cook until chicken is tender, 3 to 4 hours on low.

3. Transfer chicken to serving dish. Stir olives and parsley into sauce and season with salt and pepper to taste. Pour sauce over chicken and serve.

SMART SHOPPING PARSLEY

You've probably noticed that your neighborhood grocer offers two different varieties of this recognizable herb (though there are actually more than 30 varieties out there): curly-leaf and flat-leaf (also called Italian). Curly-leaf parsley is more popular, but in the test kitchen flat-leaf is by far the favorite. We find flat-leaf to have a sweet, bright flavor that's much preferable to the bitter, grassy tones of curly-leaf parsley. Flat-leaf parsley is also much more fragrant than its curly cousin.

Balsamic-Braised Chicken with Swiss Chard

Serves 2   **Cooking Time** 3 to 4 hours on Low   **Slow Cooker Size** 3½ to 7 Quarts

✔ **WHY THIS RECIPE WORKS:** This Italian-inspired braise offers surprising intensity and flavor, even though it takes mere minutes to get it into the slow cooker and hit the start button. Bone-in chicken thighs stayed moist and tender during the long cooking time, and removing the skin ensured that the dish wasn't greasy. Chicken broth provided a flavorful braising medium, and tomato paste, which we microwaved with our aromatics, amped up the meaty depth of the dish. A little instant tapioca thickened the sauce to the proper consistency. Finally, for more substance and to reinforce the Italian character of our braise, we added some Swiss chard and cherry tomatoes; a brief stint in the slow cooker was all they needed to soften slightly but still retain their fresh flavors. Serve with polenta.

1   **tablespoon vegetable oil**

1   **tablespoon tomato paste**

1   **teaspoon minced garlic**

½   **teaspoon dried thyme**

    Pinch red pepper flakes

½   **cup chicken broth**

2   **tablespoons balsamic vinegar**

1   **tablespoon instant tapioca**

    Salt and pepper

4   **(5- to 7-ounce) bone-in chicken thighs, skin removed**

1   **pound Swiss chard, stemmed and cut into 1-inch pieces**

4   **ounces cherry tomatoes, halved**

1. Lightly spray inside of slow cooker with vegetable oil spray. Microwave oil, tomato paste, garlic, thyme, and pepper flakes in bowl, stirring occasionally, until fragrant, about 1 minute; transfer to prepared slow cooker. Stir in broth, vinegar, tapioca, and ½ teaspoon pepper. Season chicken with salt and pepper and nestle into slow cooker. Cover and cook until chicken is tender, 3 to 4 hours on low.

2. Transfer chicken to serving dish and tent with aluminum foil. Stir Swiss chard and tomatoes into braising liquid, cover, and cook on high until chard is wilted, 15 to 20 minutes.

3. Return chicken and any accumulated juices to slow cooker and season with salt and pepper to taste. Let chicken heat through, about 5 minutes. Serve.

QUICK PREP TIP JUDGING FRESHNESS OF DRIED HERBS

If you are questioning the age and freshness of an already-opened jar of dried herbs, crumble a small amount between your fingers and take a whiff. If it releases a lively aroma, it's good to use. If the fragrance is present but relatively mild, consider using more than you normally would.

Penne with Chicken and Broccoli

Serves 2   **Cooking Time** 2 to 3 hours on High   **Slow Cooker Size** 3½ to 7 Quarts

✔ **WHY THIS RECIPE WORKS:** Penne with chicken and broccoli offers an appealing mix of flavors and textures, making this dish a dinnertime favorite. But move it to a slow cooker, and the result is a huge letdown, with flabby pasta, drab broccoli, and dry chicken. To ensure that our pasta didn't become overcooked and blown out in the slow cooker, we toasted it briefly in the microwave. Adding it to the slow cooker with hot liquid jump-started its cooking; we used chicken broth rather than water to ramp up the savory depth of the dish. Considering our options when it came to the chicken, we selected tenderloins, which were already fork-friendly and required no prep—they simply needed to be stirred into the pasta at the outset of cooking. To keep our broccoli from becoming overcooked during the long stint in the slow cooker, we saved it until the end, then microwaved it briefly and stirred it into the chicken and pasta. Chopped sun-dried tomatoes helped to brighten our pasta dinner, and a small amount of grated Parmesan turned the cooking liquid into a light, creamy sauce when added at the end. For more information on cooking pasta in the slow cooker and making a foil collar, see page 180.

1¾ **cups chicken broth**

4 **ounces (1¼ cups) penne**

1 **tablespoon olive oil**

⅓ **cup oil-packed sun-dried tomatoes, chopped coarse**

Pinch red pepper flakes

Salt and pepper

8 **ounces chicken tenderloins**

6 **ounces broccoli florets, cut into 1-inch pieces**

½ **cup grated Parmesan cheese**

1. Line slow cooker with aluminum foil collar and spray with vegetable oil spray. Microwave broth in bowl until steaming, about 2 minutes. In separate bowl, microwave penne and 2 teaspoons oil at 50 percent power, stirring occasionally, until some pieces look toasted and blistered, 2 to 4 minutes. Transfer hot pasta to prepared slow cooker and immediately stir in hot broth (pasta will sizzle). Stir in tomatoes, pepper flakes, ½ teaspoon salt, and ¼ teaspoon pepper. Season chicken with salt and pepper and nestle into pasta. Cover and cook until pasta is tender, 2 to 3 hours on high.

2. Microwave broccoli and remaining 1 teaspoon oil in bowl, stirring occasionally, until tender, about 3 minutes. Remove foil collar. Gently stir in broccoli and Parmesan and season with salt and pepper to taste. Serve.

SMART SHOPPING CHICKEN TENDERLOINS
The chicken tenderloin is the piece of meat located on the inside of the breast, closest to the bone. The tenderloin is weakly attached to the breast and is easy to remove with a simple tug. Tenderloins come prepackaged in the meat section of most supermarkets, but if you have trouble finding them, it's simple to create a quick substitute. Just trim an equal amount of boneless, skinless chicken breasts and cut them crosswise into ½-inch-thick slices.

Southern-Style Chicken and Dirty Rice

Serves 2   **Cooking Time** 4 to 5 hours on Low   **Slow Cooker Size** 3½ to 7 Quarts

WHY THIS RECIPE WORKS: In the South, chicken is often paired with dirty rice—a side dish of cooked rice, cured meats, vegetables, and seasonings that give the rice a "dirty" appearance. We wanted to transform this duo into a scaled-down slow-cooker casserole—we thought the moist environment would give all the robust flavors a chance to meld, for a richer-tasting dish overall. For the chicken, we selected boneless, skinless thighs, which stayed moist, even after a few hours of cooking, and were easy enough to shred and stir back into the slow cooker once tender. Onion, bell pepper, and garlic, plus some chili powder and thyme, provided a flavorful backbone. For meaty, savory depth and richness, we included kielbasa; chopping it into small pieces ensured that every bite had some meaty oomph. Precooked rice, purchased at the supermarket, worked best and kept our recipe super-easy; starting with uncooked rice gave us underdone grains, and using leftover white rice resulted in mushy, blown-out grains. Sliced scallions added a touch of color and freshness. Store-bought precooked rice is important to the success of this dish; it consistently remains intact and retains the proper doneness. Do not use freshly made or leftover rice, as it will turn mushy and blown out in the slow cooker. See page 115 for more information on our top-rated precooked rice. Don't shred the chicken too fine in step 2; it will break up more as it is stirred back into the slow cooker.

4	ounces kielbasa sausage, cut into ½-inch pieces
1	cup chopped onion
1	red bell pepper, cored and cut into ½-inch pieces
2	teaspoons minced garlic
2	teaspoons chili powder
½	teaspoon dried thyme
2	cups cooked rice
	Salt and pepper
1	pound boneless, skinless chicken thighs, trimmed
2	scallions, sliced thin

1. Lightly spray inside of slow cooker with vegetable oil spray. Microwave kielbasa, onion, bell pepper, garlic, chili powder, and thyme in bowl, stirring occasionally, until vegetables are softened, about 5 minutes; transfer to prepared slow cooker. Stir in rice, ¼ teaspoon salt, and ½ teaspoon pepper. Season chicken with salt and pepper and nestle into slow cooker. Cover and cook until chicken is tender, 4 to 5 hours on low.

2. Transfer chicken to cutting board, let cool slightly, then shred into bite-size pieces. Gently stir shredded chicken and scallions into slow cooker and season with salt and pepper to taste. Serve.

SMART SHOPPING KIELBASA

Kielbasa, or Polish sausage, is a smoked pork sausage that sometimes has beef added and is usually sold precooked. We tested five national supermarket brands, and **Smithfield Naturally Hickory Smoked Polska Kielbasa** slightly outranked Wellshire Farms Polska Kielbasa, but both had a smoky, complex flavor and a heartier texture we preferred to the springy, hot dog-like textures of the others.

Braised Steaks with Mushrooms and Onions

Serves 2 **Cooking Time** 6 to 7 hours on Low or 4 to 5 hours on High
Slow Cooker Size 3½ to 7 Quarts

✔ **WHY THIS RECIPE WORKS:** This dish promises meltingly tender blade steaks smothered in a sauce of sweet onions and earthy mushrooms, a combination that works perfectly in the slow cooker. We found that blade steaks were ideal in this application because they have a relatively high and even distribution of fat; after hours of simmering in the slow cooker, they were supremely moist and tender. Since we weren't browning our steaks, we added a spoonful of soy sauce to enhance the meaty, savory notes of the dish. Microwaving the onions and mushrooms briefly worked to jump-start their cooking and deepen their flavor. A couple teaspoons of tapioca turned the vegetables and braising liquid into a full-fledged sauce that clung nicely to our fork-tender steaks. Serve over egg noodles or mashed potatoes.

1	onion, halved and sliced ½ inch thick
4	ounces sliced cremini or white mushrooms
1	tablespoon vegetable oil
1½	teaspoons packed brown sugar
1	teaspoon minced garlic
¼	teaspoon dried thyme
½	cup beef broth
1	tablespoon soy sauce
2	teaspoons instant tapioca
2	(8-ounce) beef blade steaks, ¾ to 1 inch thick
	Salt and pepper

1. Lightly spray inside of slow cooker with vegetable oil spray. Microwave onion, mushrooms, oil, sugar, garlic, and thyme in bowl, stirring occasionally, until vegetables are softened, about 5 minutes; transfer to prepared slow cooker. Stir in broth, soy sauce, and tapioca. Season steaks with salt and pepper and nestle into slow cooker. Cover and cook until beef is tender, 6 to 7 hours on low or 4 to 5 hours on high.

2. Transfer steaks to serving dish, tent with aluminum foil, and let rest for 5 minutes. Using large spoon, skim excess fat from surface of sauce. Season with salt and pepper to taste. Pour sauce over steaks and serve.

SMART SHOPPING YELLOW VERSUS WHITE ONIONS
In our recipes, unless otherwise specified, we always use yellow onions, the kind that come in 5-pound bags at the supermarket. But wondering if there was any difference between these onions and white onions (color aside, of course), we decided to hold a blind taste test to find out. We tried them raw in pico de gallo, cooked in a simple tomato sauce, and caramelized. More than half a dozen tasters could not tell the difference between the two types; the others tasted only minor variations in sweetness and pungency. Our conclusion? Since we go through onions quickly, we find it easiest to buy a big bag of yellow onions, but you can use white and yellow onions interchangeably in any recipe calling for "onions."

Asian-Style Braised Short Ribs

Serves 2   **Cooking Time** 8 to 9 hours on Low or 5 to 6 hours on High
Slow Cooker Size 3½ to 7 Quarts

✔ **WHY THIS RECIPE WORKS:** For a boldly flavored, ultrasatisfying dinner for two, we slow-cooked short ribs until meltingly tender in an Asian-style sauce that tasted sweet, spicy, and savory all at once. The well-marbled ribs cooked down significantly, so to compensate we started with over a pound of ribs for two diners. The duo of hoisin sauce and chili-garlic sauce provided an intensely flavored sauce with a nice sweetness and subtle heat, and a small pour of chicken broth worked to thin the mixture slightly. To ensure an ultraclingy sauce by the end of the cooking time, we stirred in 2 teaspoons of tapioca. Thinly sliced scallion whites gave the sauce an aromatic presence. Once the ribs were tender, we defatted the sauce, then stirred the ribs back in and sprinkled the finished dish with scallion greens for freshness and a burst of color. Look for boneless short ribs that are well marbled and measure about 2 inches wide and 1 inch thick. Serve over egg noodles or rice.

½   **cup chicken broth**

⅓   **cup hoisin sauce**

3   **scallions, white parts minced, green parts sliced thin**

1   **tablespoon Asian chili-garlic sauce**

2   **teaspoons instant tapioca**

2   **(10-ounce) boneless beef short ribs**

   Salt and pepper

1. Lightly spray inside of slow cooker with vegetable oil spray. Combine broth, hoisin, scallion whites, chili-garlic sauce, and tapioca in prepared slow cooker. Trim fat from top and bottom of short ribs, season with salt and pepper, and nestle into slow cooker. Cover and cook until beef is tender, 8 to 9 hours on low or 5 to 6 hours on high.

2. Transfer short ribs to serving dish, tent with aluminum foil, and let rest for 5 minutes. Using large spoon, skim excess fat from surface of sauce. Pour sauce over short ribs and sprinkle with scallion greens. Serve.

SMART SHOPPING HOT CHILE SAUCES
Used both in cooking and as a condiment, these sauces come in a variety of styles. Sriracha (right) contains garlic and is made from chiles that are ground into a smooth paste. Chili-garlic sauce (left) also contains garlic and is similar to Sriracha but the chiles are coarsely ground. Sambal oelek (middle) is made purely from ground chiles without the addition of garlic or other spices, thus adding heat but not additional flavor. Once opened, these sauces will keep for several months in the refrigerator.

Pesto Meatballs and Marinara

Makes 4 meatballs and 2 cups sauce; enough for 6 ounces pasta
Cooking Time 3 to 4 hours on Low   **Slow Cooker Size** 3½ to 7 Quarts

✔ **WHY THIS RECIPE WORKS:** To streamline our meatballs and marinara for two, we cut back on the prep but amped up the flavor by adding store-bought pesto. The pesto offered big garlic and herb notes to the meatballs—no chopping needed—and ensured that they were moist. Using meatloaf mix (a combination of ground beef, veal, and pork) kept shopping easy, and a bit of panko helped hold the mixture together. Microwaving the meatballs briefly before placing them in the slow cooker helped to get rid of excess fat and firmed them up. For an effortless but flavor-packed sauce, we reached for the duo of tomato puree and tomato paste; the puree ensured that our sauce had the right consistency, and the paste offered depth and intensity. A bit of sugar balanced the acidity of the sauce. A few spoonfuls of pesto stirred into our sauce at the end punched up its flavor and added freshness. Meatloaf mix is a prepackaged mix of ground beef, pork, and veal; if it's unavailable, use 4 ounces each of ground pork and 85 percent lean ground beef. You can make your own pesto or use your favorite store-bought brand from the refrigerated section of the supermarket—they have a fresher flavor than the jarred pesto sold in the grocery aisles.

8	**ounces meatloaf mix**
½	**cup prepared basil pesto**
¼	**cup panko bread crumbs**
2	**tablespoons grated Parmesan cheese**
	Salt and pepper
1	**(28-ounce) can tomato puree**
1	**tablespoon tomato paste**
½	**teaspoon sugar**

1. Using hands, mix meatloaf mix, ¼ cup pesto, panko, Parmesan, and ¼ teaspoon pepper together in bowl until uniform. Pinch off and roll mixture into 2-inch meatballs (about 4 meatballs total) and arrange on large plate. Microwave meatballs until fat renders and meatballs are firm, about 2 minutes.

2. Lightly spray inside of slow cooker with vegetable oil spray. Combine tomato puree, tomato paste, sugar, and ½ teaspoon pepper in prepared slow cooker. Transfer microwaved meatballs to slow cooker, discarding rendered fat. Cover and cook until meatballs are tender, 3 to 4 hours on low.

3. Using large spoon, skim excess fat from surface of sauce. Before serving, stir in remaining ¼ cup pesto and season with salt and pepper to taste.

QUICK PREP TIP **STORING CHEESE**
Storing cheese presents a conundrum: As it sits, it releases moisture. If this moisture evaporates too quickly, the cheese dries out. But if the moisture is trapped on the cheese's surface, it encourages mold. Specialty cheese paper prevents this problem with a two-ply construction that lets cheese breathe without drying out, but it usually requires mail-ordering. For a more accessible method, we found that wrapping our cheese with waxed or parchment paper, then loosely wrapping around the parchment with aluminum foil, did the trick. Both papers wick moisture away, and the foil traps just enough water to keep the cheese from drying out.

Smothered Pork Chops

Serves 2   **Cooking Time** 2 to 3 hours on Low   **Slow Cooker Size** 3½ to 7 Quarts

✓ **WHY THIS RECIPE WORKS:** Pork chops are a convenient cut of pork when cooking for two, and smothering them in a rich, hearty gravy adds richness to an otherwise lean dish. For ours, we started with blade-cut chops, which are cut from the shoulder end of the loin and contain a good amount of fat and connective tissue that helps them stay juicy in the slow cooker. Chicken broth provided a savory base for our onion gravy. Soy sauce added meaty notes, and tapioca helped to thicken it. A splash of cider vinegar and parsley offered brightness, and chopped bacon, microwaved briefly, gave us a crispy garnish. Often, blade chops aren't labeled as such; be sure to look for bone-in chops with a good streak of dark meat running through the center of the chop or for chops with as much dark meat as possible. See page 125 for more information on blade chops. Serve over egg noodles or mashed potatoes.

1	onion, halved and sliced ½ inch thick
1	tablespoon vegetable oil
2	teaspoons minced garlic
¼	teaspoon dried thyme
½	cup chicken broth
1	tablespoon soy sauce
2	teaspoons instant tapioca
	Salt and pepper
2	(8-ounce) bone-in blade-cut pork chops, ¾ inch thick
4	slices bacon, chopped
2	tablespoons minced fresh parsley
1½	teaspoons cider vinegar

1. Lightly spray inside of slow cooker with vegetable oil spray. Microwave onion, oil, garlic, and thyme in bowl, stirring occasionally, until onion is softened, about 5 minutes; transfer to prepared slow cooker. Stir in broth, soy sauce, tapioca, and ½ teaspoon pepper. Cut 2 slits, about 2 inches apart, through outer layer of fat and silverskin on each chop. Season chops with salt and pepper and nestle into slow cooker. Cover and cook until pork is tender, 2 to 3 hours on low.

2. Transfer chops to serving dish and tent with aluminum foil. Line plate with double layer of coffee filters. Spread bacon in even layer over filters and microwave until crisp, about 5 minutes. Using large spoon, skim excess fat from surface of sauce. Stir in parsley and vinegar and season with salt and pepper to taste. Pour sauce over chops and sprinkle with bacon. Serve.

SMART SHOPPING CIDER VINEGAR

To see whether cider vinegar varies from brand to brand, we rounded up 10 vinegars—domestic as well as a couple from France and Canada—and it was immediately clear they were not identical. They ranged in color from pale straw to deep gold, in flavor from sweet to puckeringly tart, and in appearance from crystal clear to clouded with particulate matter. After tasting the vinegars straight, in a vinaigrette, in a cooked sauce, and in a vinegar-based barbecue sauce, one thing was clear: Sweet vinegars stole the show. Our favorite, California-made **Spectrum Naturals Organic Apple Cider Vinegar**, was praised not only for its sweetness, but also for its "distinct apple flavor" and "assertive, tangy" qualities.

Sweet and Sour Sticky Ribs

Serves 2   **Cooking Time** 3 to 6 hours on Low   **Slow Cooker Size** 3½ to 7 Quarts

✔ **WHY THIS RECIPE WORKS:** Chinese-style sweet and sour ribs are a bar and party favorite, but we wanted to scale this irresistible dish down for two. Leaving the membrane attached to the underside of our baby back ribs helped the rack hold together as it cooked and, as a bonus, shortened our prep time. Rubbing the ribs with a mixture of granulated garlic and ground ginger infused them with flavor. Once the ribs were tender, we brushed them with a tangy sauce and broiled them to develop a caramelized, lightly charred exterior. Avoid racks of baby back ribs that are larger than 2 pounds; they will be difficult to maneuver into the slow cooker.

1½ teaspoons granulated garlic

1 teaspoon ground ginger

Salt and pepper

1 (1½- to 2-pound) rack baby back ribs

⅓ cup apricot preserves

2 tablespoons ketchup

2 tablespoons soy sauce

2 tablespoons rice vinegar

1 tablespoon minced fresh cilantro

1. Mix garlic, ginger, 1 teaspoon salt, and 1 teaspoon pepper together in bowl and rub evenly over ribs.

2A. FOR A 3½- TO 4½-QUART SLOW COOKER: Lightly spray inside of slow cooker with vegetable oil spray. Arrange ribs along bottom and sides of prepared slow cooker, meaty side facing down. Cover and cook until ribs are tender, 5 to 6 hours on low.

2B. FOR A 5- TO 7-QUART SLOW COOKER: Lightly spray inside of slow cooker with vegetable oil spray. Arrange ribs along bottom and sides of prepared slow cooker, meaty side facing down. Cover and cook until ribs are tender, 3 to 4 hours on low.

3. Adjust oven rack 10 inches from broiler element and heat broiler. Place wire rack in aluminum foil–lined rimmed baking sheet; spray with vegetable oil spray. Whisk preserves, ketchup, soy sauce, and vinegar together. Transfer ribs, meaty side up, to sheet. Brush ribs with sauce, then broil until browned and sticky, 10 to 15 minutes, flipping and brushing with additional sauce every few minutes. Sprinkle with cilantro. Serve with remaining sauce.

QUICK PREP TIP **ARRANGING A SINGLE RACK OF RIBS IN SLOW COOKER**
To ensure that a single rack of ribs cooks evenly in a small or large slow cooker, arrange the rack with the meaty side down across the bottom of the slow cooker. The ends of the rack will come up against the sides of the slow cooker.

Easy Pulled Pork

Serves 2   **Cooking Time** 5 to 6 hours on Low or 3 to 4 hours on High
Slow Cooker Size 3½ to 7 Quarts

✓ **WHY THIS RECIPE WORKS:** To revamp this cookout classic for two, we ditched the usual pork shoulder in favor of boneless country-style ribs, which have plenty of marbling to keep the meat tender and are easy to purchase in smaller quantities. Bottled barbecue sauce ensured that our recipe was effortless and we didn't have to bother assembling umpteen ingredients for a simple sauce. To guarantee that our pork offered the big flavor of authentic recipes, we applied a dry spice rub (brown sugar, paprika, and chili powder) to our ribs. Two slices of bacon, tossed into the slow cooker whole, infused the pork with smoky flavor. Adding the leftover braising liquid to the barbecue sauce enhanced its flavor and added meaty depth and richness. Try to buy country-style pork ribs with lots of fat and dark meat, and stay away from ribs that look overly lean with pale meat, as they will taste very dry after the extended cooking time. Don't shred the pork too fine in step 2; it will break up more as it is combined with the sauce. Serve on hamburger buns with pickle chips.

½	**cup chicken broth**
2	**slices bacon**
1	**tablespoon packed brown sugar**
1	**tablespoon paprika**
1½	**teaspoons chili powder**
	Salt and pepper
1	**pound boneless country-style pork ribs, trimmed**
¾	**cup barbecue sauce**

1. Lightly spray inside of slow cooker with vegetable oil spray. Combine broth and bacon in prepared slow cooker. Mix sugar, paprika, chili powder, ½ teaspoon salt, and ½ teaspoon pepper together in bowl and rub evenly over ribs. Nestle ribs into slow cooker, cover, and cook until pork is tender, 5 to 6 hours on low or 3 to 4 hours on high.

2. Transfer ribs to bowl and let cool slightly. Shred into bite-size pieces, discarding excess fat.

3. Discard bacon. Strain cooking liquid into fat separator and let sit for 5 minutes; reserve ½ cup defatted liquid. Combine reserved liquid and barbecue sauce in separate bowl. Stir ½ cup sauce into shredded pork, adding more sauce as needed to keep meat moist. Season with salt and pepper to taste and serve with remaining sauce.

ON THE SIDE SWEET AND TANGY COLESLAW
Toss 4 cups shredded green cabbage (½ small head) and 1 small shredded carrot with 1 teaspoon salt and let drain in colander until wilted, about 1 hour. Rinse cabbage and carrot with cold water, then dry thoroughly with paper towels. Whisk 2 tablespoons cider vinegar, 2 tablespoons sugar, 1 tablespoon vegetable oil, 1 tablespoon minced fresh parsley, and pinch celery seeds together in large bowl. Add rinsed cabbage mixture and toss to combine. Season with extra vinegar, extra sugar, and salt to taste and refrigerate until chilled. Serves 2.

Poached Salmon

Serves 2   **Cooking Time** 1 to 2 hours on Low   **Slow Cooker Size** 3½ to 7 Quarts

WHY THIS RECIPE WORKS: Poaching is a gentle cooking method that promises to deliver tender, delicately flavored salmon, thanks to a longer stint in a moist, gentle cooking environment. Rather than poach our salmon on the stovetop, where we'd have to carefully monitor the heat level, we decided to move this dish to the slow cooker to take advantage of its walk-away convenience. We started with two salmon fillets and kept the flavor profile simple, pairing our fish with lemon and dill for subtle flavor. To prevent the bottom of our salmon from overcooking, we rested our fillets on lemon slices and dill stems, then added a small amount of water to the slow cooker to create a moist cooking environment. A foil sling made it easy to remove the delicate salmon from the slow cooker without the fillets breaking apart. For a simple serving sauce, we combined sour cream and Dijon mustard with more lemon and dill. To ensure even cooking, be sure to buy salmon fillets of equal size and thickness. Because delicate fish can easily overcook in the slow cooker, it requires some monitoring (at least the first time you make it). Check the temperature of the salmon after 1 hour of cooking and continue to monitor until it registers 135 degrees. For more information on making a foil sling for fish, see page 144.

1   lemon, sliced ¼ inch thick, plus
      1 tablespoon juice

1½   teaspoons minced fresh dill,
      stems reserved

2   (6- to 8-ounce) skin-on salmon
      fillets, about 1½ inches thick
      Salt and pepper

¼   cup sour cream

1   teaspoon Dijon mustard

1. Fold sheet of aluminum foil into 12 by 9-inch sling and press widthwise into slow cooker. Arrange lemon slices in tight single layer in bottom of prepared slow cooker. Scatter dill stems over lemon slices. Pour water into slow cooker until it is even with lemon slices (about ½ cup water). Season fillets with salt and pepper and place skin side down on top of lemon slices. Cover and cook until salmon is opaque throughout when checked with tip of paring knife and registers 135 degrees, 1 to 2 hours on low.

2. Combine sour cream, mustard, lemon juice, and minced dill in bowl and season with salt and pepper to taste. Using sling, transfer fillets to baking sheet. Gently lift and tilt fillets with spatula to remove dill stems and lemon slices and transfer fillets to individual plates; discard dill stems, lemon slices, and poaching liquid. Serve with sauce.

SMART SHOPPING WILD VERSUS FARMED SALMON
In season, we've always preferred the more pronounced flavor of wild-caught salmon to that of farmed Atlantic salmon, traditionally the main farm-raised variety in this country. But with more wild and farmed species now available, we decided to reevaluate. We tasted three kinds of wild Pacific salmon and two farmed. While we love the stronger flavor of wild-caught fish, if you're going to spend the extra money, make sure it looks and smells fresh, and realize that high quality is available only from late spring through the end of summer.

Easy Sides

Braised Artichokes

Serves 4   **Cooking Time** 8 to 9 hours on Low or 5 to 6 hours on High
Slow Cooker Size 5½ to 7 Quarts

✓ **WHY THIS RECIPE WORKS:** Whole artichokes with drawn butter make for an impressive side dish or starter. To ensure that we didn't have to prep or cook it while also getting dinner going, we moved it to the slow cooker, so the leaves could simmer unattended until tender. Prep was easy: We simply trimmed the artichokes and placed them upright in the slow cooker with a little water. Tossing them with a bit of lemon juice and olive oil beforehand helped to preserve their color. For a simple yet boldly flavored dipping sauce, we melted some butter with more lemon juice and minced garlic. Try to purchase artichokes that weigh about 8 ounces each; if the artichokes are larger or smaller, you may need to adjust the cooking time.

4	whole artichokes (8 ounces each)
¼	cup lemon juice (2 lemons)
1	tablespoon olive oil
½	cup water
6	tablespoons unsalted butter
1	tablespoon minced garlic
¼	teaspoon salt

1. Using chef's knife, cut off stems so artichokes sit upright, then trim off top quarter of each artichoke. Using kitchen shears, trim off top portion of outer leaves. Toss artichokes with 2 tablespoons lemon juice and oil, then place right side up in slow cooker. Add water, cover, and cook until outer leaves of artichokes pull away easily and tip of paring knife inserted into stem end meets no resistance, 8 to 9 hours on low or 5 to 6 hours on high.

2. Microwave remaining 2 tablespoons lemon juice, butter, garlic, and salt together in bowl until butter is melted, about 30 seconds. Whisk butter mixture to combine, then divide evenly among 4 serving bowls. Remove artichokes from slow cooker, letting any excess water drain back into insert, and place artichokes in bowls with butter; discard water. Serve.

QUICK PREP TIP **TRIMMING ARTICHOKES**

Cut stem off each artichoke with chef's knife so that base is even, then trim off top quarter of artichoke. Using kitchen shears, cut off dry, sharp tips from remaining outer leaves.

Honey-Rosemary Glazed Carrots

Serves 4 to 6   **Cooking Time** 5 to 6 hours on Low or 3 to 4 hours on High
Slow Cooker Size 5½ to 7 Quarts

✓ **WHY THIS RECIPE WORKS:** Moving our glazed carrots to the slow cooker gave us a family-friendly side dish that was also fuss-free. Cooking the carrots in chicken broth detracted from their delicate flavor, so we stuck with water, seasoned with a little sugar and salt. Once they were tender, we simply drained them and tossed them with a bit of honey, a pat of butter, and fresh rosemary. This recipe can easily be doubled.

2	**pounds carrots, peeled and sliced ¼ inch thick on bias**
¾	**cup water**
2	**teaspoons sugar**
	Salt and pepper
3	**tablespoons honey**
1	**tablespoon unsalted butter**
1	**teaspoon minced fresh rosemary**

1. Combine carrots, water, sugar, and ½ teaspoon salt in slow cooker. Cover and cook until carrots are tender, 5 to 6 hours on low or 3 to 4 hours on high.

2. Drain carrots and return to now-empty slow cooker. Stir in honey, butter, and rosemary, cover, and cook on high until fragrant, about 5 minutes. Season with salt and pepper to taste. Serve. (Carrots can be held on warm or low setting for up to 2 hours; loosen glaze with hot water as needed.)

Curried Carrots with Pistachios and Dried Cherries

Serves 4 to 6   **Cooking Time** 5 to 6 hours on Low or 3 to 4 hours on High
Slow Cooker Size 5½ to 7 Quarts

✓ **WHY THIS RECIPE WORKS:** For another riff on slow-cooked carrots, we added curry powder, which worked well with the vegetable's sweet flavor. Toasted pistachios added a nice crunch, and tart dried cherries balanced the sweet notes of the carrots. This recipe can easily be doubled.

2	**pounds carrots, peeled and sliced ¼ inch thick on bias**
¾	**cup water**
2	**teaspoons sugar**
1	**teaspoon curry powder**
	Salt and pepper
3	**tablespoons unsalted butter**
¼	**cup dried cherries, chopped**
¼	**cup toasted chopped pistachios**

1. Combine carrots, water, sugar, curry powder, and ½ teaspoon salt in slow cooker. Cover and cook until carrots are tender, 5 to 6 hours on low or 3 to 4 hours on high.

2. Drain carrots and return to now-empty slow cooker. Stir in butter and cherries and season with salt and pepper to taste. Sprinkle with pistachios and serve. (Carrots can be held on warm or low setting for up to 2 hours. Before serving, sprinkle with pistachios.)

Beets with Blue Cheese and Walnuts

Serves 4 to 6 **Cooking Time** 6 to 7 hours on Low or 4 to 5 hours on High
Slow Cooker Size 5½ to 7 Quarts

✔ **WHY THIS RECIPE WORKS:** Roasting beets can take up to an hour, which is a long time for the oven to be occupied by a simple side, and steaming them can lead to a loss in flavor. Moving ours to the slow cooker both freed up the oven and guaranteed beets with an undiluted, earthy flavor. Wrapping the beets in aluminum foil and including half a cup of water in the slow cooker ensured that they cooked through evenly. Coating them with vegetable oil spray helped a bit of salt and pepper to adhere. Rather than skin the beets when they were raw—which can be a messy endeavor—we waited until they were cooked and simply rubbed the skins off with paper towels. Cutting our beets into fork-friendly wedges ensured that they were easy to eat, and a simple balsamic vinaigrette added brightness. Crumbled blue cheese, toasted walnuts, and fresh mint turned our slow-cooked veggie into an impressive bistro-style side dish. To ensure even cooking, we recommend using beets that are similar in size—roughly 3 inches in diameter.

2	pounds beets, trimmed
	Vegetable oil spray
	Salt and pepper
½	cup water
¼	cup balsamic vinegar
3	tablespoons extra-virgin olive oil
¼	cup chopped fresh mint
½	cup crumbled blue cheese
½	cup walnuts, toasted and chopped coarse

1. Spray beets with vegetable oil spray and season with salt and pepper. Wrap beets individually in aluminum foil and place in slow cooker. Add water, cover, and cook until beets are tender, 6 to 7 hours on low or 4 to 5 hours on high.

2. Transfer beets to cutting board and carefully remove foil (watch for steam); discard water. When beets are cool enough to handle, rub off skins with paper towels or dish towel and cut into ½-inch-thick wedges.

3. Whisk vinegar, oil, and mint together in large bowl. Add beets and toss to coat. Season with salt and pepper to taste. Sprinkle with blue cheese and walnuts and serve.

QUICK PREP TIP REMOVING BEET SKINS
Cradle beet in several layers of paper towels or dish towel in your hands, then gently rub off skin.

Italian-Style Braised Green Beans

Serves 4 to 6   **Cooking Time** 8 to 9 hours on Low or 5 to 6 hours on High
Slow Cooker Size 5½ to 7 Quarts

WHY THIS RECIPE WORKS: Slowly braising green beans turns them incredibly tender and infuses them with big flavor. The Italian take on this method calls for adding tomatoes, garlic, and onion for a robustly flavored side dish. We found that a can of crushed tomatoes provided a bold tomato presence and guaranteed a sauce with the right consistency. Chopped onion and minced garlic gave the dish an aromatic backbone, and dried thyme offered woodsy notes. For a subtle heat, we included a small amount of red pepper flakes. Microwaving our aromatics briefly worked to jump-start their cooking and deepen their flavor in short order. For meaty richness and smoky notes, we included two strips of bacon; microwaving them with the aromatics helped to render some of their fat so we didn't need any oil. We then removed the spent bacon slices at the end of the cooking time. Our Italian-style braised green beans boast a velvety texture and deep flavor, and best of all, they are practically effortless.

1   **cup chopped onion**

2   **slices bacon**

1   **tablespoon minced garlic**
    Salt and pepper

½   **teaspoon dried thyme**

⅛   **teaspoon red pepper flakes**

1   **(28-ounce) can crushed tomatoes**

2   **pounds green beans, trimmed**

1. Microwave onion, bacon, garlic, ½ teaspoon salt, thyme, and pepper flakes in bowl, stirring occasionally, until onion is softened, about 5 minutes; transfer to slow cooker. Stir in tomatoes, then add green beans and toss to coat. Cover and cook until green beans are tender, 8 to 9 hours on low or 5 to 6 hours on high.

2. Remove bacon. Season with salt and pepper to taste. Serve. (Green beans can be held on warm or low setting for up to 2 hours.)

QUICK PREP TIP TRIMMING GREEN BEANS QUICKLY
Instead of trimming the ends from one green bean at a time, line up the beans on a cutting board and trim all the ends with just one slice.

Spanish-Style Braised Green Beans

Serves 4 to 6   **Cooking Time** 8 to 9 hours on Low or 5 to 6 hours on High
Slow Cooker Size 5½ to 7 Quarts

✔ WHY THIS RECIPE WORKS: For another satisfying take on braised green beans, we looked to Spanish cuisine for inspiration. Sweet, piquant paprika was a given in this dish. Chopped green olives added more flavor and meaty bites, and olive oil provided richness. To preserve the texture of the olives, we waited until the end to stir them in. As for the braising liquid, we tried using water, but it didn't provide enough flavor; tasters much preferred chicken broth, which infused our green beans with a deep, savory character. For a bit of crunch, we stirred in a good amount of slivered almonds just before serving. A dash of sherry vinegar contributed brightness and amped up the Spanish feel of our dish.

2	**tablespoons minced garlic**
2	**tablespoons extra-virgin olive oil**
1	**tablespoon paprika**
	Salt and pepper
¼	**teaspoon red pepper flakes**
½	**cup chicken broth**
2	**pounds green beans, trimmed**
1	**cup slivered almonds, toasted**
½	**cup pitted green olives, chopped**
2	**tablespoons sherry vinegar**

1. Microwave garlic, 1 tablespoon oil, paprika, ½ teaspoon salt, and pepper flakes in bowl, stirring occasionally, until fragrant, about 1 minute; transfer to slow cooker. Stir in broth, then add green beans and toss to coat. Cover and cook until green beans are tender, 8 to 9 hours on low or 5 to 6 hours on high.

2. Stir in almonds, olives, vinegar, and remaining 1 tablespoon oil. Season with salt, pepper, and extra vinegar to taste. Serve. (Green beans can be held on warm or low setting for up to 2 hours. Before serving, stir in almonds.)

SMART SHOPPING SHERRY VINEGAR
Sherry vinegar is a great addition to any pantry because it has a lively, complex flavor, and a little of it can brighten up just about any sauce, salad, or soup. Unlike the complex and slightly sweet balsamic vinegar that Italian cooking favors, sherry vinegar, made from the Spanish fortified wine for which it is named, is smoother and a bit more potent. Sherry vinegar, which is popular in Spanish cuisine, works well in sauces paired with hearty meats or in any dish where a bright and lively finishing touch would be welcome.

Balsamic-Glazed Brussels Sprouts with Pine Nuts

Serves 4 to 6   **Cooking Time** 2 to 3 hours on High   **Slow Cooker Size** 5½ to 7 Quarts

✔ **WHY THIS RECIPE WORKS:** These dressed-up Brussels sprouts are perfect for the holiday table—and they leave the oven open for the main course. Chicken broth added savory depth, and a drizzle of balsamic glaze and olive oil contributed intense flavor and richness. Pine nuts lent a delicate crunch. You can find balsamic glaze with the vinegar and salad dressings in most well-stocked supermarkets.

2	**pounds Brussels sprouts, trimmed and halved**
2	**cups chicken broth**
	Salt and pepper
2	**tablespoons balsamic glaze**
2	**tablespoons extra-virgin olive oil**
¼	**cup pine nuts, toasted**
¼	**cup grated Parmesan cheese**

1. Combine Brussels sprouts, broth, and ½ teaspoon salt in slow cooker. Cover and cook until Brussels sprouts are tender, 2 to 3 hours on high.

2. Drain Brussels sprouts and transfer to serving dish. Season with salt and pepper to taste. Drizzle with balsamic glaze and oil, then sprinkle with pine nuts and Parmesan. Serve.

Brussels Sprouts with Lemon, Thyme, and Bacon

Serves 4 to 6   **Cooking Time** 2 to 3 hours on High   **Slow Cooker Size** 5½ to 7 Quarts

✔ **WHY THIS RECIPE WORKS:** For a variation on our braised Brussels sprouts, we added a bit of lemon juice for brightness and grated lemon zest for sweet, citrusy flavor. Thyme contributed woodsy notes. For smoky, savory depth, we included some bacon, which we quickly crisped in the microwave.

2	**pounds Brussels sprouts, trimmed and halved**
2	**cups chicken broth**
	Salt and pepper
4	**slices bacon, chopped**
2	**tablespoons unsalted butter, melted**
2	**teaspoons grated lemon zest plus 1 tablespoon juice**
1	**teaspoon minced fresh thyme**

1. Combine Brussels sprouts, broth, and ½ teaspoon salt in slow cooker. Cover and cook until Brussels sprouts are tender, 2 to 3 hours on high.

2. Line plate with double layer of coffee filters. Spread bacon in even layer on filters and microwave until crisp, about 5 minutes. Drain Brussels sprouts and return to now-empty slow cooker. Stir in melted butter, lemon zest and juice, and thyme. Season with salt and pepper to taste. Sprinkle with bacon and serve.

Hearty Braised Greens with Garlic and Chorizo

Serves 4 to 6   **Cooking Time** 5 to 6 hours on Low or 3 to 4 hours on High
Slow Cooker Size 5½ to 7 Quarts

✔ **WHY THIS RECIPE WORKS:** Using the slow cooker to prepare our hearty greens was a no-brainer—after all, a long cooking time helps to turn kale and collard greens meltingly tender and tempers their assertive flavor. Braising the greens with chorizo and garlic gave these simple greens a meaty, spicy kick.

2 **pounds kale or collard greens, stemmed and sliced into 1-inch-wide strips**	**1.** Combine kale, chorizo, water, and garlic in slow cooker. Cover and cook until kale is tender, 5 to 6 hours on low or 3 to 4 hours on high.
8 **ounces chorizo sausage, halved and sliced ½ inch thick**	**2.** Season with salt and pepper to taste. Serve. (Braised greens can be held on warm or low setting for up to 2 hours.)
½ **cup water**	
2 **tablespoons minced garlic**	
Salt and pepper	

Hearty Braised Greens with Coconut and Curry

Serves 4 to 6   **Cooking Time** 5 to 6 hours on Low or 3 to 4 hours on High
Slow Cooker Size 5½ to 7 Quarts

✔ **WHY THIS RECIPE WORKS:** For braised greens with an exotic flavor profile, we added curry powder and fresh ginger. Coconut milk, plus chicken broth, gave us a velvety sauce with savory depth.

1 **cup chopped onion**	**1.** Microwave onion, oil, garlic, ginger, and curry powder in bowl, stirring occasionally, until onion is softened, about 5 minutes; transfer to slow cooker. Stir in kale and broth. Cover and cook until kale is tender, 5 to 6 hours on low or 3 to 4 hours on high.
1 **tablespoon vegetable oil**	
1 **tablespoon minced garlic**	
1 **tablespoon grated ginger**	
1 **tablespoon curry powder**	
2 **pounds kale or collard greens, stemmed and sliced into 1-inch-wide strips**	**2.** Microwave coconut milk in bowl until hot, about 2 minutes; stir into kale with lime juice. Season with salt, pepper, and extra lime juice to taste. Serve. (Braised greens can be held on warm or low setting for up to 2 hours.)
½ **cup chicken broth**	
1 **cup canned coconut milk**	
1 **tablespoon lime juice**	
Salt and pepper	

Maple Mashed Butternut Squash

Serves 6   **Cooking Time** 4 to 5 hours on Low or 3 to 4 hours on High
Slow Cooker Size 5½ to 7 Quarts

✔ WHY THIS RECIPE WORKS: With its silky-smooth texture and earthy, slightly sweet flavor, mashed butternut squash is one of our favorite side dishes. But because its flavor is so delicate, it can be easily overwhelmed. Using chicken broth for the braising liquid led to a chicken-flavored side dish, so we switched to water. But now the squash's subtle flavor was washed away, and its texture, once it was mashed, was watery. After a number of tests, we realized that the squash exuded a good amount of moisture during cooking, so we wondered if we needed to include any braising liquid at all. In the end it, we found that simply adding the squash pieces and a little salt to the slow cooker was all we needed to do to get properly cooked squash that tasted great. A small amount of maple syrup enhanced its sweetness without overpowering it, and a few pats of butter, plus two spoonfuls of heavy cream, ensured that our mash was plenty rich and had a creamy texture. This recipe can easily be doubled.

3   **pounds peeled and seeded butternut squash, cut into 1-inch pieces**
      Salt and pepper
¼   **cup maple syrup**
4   **tablespoons unsalted butter, melted**
2   **tablespoons heavy cream**

1. Combine squash and ½ teaspoon salt in slow cooker. Cover and cook until squash is tender, 4 to 5 hours on low or 3 to 4 hours on high.

2. Mash squash with potato masher until smooth. Fold in maple syrup, melted butter, and cream. Season with salt, pepper, and extra maple syrup to taste. Serve. (Squash can be held on warm or low setting for up to 2 hours; loosen with hot water as needed before serving.)

SMART SHOPPING BUTTERNUT SQUASH

It certainly saves prep time to buy precut, peeled butternut squash, but how do the flavor and texture of this timesaver squash stand up to a whole squash you cut up yourself? The test kitchen has found that whole squash that you peel and cube yourself can't be beat in terms of flavor or texture, but when you are trying to make the most of every minute, already peeled, halved squash is perfectly acceptable. Avoid the precut chunks; test kitchen tasters agree they are dry and stringy, with barely any squash flavor.

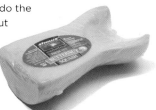

Creamy Garlic and Parmesan Mashed Potatoes

Serves 6   **Cooking Time** 4 to 5 hours on Low or 3 to 4 hours on High
Slow Cooker Size 5½ to 7 Quarts

☑ **WHY THIS RECIPE WORKS:** Infusing mashed potatoes with the sweet, nutty flavor of roasted garlic is easy—if you don't mind taking an extra hour to roast a head of garlic. We found that simply tossing peeled garlic cloves right into the slow cooker with the spuds guaranteed a deeply flavored dish—with a lot less hassle. Cooking the potatoes and garlic in a few cups of water ensured that they cooked through gently. After draining them, we reached for a potato masher and mashed them together right in the slow cooker—no need to dirty a bowl. When it came to the dairy, we found that milk, plus a bit of melted butter, gave our potatoes a nicely creamy texture. A cup of grated Parmesan added to our mash enhanced the nutty notes of the roasted garlic and guaranteed that our spuds were ultrarich. This recipe can easily be doubled.

3	**pounds russet potatoes, peeled and cut into 1-inch pieces**
3	**cups water**
4	**garlic cloves, peeled**
	Salt and pepper
3	**tablespoons unsalted butter, melted**
1	**cup milk, warmed**
1	**cup grated Parmesan cheese**

1. Combine potatoes, water, garlic, and ½ teaspoon salt in slow cooker. Cover and cook until potatoes are tender, 4 to 5 hours on low or 3 to 4 hours on high.

2. Drain potatoes and return to now-empty slow cooker. Mash potatoes with potato masher until smooth. Fold in melted butter, then fold in milk and Parmesan, adjusting consistency with extra warm milk as needed. Season with salt and pepper to taste and serve. (Mashed potatoes can be held on warm or low setting for up to 2 hours; loosen with extra warm milk as needed before serving.)

SMART SHOPPING PREPEELED VERSUS FRESH GARLIC

Many supermarkets carry jars or deli containers of prepeeled garlic cloves, but how do they compare to fresh garlic bought by the head? We tasted both kinds of garlic in various recipes, both raw and cooked, and, in all cases, results were mixed. However, we did notice a difference in shelf life: A whole head of garlic stored in a cool, dry place will last for at least a few weeks, while prepeeled garlic in a jar (which must be kept refrigerated) lasts for only about two weeks before turning yellowish and developing an overly pungent aroma, even if kept unopened in its original packaging. (In fact, in several instances we found containers of garlic that had started to develop this odor and color on the supermarket shelf.) But if you go through a lot of garlic, prepeeled cloves can be a fine alternative. Just make sure they look firm and white and have a matte finish when you purchase them.

Bourbon and Brown Sugar Mashed Sweet Potatoes

Serves 6 **Cooking Time** 4 to 5 hours on Low or 3 to 4 hours on High
Slow Cooker Size 5½ to 7 Quarts

✓ **WHY THIS RECIPE WORKS:** Mashed sweet potatoes are often overdressed as a marshmallow-topped casserole at Thanksgiving. But for an everyday side, you can't beat an honest sweet potato mash. Braising the sweet potatoes in the slow cooker makes cooking them virtually effortless, and there's a world of options when it comes to dressing them up once cooked. For ours, we decided to include some bourbon, for an intensely flavored dish with a sophisticated feel. Once our sweet potatoes were tender, we mashed them and folded in a full quarter-cup of bourbon, which imparted a rich, caramelly flavor that we enhanced with a bit of brown sugar. A good amount of butter and some heavy cream ensured that they were plenty creamy. At last, we had a richly flavored sweet potato mash that actually tasted of sweet potatoes. This recipe can easily be doubled.

3 **pounds sweet potatoes, peeled and cut into 1-inch pieces**

3 **cups water**

Salt and pepper

6 **tablespoons unsalted butter, melted**

¼ **cup bourbon**

3 **tablespoons heavy cream, warmed**

1½ **tablespoons packed brown sugar**

1. Combine potatoes, water, and ½ teaspoon salt in slow cooker. Cover and cook until potatoes are tender, 4 to 5 hours on low or 3 to 4 hours on high.

2. Drain potatoes and return to now-empty slow cooker. Mash potatoes with potato masher until smooth. Fold in melted butter, bourbon, cream, and sugar, adjusting consistency with extra warm cream as needed. Season with salt and pepper to taste and serve. (Mashed sweet potatoes can be held on warm or low setting for up to 2 hours; loosen with extra warm cream as needed before serving.)

SMART SHOPPING SWEET POTATO OR YAM?
You often hear "yam" and "sweet potato" used interchangeably, but they actually belong to completely different botanical families. Yams, generally sold in Latin and Asian markets, are often sold in chunks (they can grow to be several feet long) and can be found in dozens of varieties, with flesh ranging from white to light yellow to pink, and skin from off-white to brown. They all have very starchy flesh. Sweet potatoes are also found in several varieties and can have firm or soft flesh, but it's the soft varieties that have in the past been mislabeled as "yams," and the confusion continues to this day. In an attempt to remedy this, the USDA now requires labels with the term "yam" to be accompanied by the term "sweet potato" when appropriate. We typically buy the conventional sweet potato, a longish, knobby tuber with dark, orangey-brown skin and vivid flesh that cooks up moist and sweet. The buttery-sweet Beauregard is our favorite variety.

Easy "Baked" Potatoes

Serves 4 to 6   **Cooking Time** 6 to 7 hours on Low or 4 to 5 hours on High
Slow Cooker Size 5½ to 7 Quarts

✔ **WHY THIS RECIPE WORKS:** Forget about preheating the oven to achieve perfectly cooked baked potatoes with a creamy interior—we moved this dish to the slow cooker, leaving the oven available for other things (like the main course). Wrapping the potatoes in foil and including a little water in the slow cooker helped them cook through more evenly. Spritzing the potatoes with vegetable oil spray ensured that our seasonings adhered (salt and pepper did the trick). Serve with your favorite baked potato toppings.

4–6	**russet potatoes**
	Vegetable oil spray
	Salt and pepper
½	**cup water**

1. Spray potatoes with vegetable oil spray and season with salt and pepper. Wrap potatoes individually in aluminum foil and place in slow cooker. Add water, cover, and cook until potatoes are tender, 6 to 7 hours on low or 4 to 5 hours on high.

2. Transfer potatoes to serving dish and carefully remove foil (watch for steam); discard water. Serve.

Braised Red Potatoes with Rosemary and Garlic

Serves 4 to 6   **Cooking Time** 4 to 5 hours on Low or 3 to 4 hours on High
Slow Cooker Size 5½ to 7 Quarts

✔ **WHY THIS RECIPE WORKS:** Moving our baby red potatoes to the slow cooker gave us another simple side that goes well with any number of entrées. Since our spuds were small, they cooked through evenly on their own—no need to wrap them in foil. We simply tossed them with olive oil and minced garlic for richness and flavor. A sprig of rosemary, steeped in the slow cooker for the last 10 minutes of cooking, infused our super-tender, ultracreamy spuds with woodsy notes. Look for small red potatoes measuring 1 to 2 inches in diameter. This recipe can easily be doubled, but you will need to increase the cooking time by 1 hour.

2	**pounds small red potatoes**
3	**tablespoons olive oil**
1	**tablespoon minced garlic**
	Salt and pepper
1	**sprig fresh rosemary**

1. Combine potatoes, oil, garlic, ½ teaspoon salt, and ¼ teaspoon pepper in slow cooker. Cover and cook until potatoes are tender, 4 to 5 hours on low or 3 to 4 hours on high.

2. Stir in rosemary, cover, and cook on high until fragrant, about 10 minutes. Discard rosemary. Season with salt and pepper to taste and serve. (Potatoes can be held on warm or low setting for up to 2 hours.)

Scalloped Potatoes with Root Vegetables

Serves 6 to 8   **Cooking Time** 5 to 6 hours on Low or 3 to 4 hours on High
Slow Cooker Size 5½ to 7 Quarts

✓ **WHY THIS RECIPE WORKS:** While scalloped potatoes pair well with baked ham, roast leg of lamb, and many other holiday classics, the problem is that they take up to an hour to cook through in the oven, often at a different temperature from the main course. Moving our scalloped potatoes to the slow cooker solved this problem, yet still ensured an elegant casserole with tender vegetables and a luxurious sauce. Cream and broth, plus butter, thyme, and garlic, guaranteed that the sauce was rich and flavorful. To thicken it, we tried adding flour, but this led to a pasty sauce that separated. Thickening the sauce with cornstarch, which remained consistently stable over the long cooking time, worked much better; shredded cheddar melted into the sauce and ensured that it was smooth and robustly flavored. For the vegetables, we began with russets for their fluffy texture, then supplemented them with parsnips and carrots for complexity. Adding the sliced vegetables raw resulted in a dish with a mix of tender and crunchy bites, so we gave the veggies a head start in the microwave; tossing them with a little cream prevented them from sticking together. Lining the side of the slow cooker with foil also ensured that our easy casserole was evenly cooked throughout. Extra-sharp cheddar, which becomes grainy during slow cooking, should not be substituted for the sharp cheddar. Don't soak the potatoes in water before using or the scalloped potatoes will be watery. For more information on making a foil collar, see page 180. For a crisp, buttery topping, sprinkle with our Toasted Bread-Crumb Topping; page 184.

1	**pound russet potatoes, peeled and halved lengthwise**
1	**pound carrots, peeled**
1	**pound parsnips, peeled**
1¼	**cups heavy cream**
1¼	**cups chicken broth**
4½	**tablespoons cornstarch**
1	**tablespoon unsalted butter**
1	**tablespoon minced garlic**
1	**teaspoon salt**
½	**teaspoon pepper**
½	**teaspoon dried thyme**
1¼	**cups shredded sharp cheddar cheese**

1. Line slow cooker with aluminum foil collar and spray with vegetable oil spray. Using food processor fitted with ¼-inch slicing disk, slice potatoes, carrots, and parsnips. Microwave sliced vegetables and 2 tablespoons cream in covered bowl, stirring occasionally, until vegetables are almost tender, 6 to 8 minutes.

2. In large bowl, microwave remaining cream, broth, cornstarch, butter, garlic, salt, pepper, and thyme, stirring occasionally, until thickened, about 1 minute. Slowly whisk in ¾ cup cheddar until evenly melted.

3. Spread half of sauce in prepared slow cooker. Arrange vegetable mixture over sauce into even thickness and press gently to compress layers. Spread remaining sauce over top. Cover and cook until vegetables are tender, 5 to 6 hours on low or 3 to 4 hours on high.

4. Remove foil collar. Sprinkle with remaining ½ cup cheddar and let sit until cheese is melted and casserole is cooled slightly, about 20 minutes. Serve.

Corn Pudding

Serves 6   **Cooking Time** 2½ to 3½ hours on Low   **Slow Cooker Size** 5½ to 7 Quarts

WHY THIS RECIPE WORKS: Boasting a sweet, nutty corn flavor and tender, spoonable texture, corn pudding is incredibly satisfying and addictive. But this simple recipe can be quite finicky, with most versions calling for a roasting pan and water bath, which works to keep the dish moist. We decided to swap these for the slow cooker, where the low, slow heat would guarantee a creamy, flavorful corn pudding that was also fuss-free. We started with convenient frozen corn, which offers consistently sweet flavor and good quality year-round. We found that the secret to big corn flavor was processing a portion of the corn; this simple move infused the custard with richer flavor and guaranteed a more cohesive casserole. Three eggs and heavy cream ensured that our corn pudding was plenty rich and set up nicely. Shredded cheddar added deep, savory flavor, and cayenne pepper and chopped basil helped balance the sweetness and creaminess of the pudding. Simmering the corn pudding in a soufflé dish surrounded by water ensured that it cooked through gently and evenly, so that every flavor-packed bite was tender and creamy. We prefer the convenience of frozen corn here, but you can substitute fresh corn, if desired; note that you will need about 4 ears of corn.

3	cups frozen corn, thawed and patted dry
¾	cup heavy cream
¾	cup shredded sharp cheddar cheese
3	large eggs, lightly beaten
2	tablespoons chopped fresh basil
1½	teaspoons sugar
½	teaspoon salt
⅛	teaspoon cayenne pepper

1. Grease 1½-quart soufflé dish. Pulse 2 cups corn in food processor until coarsely ground, about 10 pulses.

2. Mix remaining 1 cup corn, processed corn, cream, cheddar, eggs, basil, sugar, salt, and cayenne together in bowl until well combined; transfer to prepared dish. Set dish in slow cooker and pour water into slow cooker until it reaches about one-third up sides of dish (about 2 cups water). Cover and cook until pudding is set, 2½ to 3½ hours on low. Remove dish from slow cooker and let pudding cool for 10 minutes before serving.

SMART SHOPPING SHARP CHEDDAR CHEESE

Traditionally, cheddar is made by a process called cheddaring: The curd (made by adding acid-producing cultures and clotting agents to unpasteurized whole milk) is cut into slabs, then stacked, cut, pressed, and stacked again. Along the way a large amount of liquid, called whey, is extracted. The remaining compacted curd is what gives farmhouse cheddars their hard and fine-grained characteristics. When it comes to flavor and sharpness, the longer a cheddar is aged, which can be anywhere from a couple of months to a couple of years, the firmer in texture and more concentrated in flavor (and sharper) it gets. In a recent taste test, **Cabot Sharp Vermont Cheddar Cheese** came out on top. This cheese, which is aged for five to eight months, was praised for its "sharp," "clean," and "tangy" flavor.

Sun-Dried Tomato and Basil Polenta

Serves 6 to 8   **Cooking Time** 4 to 5 hours on Low or 3 to 4 hours on High
Slow Cooker Size 5½ to 7 Quarts

✔ **WHY THIS RECIPE WORKS:** Polenta makes a hearty yet creamy bed for saucy braises and stews, but it usually requires a fairly lengthy cooking time and lots of stirring to achieve a nicely creamy texture and deep corn flavor. In translating this recipe to the slow cooker, we weren't concerned with the cooking time, but we did want this version to be essentially hands-free. We started by whisking coarse-ground polenta together with water, plus some salt, in the slow cooker (we used the typical ratio found in the stovetop versions). After a few hours, the polenta was perfectly tender—no stirring necessary. To amp up its flavor, we included sun-dried tomatoes at the beginning of the cooking time, then finished the dish with a good amount of grated Parmesan and some chopped basil. Be sure to use traditional polenta, not instant polenta.

7½	**cups water**
1½	**cups coarse-ground polenta**
⅓	**cup oil-packed sun-dried tomatoes, rinsed and chopped**
	Salt and pepper
1	**cup grated Parmesan cheese**
¼	**cup chopped fresh basil**

1. Lightly spray inside of slow cooker with vegetable oil spray. Whisk water, polenta, tomatoes, and 1½ teaspoons salt together in slow cooker. Cover and cook until polenta is tender, 4 to 5 hours on low or 3 to 4 hours on high.

2. Stir in Parmesan and basil and season with salt and pepper to taste. Serve. (Polenta can be held on warm or low setting for up to 2 hours; loosen with extra hot water as needed before serving.)

SMART SHOPPING POLENTA

Buying polenta can be confusing. Not only are several different types of polenta widely available at the market—traditional, instant, and precooked—but they all are simply labeled "polenta." Here's how to tell them apart. The real deal (left) is labeled as either "polenta" or "traditional polenta," and it is nothing more than a package of coarse-ground cornmeal with a very even grind and no small floury bits; it is often sold in clear bags so you can inspect it. Don't be tempted to buy coarse-grain cornmeal without the term "polenta" clearly listed on the package, as it often includes a portion of fine, floury bits that will make the polenta taste gluey. Instant polenta (center) and precooked tubes of polenta (right) are parcooked convenience products that have short cooking times (much like instant rice). Precooked polenta is easy to spot thanks to its tubelike packaging. Instant polenta, on the other hand, can look just like traditional polenta at the store and is identifiable only by the word "instant" in its title (which can be slightly hidden, in our experience).

Warm Wheat Berry Salad with Arugula and Dried Cherries

Serves 6 **Cooking Time** 10 to 11 hours on Low or 7 to 8 hours on High
Slow Cooker Size 5½ to 7 Quarts

✔ **WHY THIS RECIPE WORKS:** Because wheat berries, which are whole, husked wheat kernels, remain firm and distinct when cooked, they work especially well in salads, and they have a nutty flavor that pairs nicely with many ingredients. We thought the slow cooker would be the perfect vessel to prepare our wheat berries; because they are so hearty, they tend to require a lengthy simmer to become tender and chewy. Cooking our wheat berries in a large amount of water, much as we would cook pasta, worked best. Minced garlic and thyme, added right to the slow cooker, provided an aromatic backbone. A bit of salt boosted the flavor of the grains as well, but because salt affects the wheat berries' ability to absorb water, we had to be careful not to use more than ½ teaspoon or we ended up with hard, crunchy grains. Once the wheat berries were tender, we drained them and dressed them with a simple red wine vinaigrette. Baby arugula and dried cherries rounded out our salad and contributed bitter and sweet-tart notes. Crumbled goat cheese provided a creamy, tangy counterpoint to the nutty, chewy wheat berries.

5	cups water
1½	cups wheat berries
1	tablespoon minced garlic
½	teaspoon dried thyme
	Salt and pepper
3	tablespoons extra-virgin olive oil
3	tablespoons red wine vinegar
	Pinch sugar
4	ounces (4 cups) baby arugula
½	cup dried cherries
1	cup crumbled goat cheese

1. Combine water, wheat berries, garlic, thyme, and ½ teaspoon salt in slow cooker. Cover and cook until wheat berries are tender, 10 to 11 hours on low or 7 to 8 hours on high.

2. Drain wheat berries and return to now-empty slow cooker. Whisk oil, vinegar, sugar, and ¼ teaspoon salt together in bowl; stir into wheat berries. Stir in arugula and cherries and season with salt and pepper to taste. Sprinkle with goat cheese and serve.

SMART SHOPPING GOAT CHEESE
Goat cheese boasts an assertive, tangy flavor and a creamy yet crumbly texture that works well in many dishes, from salads and appetizers to pastas and pizza. To find the best one, we tasted nine brands plain and baked, rating them on flavor, texture, and tanginess. Our favorite goat cheese is **Laura Chenel's Chèvre Fresh Chèvre Log**, which tasters found to be "rich-tasting" with a "grassy" and "tangy" finish. It was "smooth" and "creamy" both unheated and baked, and it kept its "lemony, bright flavor."

Creamy Orzo with Parmesan and Peas

Serves 4 to 6   **Cooking Time** 1½ to 2½ hours on High   **Slow Cooker Size** 5½ to 7 Quarts

✔ **WHY THIS RECIPE WORKS:** For a side dish of tender—not mushy—orzo, we toasted our pasta in oil in the microwave before moving it to the slow cooker, then added hot broth to jump-start its cooking. Grated Parmesan and a couple of pats of butter, added at the end, gave us a rich-tasting dish with a creamy texture.

2	**cups chicken broth**
1	**cup orzo**
1	**cup chopped onion**
2	**tablespoons minced garlic**
3	**tablespoons unsalted butter**
¼	**cup dry white wine**
	Salt and pepper
1	**cup frozen peas**
1	**cup grated Parmesan cheese**

1. Microwave broth in bowl until steaming, about 2 minutes. In separate bowl, microwave orzo, onion, garlic, and 1 tablespoon butter, stirring occasionally, until orzo is lightly toasted, 5 to 7 minutes. Transfer hot orzo to slow cooker, immediately stir in wine, and let sit until wine is almost completely absorbed, about 2 minutes. Stir in hot broth and ½ teaspoon salt. Cover and cook until orzo is tender, 1½ to 2½ hours on high.

2. Stir in peas and let sit until heated through, about 5 minutes. Stir in Parmesan and remaining 2 tablespoons butter. Season with salt and pepper to taste and serve.

Orzo with Cherry Tomatoes, Mozzarella, and Basil

Serves 4 to 6   **Cooking Time** 1½ to 2½ hours on High   **Slow Cooker Size** 5½ to 7 Quarts

✔ **WHY THIS RECIPE WORKS:** For a summery, fresh-tasting pasta salad, we added halved cherry tomatoes, chunks of fresh mozzarella, and chopped basil to our tender slow-cooked orzo.

2	**cups chicken broth**
1	**cup orzo**
1	**cup chopped onion**
2	**tablespoons minced garlic**
3	**tablespoons extra-virgin olive oil**
¼	**cup dry white wine**
	Salt and pepper
6	**ounces cherry tomatoes, halved**
4	**ounces fresh mozzarella cheese, cut into ½-inch pieces**
½	**cup coarsely chopped fresh basil**

1. Microwave broth in bowl until steaming, about 2 minutes. In separate bowl, microwave orzo, onion, garlic, and 1 table-spoon oil, stirring occasionally, until orzo is lightly toasted, 5 to 7 minutes. Transfer hot orzo to slow cooker, immediately stir in wine, and let sit until wine is almost completely absorbed, about 2 minutes. Stir in hot broth and ½ teaspoon salt. Cover and cook until orzo is tender, 1½ to 2½ hours on high.

2. Stir in tomatoes and let sit until heated through, about 5 minutes. Stir in mozzarella, basil, and remaining 2 tablespoons oil. Season with salt and pepper to taste and serve.

Refried Beans

Serves 6 to 8 **Cooking Time** 9 to 10 hours on Low or 6 to 7 hours on High
Slow Cooker Size 5½ to 7 Quarts

✔ **WHY THIS RECIPE WORKS:** Homemade refried beans, infused with rich pork flavor, a subtle heat, and warm spice notes, are worlds apart from the canned stuff, but making them takes time. For great refried beans for our tacos, tostadas, and nachos, we put our slow cooker to work and developed a recipe that was flavor-packed but hands-off. We started with dried pintos (the usual pick for refried beans) and added them right to the slow cooker—no advance soaking or simmering needed. Chicken broth provided a flavorful cooking liquid, and garlic, onion, and cumin offered the requisite aromatic and warm spice notes. A poblano chile upped the heat level, and two slices of bacon infused the beans with smoky, savory depth. To jump-start the cooking of the aromatics and spices and deepen their flavor, we microwaved them briefly with the bacon, which rendered some fat and took the place of any vegetable oil. Once the beans were tender, we discarded the spent bacon strips and mashed the beans. Cilantro and lime juice added brightness and gave our dish authentic south-of-the-border flavor.

1   **cup chopped onion**

1   **poblano chile, stemmed, seeded, and minced**

2   **slices bacon**

1   **tablespoon minced garlic**

1   **tablespoon ground cumin**

1   **pound (2½ cups) dried pinto beans, picked over and rinsed**

5   **cups chicken broth**

3   **tablespoons minced fresh cilantro**

1   **tablespoon lime juice**
    Salt and pepper

1. Microwave onion, poblano, bacon, garlic, and cumin in bowl, stirring occasionally, until vegetables are softened, about 5 minutes; transfer to slow cooker. Stir in beans and broth. Cover and cook until beans are tender, 9 to 10 hours on low or 6 to 7 hours on high.

2. Remove bacon. Mash beans with potato masher until smooth. Stir in cilantro and lime juice and season with salt, pepper, and extra lime juice to taste. Serve. (Beans can be held on warm or low setting for up to 2 hours; loosen with hot water as needed before serving.)

SMART SHOPPING DRIED BEANS

When shopping for beans, it is imperative to select "fresh" dried beans. Buy those that are uniform in size and have a smooth exterior. When dried beans are fully hydrated and cooked, they should be plump with a taut skin and have creamy insides; spent beans will have wrinkled skins and a dry, almost gritty texture. Uncooked beans should be stored in a cool, dry place in a sealed plastic or glass container. Though dried beans can be stored for up to one year, it is best to use them within a month or two of purchase.

Campfire Beans

Serves 6 to 8   **Cooking Time** 9 to 10 hours on Low or 6 to 7 hours on High
Slow Cooker Size 5½ to 7 Quarts

✔ **WHY THIS RECIPE WORKS:** Perfect alongside a slab of ribs or a mound of pulled pork, these slow-cooked beans deliver deep, smoky flavor and a creamy, tender texture. The beans themselves—we found that either pinto or navy beans worked well here—required no prep, other than being picked over and rinsed. For a sauce with sweet and tangy flavor, we combined ketchup, molasses, and cider vinegar. A bit of Dijon mustard added heat, and brown sugar echoed the rich, caramelly notes of the molasses. We waited until the beans were tender to add the sauce because its acidity prevented them from cooking through all the way. To ensure that the beans took on rich flavor during their long stint in the slow cooker, we simmered them with onion, chili powder, and a dash of liquid smoke. Allowing the beans to cook with the sauce for an extra 30 minutes guaranteed that they picked up the sweet and tangy flavors and gave the sauce plenty of time to thicken.

1	cup chopped onion
1	teaspoon chili powder
1	tablespoon vegetable oil
1	pound (2½ cups) dried pinto or navy beans, picked over and rinsed
5	cups water
½	teaspoon liquid smoke
¾	cup ketchup
¼	cup molasses
3	tablespoons cider vinegar
3	tablespoons Dijon mustard
1	tablespoon packed brown sugar
	Salt and pepper

1. Microwave onion, chili powder, and oil in bowl, stirring occasionally, until onion is softened, about 5 minutes; transfer to slow cooker. Stir in beans, water, and liquid smoke. Cover and cook until beans are tender, 9 to 10 hours on low or 6 to 7 hours on high.

2. Stir in ketchup, molasses, vinegar, mustard, and sugar, cover, and cook on high until flavors meld and sauce is thickened, about 30 minutes. Season with salt and pepper to taste and serve. (Beans can be held on warm or low setting for up to 2 hours; loosen with extra hot water as needed before serving.)

SMART SHOPPING LIQUID SMOKE
We were among the many people who assume that there must be some kind of synthetic chemical chicanery going on in the making of "liquid smoke" flavoring, but that's not the case. Liquid smoke is made by channeling smoke from smoldering wood chips through a condenser, which quickly cools the vapors, causing them to liquefy (just like the drops that form when you breathe on a piece of cold glass). The water-soluble flavor compounds in the smoke are trapped within this liquid, and the nonsoluble, carcinogenic tars and resins are removed by a series of filters, resulting in a clean, smoke-flavored liquid. When buying liquid smoke, be sure to avoid brands with additives such as salt, vinegar, and molasses. Our top-rated brand, **Wright's Liquid Smoke**, contains nothing but smoke and water.

Desserts

Fudgy Brownie Wedges

Serves 6   **Cooking Time** 3 to 4 hours on High   **Slow Cooker Size** 5½ to 7 Quarts

✓ **WHY THIS RECIPE WORKS:** The low heat and moist environment of the slow cooker aren't just good for preparing richly flavored stews and braises—we found we could also take advantage of this appliance to make easy, from-scratch brownies. And because the flavor compounds in chocolate are extremely volatile and cook off easily in a hot oven, using the gentle heat of the slow cooker preserves more chocolate flavor and practically guarantees a fudgy texture. In fact, when we made our classic brownies in a slow cooker they were too fudgy, so we cut back on the sugar and omitted an egg yolk. Simply pouring the batter into the slow cooker led to unevenly cooked brownies that were hard to remove. Instead, we "baked" our brownies in a small springform pan, which fit nicely in the slow cooker and was easy to pull out when the brownies were done. A water bath ensured that they cooked through gently and evenly, and using a foil rack elevated the pan so no water seeped in. You will need a 6-inch springform pan for this recipe, or you can substitute a 6-inch round cake pan. For more information on making a foil rack, see page 292.

2	ounces unsweetened chocolate, chopped
5	tablespoons unsalted butter
½	cup (2½ ounces) all-purpose flour
½	teaspoon baking powder
⅛	teaspoon salt
⅔	cup packed (4⅔ ounces) brown sugar
1	large egg plus 1 large yolk, room temperature
½	teaspoon vanilla extract
⅓	cup pecans or walnuts, toasted and chopped coarse (optional)

1. Fill slow cooker with ½ inch water (about 2 cups water) and place aluminum foil rack in bottom. Grease 6-inch springform pan and line with parchment paper.

2. Microwave chocolate in large bowl at 50 percent power for 1 to 2 minutes. Stir, add butter, and continue to heat until melted, stirring once every 30 seconds; let cool slightly. In separate bowl, whisk flour, baking powder, and salt together. Whisk sugar, egg and yolk, and vanilla into cooled chocolate mixture until well combined. Stir in flour mixture until just incorporated.

3. Scrape batter into prepared pan, smooth top, and sprinkle with pecans, if using. Set pan on prepared rack, cover, and cook until toothpick inserted into center comes out with few moist crumbs attached, 3 to 4 hours on high.

4. Let brownies cool completely in pan on wire rack, 1 to 2 hours. Run small knife around edge of brownies, then remove sides of pan. Remove brownies from pan bottom, discarding parchment, and transfer to cutting board. Cut brownies into wedges and serve.

Carrot Cake

Serves 6   **Cooking Time** 3 to 4 hours on High   **Slow Cooker Size** 5½ to 7 Quarts

☑ **WHY THIS RECIPE WORKS:** This humble cake really shines when the balance of sweet shredded carrots and vegetable oil is just right, ensuring a moist, tender crumb. All too often, however, this cake dries out in the oven, unless you use a lot of oil. It turns out the slow cooker makes it far easier to produce a moist carrot cake without using all that oil. For a flavorful carrot cake with a moist, but not wet, texture, we tested different amounts of grated carrots and oil, both of which can weigh down the batter. In the end, ¾ cup of shredded carrots and 7 tablespoons of oil provided enough flavor and richness without making the cake soggy or greasy. As for the spices, we found that a small amount of cinnamon and a pinch of cloves offered ample spice notes. Finally, the combination of baking powder and baking soda gave our cake the right amount of lift. You will need a 6-inch springform pan for this recipe, or you can substitute a 6-inch round cake pan. For more information on making a foil rack, see page 292. This cake is great dusted with confectioners' sugar, or it can be topped with our Cream Cheese Frosting before serving.

¾	**cup (3¾ ounces) plus**
	2 tablespoons all-purpose flour
½	**teaspoon baking powder**
½	**teaspoon baking soda**
½	**teaspoon ground cinnamon**
	Pinch ground cloves
	Pinch salt
½	**cup packed (3½ ounces)**
	brown sugar
1	**large egg, room temperature**
7	**tablespoons vegetable oil**
¾	**cup shredded carrots**
	Confectioners' sugar (optional)

1. Fill slow cooker with ½ inch water (about 2 cups water) and place aluminum foil rack in bottom. Grease 6-inch springform pan and line with parchment paper.

2. Whisk flour, baking powder, baking soda, cinnamon, cloves, and salt together in bowl. In large bowl, whisk sugar and egg together until smooth, then slowly whisk in oil. Stir in flour mixture until just incorporated. Gently fold in carrots.

3. Scrape batter into prepared pan and smooth top. Gently tap pan on counter to release air bubbles. Set cake on prepared rack, cover, and cook until toothpick inserted in center comes out clean, 3 to 4 hours on high.

4. Let cake cool completely in pan on wire rack, 1 to 2 hours. Run small knife around edge of cake, then remove sides of pan. Remove cake from pan bottom, discarding parchment, and transfer to serving dish. Dust with confectioners' sugar, if using. Serve.

ON THE SIDE CREAM CHEESE FROSTING
Using electric mixer set at medium-high speed, beat 4 ounces softened cream cheese, 2 tablespoons softened unsalted butter, 1 teaspoon vanilla extract, and pinch salt until smooth, 2 to 4 minutes. Reduce speed to medium-low, slowly add ½ cup confectioners' sugar, and beat until smooth, 4 to 6 minutes. Increase speed to medium-high and beat until frosting is light and fluffy, 2 to 4 minutes. Makes about ¾ cup.

Applesauce Spice Cake

Serves 6   **Cooking Time** 3 to 4 hours on High   **Slow Cooker Size** 5½ to 7 Quarts

✔ **WHY THIS RECIPE WORKS:** For a simple dessert that would also satisfy that afternoon craving, we set our sights on a moist snack cake permeated with the sweet flavor of apples and infused with warm spice notes. A water bath ensured that it cooked through gently and evenly. Half a cup of applesauce guaranteed robust apple flavor throughout, and small amounts of cinnamon, nutmeg, and cloves offered subtle spice flavor. To finish our easy cake, we dusted it with a bit of confectioners' sugar. You will need a 6-inch springform pan for this recipe, or you can substitute a 6-inch round cake pan.

1	cup (5 ounces) all-purpose flour
½	teaspoon baking soda
¼	teaspoon ground cinnamon
	Pinch ground nutmeg
	Pinch ground cloves
½	cup (3½ ounces) granulated sugar
½	cup unsweetened applesauce, room temperature
1	large egg, room temperature
½	teaspoon vanilla extract
¼	teaspoon salt
6	tablespoons unsalted butter, melted and cooled
	Confectioners' sugar

1. Fill slow cooker with ½ inch water (about 2 cups water) and place aluminum foil rack in bottom. Grease 6-inch springform pan and line with parchment paper.

2. Whisk flour, baking soda, cinnamon, nutmeg, and cloves together in bowl. In large bowl, whisk granulated sugar, applesauce, egg, vanilla, and salt together until smooth. Slowly whisk in melted butter. Stir in flour mixture until just incorporated.

3. Scrape batter into prepared pan and smooth top. Gently tap pan on counter to release air bubbles. Set cake on prepared rack, cover, and cook until toothpick inserted in center comes out clean, 3 to 4 hours on high.

4. Let cake cool completely in pan on wire rack, 1 to 2 hours. Run small knife around edge of cake, then remove sides of pan. Remove cake from pan bottom, discarding parchment, and transfer to serving dish. Dust with confectioners' sugar and serve.

QUICK PREP TIP **MAKING A FOIL RACK**

To make an aluminum foil rack to elevate your baking pan so water doesn't seep in, loosely roll a 24 by 12-inch piece of foil into a 1-inch cylinder. Then bend the sides in to form an oval ring that measures 8 inches long by 5 inches wide. After adding water to the slow cooker, place the foil rack in the center, then place the pan on top.

Flourless Chocolate Cake

Serves 8   **Cooking Time** 1 to 2 hours on High   **Slow Cooker Size** 5½ to 7 Quarts

✔ **WHY THIS RECIPE WORKS:** This decadent cake requires just a handful of ingredients (chocolate, butter, eggs, and coffee) and can be made ahead of time, for an elegant and fuss-free finale. Removing the cake from the slow cooker when it was just slightly underdone (when it registered 140 degrees on an instant-read thermometer) was key because the cake continues to cook and firms up as it cools. You will need a 6-inch springform pan for this recipe. For more information on making a foil rack, see page 292. You can substitute ½ teaspoon of instant espresso powder dissolved in 2 tablespoons of boiling water for the brewed coffee, if desired. Check the temperature of the cake after 1 hour of cooking and continue to monitor until it registers 140 degrees. To make neat slices, dip the knife blade into hot water and wipe it clean with a dish towel after each cut.

8   **ounces bittersweet or semisweet chocolate, chopped**
8   **tablespoons unsalted butter**
2   **tablespoons brewed coffee**
4   **large eggs**
    Confectioners' sugar

1. Fill slow cooker with ½ inch water (about 2 cups water) and place aluminum foil rack in bottom. Grease 6-inch springform pan and line with parchment paper. Microwave chocolate in large bowl at 50 percent power for 1 to 2 minutes; stir, add butter, and continue to heat until melted, stirring once every 30 seconds. Stir in coffee and let chocolate mixture cool slightly.

2. Using electric mixer set at medium-low speed, whip eggs until foamy, about 1 minute. Increase speed to medium-high and whip eggs until very thick and pale yellow, 5 to 10 minutes. Gently fold one-third of whipped eggs into chocolate mixture until few streaks remain. Repeat folding twice more with remaining whipped eggs and continue to fold batter until no streaks remain.

3. Scrape batter into prepared pan and smooth top. Set cake on prepared rack, cover, and cook until cake registers 140 degrees, 1 to 2 hours on high.

4. Transfer cake to wire rack. Run small knife around edge of cake; gently blot away condensation using paper towels. Let cool in pan to room temperature, about 1 hour. Cover with plastic wrap; refrigerate until well chilled, at least 3 hours or up to 3 days.

5. About 30 minutes before serving, run small knife around edge of cake, then remove sides of pan. Slide thin metal spatula between parchment and pan bottom to loosen, then slide cake onto serving dish. Dust with confectioners' sugar and serve.

Individual Chocolate Fudge Cakes

Serves 4   **Cooking Time** 1 to 2 hours on Low   **Slow Cooker Size** 5½ to 7 Quarts

✔ **WHY THIS RECIPE WORKS:** With a flavor that's intense and rich and a texture that's cakey yet soufflé-like, these little desserts are utterly satisfying. Plus they're easy enough to get into the slow cooker for a sweet finish on a busy weeknight. For ours, we whipped two eggs and an egg yolk, then added sugar, melted chocolate and butter, vanilla, and a single tablespoon of flour before portioning our batter into four ramekins. To ensure that each cake had a dense, super-fudgy center, we simply pressed a small piece of chocolate into the middle of each ramekin before cooking. You will need an oval slow cooker and four 6-ounce round ramekins for this recipe. Serve these cakes warm in their ramekins.

6   ounces semisweet chocolate,
    4 ounces chopped and 2 ounces
    broken into 4 (½-ounce) pieces

4   tablespoons unsalted butter

½   teaspoon vanilla extract

2   large eggs plus 1 large yolk

¼   cup (1¾ ounces) granulated
    sugar

⅛   teaspoon salt

1   tablespoon all-purpose flour
    Confectioners' sugar

1. Fill slow cooker with ½ inch water (about 2 cups water). Microwave chopped chocolate in large bowl at 50 percent power for 1 to 2 minutes; stir, add butter, and continue to heat until melted, stirring once every 30 seconds. Stir in vanilla and let chocolate mixture cool slightly.

2. Using electric mixer set at medium-low speed, whip eggs and yolk until foamy, about 1 minute. Increase speed to medium and gradually whip in granulated sugar and salt, about 30 seconds. Increase speed to medium-high and continue to whip eggs until very thick and pale yellow, 5 to 10 minutes. Scrape whipped egg mixture on top of cooled chocolate mixture, then sift flour over top. Gently fold mixtures together until no streaks remain.

3. Portion batter into four 6-ounce ramekins. Gently press 1 piece broken chocolate into center of each ramekin to submerge and smooth tops. Set ramekins in prepared slow cooker, cover, and cook until cakes are domed, tops are just firm to touch, and centers are gooey when pierced with toothpick, 1 to 2 hours on low. Using tongs and sturdy spatula, remove ramekins from slow cooker. Dust with confectioners' sugar and serve warm. (Cakes can be held in water bath with slow cooker turned off for up to 30 minutes.)

ON THE SIDE WHIPPED CREAM
Using electric mixer set at medium-low speed, whip 1 cup heavy cream, 1 tablespoon sugar, and 1 teaspoon vanilla extract until foamy, about 1 minute. Increase speed to high and whip until soft peaks form, 1 to 3 minutes. Makes about 2 cups.

Rich and Creamy Cheesecake

Serves 8   **Cooking Time** 1½ to 2½ hours on High   **Slow Cooker Size** 5½ to 7 Quarts

✔ **WHY THIS RECIPE WORKS:** Moving this luxurious dessert to the slow cooker ensures that it "bakes" through perfectly every time—no need to worry about cracks on the top. For a supremely creamy texture, we turned off the slow cooker once the cake registered 150 degrees on an instant-read thermometer, then let the cheesecake sit in the slow cooker for an hour so it could gently finish cooking. For more information on making a foil rack, see page 292. Check the temperature of the cheesecake after 1½ hours of cooking and continue to monitor until it registers 150 degrees. To make neat slices, dip the knife blade into hot water and wipe it clean with a dish towel after each cut. Serve with sliced strawberries, if desired.

6   **whole graham crackers, crushed**

2   **tablespoons unsalted butter, melted and cooled**

⅔   **cup (4⅔ ounces) plus 1 tablespoon sugar**

½   **teaspoon ground cinnamon**

      Salt

18   **ounces cream cheese, softened**

¼   **cup sour cream**

2   **large eggs, room temperature**

1   **teaspoon vanilla extract**

1. Fill slow cooker with ½ inch water (about 2 cups) and place aluminum foil rack in bottom. Pulse graham crackers in food processor to fine crumbs, about 20 pulses. Combine crumbs, melted butter, 1 tablespoon sugar, cinnamon, and pinch salt in bowl until evenly moistened. Transfer crumbs to 6-inch springform pan and, using bottom of dry measuring cup, press crumbs evenly into pan bottom. Wipe out processor bowl.

2. Process cream cheese, remaining ⅔ cup sugar, and ¼ teaspoon salt in now-empty food processor until combined, about 15 seconds, scraping down sides of bowl as needed. Add sour cream, eggs, and vanilla; process until just incorporated, about 15 seconds; do not overmix. Pour filling into prepared pan and smooth top. Set cheesecake on prepared rack, cover, and cook until cake registers 150 degrees, 1½ to 2½ hours on high. Turn off slow cooker and let cheesecake sit for 1 hour (keeping slow cooker covered).

3. Transfer cheesecake to wire rack. Run small knife around edge of cake; gently blot away condensation using paper towels. Let cool in pan to room temperature, about 1 hour. Cover with plastic wrap and refrigerate until well chilled, at least 3 hours or up to 3 days.

4. About 30 minutes before serving, run small knife around edge of cheesecake, then remove sides of pan. Slide thin metal spatula between crust and pan bottom to loosen, then slide cheesecake onto serving dish. Serve.

Chocolate Cheesecake

Serves 8   **Cooking Time** 1½ to 2½ hours on High   **Slow Cooker Size** 5½ to 7 Quarts

✔ **WHY THIS RECIPE WORKS:** For the ultimate in decadence, we added melted semisweet chocolate and cocoa powder to our creamy cheesecake. Swapping the graham crackers for chocolate sandwich cookies ensured a flavorful crust. Any brand of chocolate sandwich cookies will work well here, but avoid any "double-filled" cookies because the crust won't set properly. For more information on making a foil rack, see page 292. Check the temperature of the cheesecake after 1½ hours of cooking and continue to monitor until it registers 150 degrees. To make neat slices, dip the knife blade into hot water and wipe it clean with a dish towel after each cut. Serve with chocolate shavings, if desired.

4	ounces semisweet chocolate, chopped
8	chocolate sandwich cookies
2	tablespoons unsalted butter, melted and cooled
18	ounces cream cheese, softened
⅔	cup (4⅔ ounces) sugar
¼	teaspoon salt
¼	cup sour cream
2	large eggs, room temperature
2	tablespoons unsweetened cocoa powder
1	teaspoon vanilla extract

1. Fill slow cooker with ½ inch water (about 2 cups) and place aluminum foil rack in bottom. Microwave chocolate in bowl at 50 percent power, stirring occasionally, until melted, 1 to 2 minutes; let cool slightly.

2. Pulse cookies in food processor to fine crumbs, about 20 pulses. Combine crumbs and melted butter in bowl until evenly moistened. Transfer crumbs to 6-inch springform pan and, using bottom of dry measuring cup, press crumbs evenly into pan bottom. Wipe out processor bowl.

3. Process cream cheese, sugar, and salt in now-empty food processor until combined, about 15 seconds, scraping down sides of bowl as needed. Add cooled chocolate, sour cream, eggs, cocoa, and vanilla and process until just incorporated, about 15 seconds; do not overmix. Pour filling into prepared pan and smooth top. Set cheesecake on prepared rack, cover, and cook until cake registers 150 degrees, 1½ to 2½ hours on high. Turn off slow cooker and let cheesecake sit for 1 hour (keeping slow cooker covered).

4. Transfer cheesecake to wire rack. Run small knife around edge of cake; gently blot away condensation using paper towels. Let cool in pan to room temperature, about 1 hour. Cover with plastic wrap; refrigerate until well chilled, at least 3 hours or up to 3 days.

5. About 30 minutes before serving, run small knife around edge of cheesecake, then remove sides of pan. Slide thin metal spatula between crust and pan bottom to loosen, then slide cheesecake onto serving dish. Serve.

Crème Brûlée

Serves 4   **Cooking Time** 2 to 3 hours on Low   **Slow Cooker Size** 5½ to 7 Quarts

✓ **WHY THIS RECIPE WORKS:** Making crème brûlée the traditional way requires a few steps and lots of attention to detail, from making a custard and tempering eggs to pouring boiling water into a roasting pan already filled with ramekins without splashing it into the custards. Enter our easy, foolproof slow-cooker version—we simply whisked a good amount of cream and egg yolks together with some sugar and vanilla extract. These custards cook to creamy perfection thanks to the gentle heat of the slow cooker. Cooking the custards on low until the centers are just barely set and then chilling them also ensures a smooth, rich texture. Turbinado sugar, sprinkled over the top and heated with a kitchen torch, gave our crème brûlée a picture-perfect crust. You will need an oval slow cooker and four 6-ounce round ramekins for this recipe. Turbinado sugar is commonly sold as Sugar in the Raw. Be sure to caramelize the sugar topping on the custards just before serving. Check the temperature of the custards after 2 hours of cooking and continue to monitor until they register 185 degrees.

2   **cups heavy cream**

5   **large egg yolks, room temperature**

⅓   **cup (2⅓ ounces) granulated sugar**

1   **teaspoon vanilla extract**
     Pinch salt

4   **teaspoons turbinado sugar**

1. Fill slow cooker with ½ inch water (about 2 cups water). Whisk cream, egg yolks, granulated sugar, vanilla, and salt together in bowl until sugar is dissolved. Strain custard through fine-mesh strainer into 4-cup liquid measuring cup and portion into four 6-ounce ramekins. Set ramekins in prepared slow cooker, cover, and cook until centers are just barely set and register 185 degrees, 2 to 3 hours on low.

2. Using tongs and sturdy spatula, transfer ramekins to wire rack; let cool to room temperature, about 2 hours. Cover with plastic wrap; refrigerate until well chilled, at least 4 hours or up to 2 days.

3. Just before serving, gently blot away condensation using paper towels. Sprinkle 1 teaspoon turbinado sugar evenly over each custard; caramelize sugar with torch until deep golden brown. Serve.

QUICK PREP TIP
BROWNING CRÈME BRÛLÉE
After sprinkling sugar over surface of custard, tilt and tap ramekin to distribute sugar into thin, even layer. Pour out any excess sugar and wipe inside rim clean. To caramelize sugar, sweep flame of torch from perimeter of custard toward middle, keeping flame about 2 inches above ramekin, until sugar is bubbling and deep golden brown.

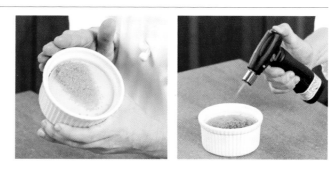

Bourbon Bread Pudding

Serves 8 to 10   **Cooking Time** 3 to 4 hours on Low   **Slow Cooker Size** 5½ to 7 Quarts

✔ **WHY THIS RECIPE WORKS:** The slow cooker works its magic on this humble dessert, keeping it moist and melding all the ingredients together perfectly, no water bath required. We took this dessert up a notch by spiking the custard with bourbon and tossing in toasted pecans for a subtle crunch. Using stale challah ensured that it didn't turn to mush when combined with the custard (a combination of egg yolks, half-and-half, brown sugar, bourbon, vanilla, and a bit of orange zest for brightness). Letting the challah sit in the custard for 10 minutes ensured that the bread really soaked it up. Cinnamon sugar and toasted pecans made the perfect topping, and lining the slow cooker with foil prevented our bread pudding from overcooking on one side. A drizzle of Bourbon Sauce added even more richness to individual servings of this homey dessert. For more information on making a foil collar and staling bread, see pages 180 and 234, respectively. Don't let this bread pudding cook longer than 4 hours or it will become dried out and rubbery.

4	**cups half-and-half**
1½	**cups packed (10½ ounces) brown sugar**
9	**large egg yolks**
½	**cup bourbon**
1	**tablespoon vanilla extract**
2	**teaspoons grated orange zest**
¼	**teaspoon salt**
14	**ounces stale challah, cut into 1-inch pieces**
⅔	**cup pecans, toasted and chopped**
1	**teaspoon ground cinnamon**

1. Line slow cooker with aluminum foil collar and spray with vegetable oil spray. Whisk half-and-half, 1¼ cups sugar, egg yolks, bourbon, vanilla, orange zest, and salt together in large bowl until sugar is dissolved. Stir in challah and let sit, pressing on bread occasionally, until custard is mostly absorbed, about 10 minutes.

2. Combine pecans, cinnamon, and remaining ¼ cup sugar in separate bowl. Transfer soaked bread mixture to prepared slow cooker and sprinkle with pecan mixture. Cover and cook until center is set, 3 to 4 hours on low. Let bread pudding cool for 20 minutes before serving.

ON THE SIDE BOURBON SAUCE
Whisk 2 tablespoons bourbon and 1½ teaspoons cornstarch together in bowl until well combined. Heat ¾ cup cream and 2 tablespoons sugar in small saucepan over medium heat until sugar dissolves. Whisk in cornstarch mixture and bring to boil. Reduce heat to low and cook until sauce thickens, 3 to 5 minutes. Off heat, stir in 1 to 2 tablespoons bourbon, 2 teaspoons unsalted butter, and pinch salt. (Sauce can be refrigerated for up to 5 days; reheat on stovetop.) Makes about 1 cup.

White Chocolate and Cherry Bread Pudding

Serves 8 to 10   **Cooking Time** 3 to 4 hours on Low   **Slow Cooker Size** 5½ to 7 Quarts

✔ WHY THIS RECIPE WORKS: For an unusual take on bread pudding, we made white chocolate the star ingredient. Rather than deal with chopping a bar of white chocolate, we opted for white chocolate chips, which we simply tossed with our stale bread cubes and dried cherries before soaking them in the custard. Once melted, the white chocolate chips ensured that our bread pudding was rich and gooey. A sprinkling of sugar and toasted pistachios lent our dessert a sweet, crunchy topping. For more information on making a foil collar and staling bread, see pages 180 and 234, respectively. Don't let this bread pudding cook longer than 4 hours or it will become dried out and rubbery.

4½	**cups half-and-half**
1	**cup (7 ounces) sugar**
9	**large egg yolks**
1	**tablespoon vanilla extract**
¼	**teaspoon salt**
14	**ounces stale challah, cut into 1-inch pieces**
¾	**cup dried cherries**
½	**cup (3 ounces) white chocolate chips**
⅔	**cup shelled pistachios, toasted and chopped**

1. Line slow cooker with aluminum foil collar and spray with vegetable oil spray. Whisk half-and-half, ¾ cup sugar, egg yolks, vanilla, and salt together in large bowl until sugar is dissolved. Stir in challah, cherries, and chocolate chips and let sit, pressing on bread occasionally, until custard is mostly absorbed, about 10 minutes.

2. Transfer soaked bread mixture to prepared slow cooker and sprinkle with pistachios and remaining ¼ cup sugar. Cover and cook until center is set, 3 to 4 hours on low. Let bread pudding cool for 20 minutes before serving.

SMART SHOPPING WHITE CHOCOLATE CHIPS
White chocolate isn't really chocolate at all. While it contains the cocoa butter of true chocolate, it lacks cocoa solids, the element responsible for milk and dark chocolate's characteristic brown color and nutty roasted flavor. Other pale confections labeled simply "white" chips or bars (these boast less than the 20 percent cocoa butter required to earn the designation "white chocolate") are just as common in the baking aisle of the supermarket. In a recent taste test, we preferred **Guittard Choc-Au-Lait White Chips** over other brands. Though these chips lack a high enough concentration of cocoa butter to qualify as true white chocolate, they impressed tasters with their smooth texture, strong vanilla flavor, and mild sweetness, beating out four real white chocolates.

Cherry Grunt

Serves 4 to 6   **Cooking Time** 3 to 4 hours on Low   **Slow Cooker Size** 5½ to 7 Quarts

WHY THIS RECIPE WORKS: A grunt is an old-fashioned summer fruit dessert topped with sweet, tender dumplings. The fruit is traditionally simmered in a pot, and the dumplings are dropped on top and steamed until fluffy and light. Starting with frozen cherries makes this rustic dessert an option even in the dead of winter, and it cuts down on prep time. For a filling that was thick and jammy, we microwaved the cherries with the flour (and sugar and other flavorings) so the released juice would be absorbed by the flour, then moved the mixture to the slow cooker. Positioning the dumplings around the perimeter of the slow cooker—where it's hottest—guaranteed that they were completely cooked through by the time the filling was done. A sprinkle of cinnamon sugar added flavor and a slight crunch to our dumplings. You will need an oval slow cooker for this recipe. Be sure to mix the cherries well after microwaving to redistribute their juice. Serve with ice cream.

2¼	**pounds frozen sweet cherries**
2	**cups (10 ounces) all-purpose flour**
1	**cup (7 ounces) plus 3 tablespoons sugar**
1	**tablespoon lemon juice**
1¼	**teaspoons ground cinnamon**
1	**teaspoon almond extract**
1	**tablespoon baking powder**
½	**teaspoon salt**
½	**cup plus 2 tablespoons milk**
4	**tablespoons unsalted butter, melted and cooled**

1. Combine cherries, ¼ cup flour, 1 cup sugar, lemon juice, 1 teaspoon cinnamon, and almond extract in bowl. Microwave until cherries begin to release their liquid, about 5 minutes, stirring halfway through microwaving. Stir cherry mixture well, transfer to slow cooker, and spread into even layer.

2. In large bowl, combine remaining 1¾ cups flour, 2 tablespoons sugar, baking powder, and salt. Stir in milk and melted butter until just combined; do not overmix. In small bowl, combine remaining 1 tablespoon sugar and ¼ teaspoon cinnamon.

3. Using greased ¼-cup measure, drop 8 dumplings around perimeter of slow cooker on top of cherries, leaving center empty. Sprinkle dumplings with cinnamon-sugar mixture. Cover and cook until toothpick inserted in center of dumplings comes out clean, 3 to 4 hours on low. Serve.

QUICK PREP TIP ARRANGING DUMPLINGS IN SLOW COOKER
Using greased ¼-cup measure, arrange dumplings around perimeter of slow cooker to ensure that they cook through.

Individual Lemon Pudding Cakes

Serves 4   **Cooking Time** 1 to 2 hours on Low   **Slow Cooker Size** 5½ to 7 Quarts

✔ **WHY THIS RECIPE WORKS:** During cooking, these magical little cakes separate into two layers: a rich pudding underneath, and a delicate, tender cake on top. For ours, we began by combining sugar, melted butter, and egg yolks, then added milk and a good amount of lemon zest and juice for brightness. Next, we folded in whipped egg whites, stabilized with cream of tartar, and portioned our batter into ramekins. A water bath ensured that they cooked through gently and evenly. After about an hour, these individual cakes offered the perfect mix of tender cake, creamy custard, and intense lemon flavor. You will need an oval slow cooker and four 6-ounce round ramekins for this recipe. Serve these cakes warm in their ramekins.

- **6** **tablespoons (2⅔ ounces) sugar**
- **2** **tablespoons unsalted butter, melted and cooled**
- **2** **large eggs, separated, plus 1 large white, room temperature**
  Pinch salt
- **2** **tablespoons all-purpose flour**
- **⅔** **cup whole milk**
- **2** **teaspoons grated lemon zest plus 3 tablespoons juice**
- **¼** **teaspoon cream of tartar**

1. Fill slow cooker with ½ inch water (about 2 cups water). In large bowl, whisk sugar, melted butter, egg yolks, and salt together until smooth. Whisk in flour, then whisk in milk and lemon zest and juice until just incorporated.

2. Using electric mixer set at medium-low speed, whip egg whites and cream of tartar until foamy, about 1 minute. Increase speed to medium-high and whip whites until stiff peaks form, 2 to 4 minutes. Gently fold one-third of whipped egg whites into batter until few streaks remain. Fold remaining egg whites into batter until no streaks remain.

3. Portion batter into four 6-ounce ramekins; smooth tops. Set in slow cooker, cover, and cook until cakes are domed, tops are just firm to touch, and toothpick inserted into center comes out clean, 1 to 2 hours on low. Using tongs and sturdy spatula, remove ramekins from slow cooker. Serve warm. (Cakes can be held in water bath with slow cooker turned off for up to 30 minutes.)

QUICK PREP TIP **WHIPPING EGG WHITES**

Lemon pudding cakes rely on perfectly whipped whites for their lightness, so it's important to whip them right. Egg whites whipped to soft peaks, which droop slightly from the tip of the whisk or beater, will not have the structure to properly support the cake. Egg whites whipped to stiff peaks (shown), standing up tall on their own on the tip of the whisk or beater, have the ideal structure to support a light-as-air pudding cake. Overwhipped egg whites, which will look curdled and separated, will not incorporate well into the cake base and often result in flat cakes. (If your whites are overwhipped, start over with new whites and a clean bowl.)

Warm Peach-Raspberry Compote

Serves 6   **Cooking Time** 3 to 4 hours on Low or 2 to 3 hours on High
Slow Cooker Size 5½ to 7 Quarts

✔ **WHY THIS RECIPE WORKS:** Ideal for entertaining, this effortless yet brightly flavored compote takes a simple bowl of vanilla ice cream from ordinary to extraordinary. Frozen sliced peaches offered consistent quality and guaranteed a compote that thickened to just the right texture with the help of a little tapioca. Raspberries, stirred in at the end, provided a lively, tart punch, and chopped mint added freshness.

2	pounds frozen sliced peaches, cut into 1-inch pieces
⅓	cup (2⅓ ounces) sugar
2	tablespoons instant tapioca
1	teaspoon lemon juice
1	teaspoon vanilla extract
⅛	teaspoon salt
10	ounces (2 cups) raspberries
¼	cup chopped fresh mint
2	pints vanilla ice cream

1. Combine peaches, sugar, tapioca, lemon juice, vanilla, and salt in slow cooker. Cover and cook until peaches are softened, 3 to 4 hours on low or 2 to 3 hours on high.

2. Stir in raspberries and let sit until heated through, about 5 minutes. Stir in mint. Portion ice cream into individual bowls, spoon warm compote over top, and serve. (Compote can be held on warm or low setting for up to 2 hours.)

Warm Pineapple-Mango Compote

Serves 6   **Cooking Time** 3 to 4 hours on Low or 2 to 3 hours on High
Slow Cooker Size 5½ to 7 Quarts

✔ **WHY THIS RECIPE WORKS:** For another flavorful, easy-prep compote, we reached for frozen mango and pineapple and added lime zest and juice. A splash of rum offered depth and rich caramel notes.

2	pounds frozen mango chunks
1	pound frozen pineapple chunks
⅓	cup packed (2⅓ ounces) brown sugar
1	tablespoon instant tapioca
1	teaspoon grated lime zest plus 1 teaspoon juice
2	tablespoons dark rum
2	pints vanilla ice cream

1. Combine mango, pineapple, sugar, and tapioca in slow cooker. Cover and cook until fruit is softened, 3 to 4 hours on low or 2 to 3 hours on high.

2. Stir in lime zest and juice and rum. Portion ice cream into individual bowls, spoon warm compote over top, and serve. (Compote can be held on warm or low setting for up to 2 hours.)

Conversions & Equivalencies

Some say cooking is a science and an art. We would say that geography has a hand in it, too. Flour milled in the United Kingdom and elsewhere will feel and taste different from flour milled in the United States. So we cannot promise that the loaf of bread you bake in Canada or England will taste the same as a loaf baked in the States, but we can offer guidelines for converting weights and measures. We also recommend that you rely on your instincts when making our recipes. Refer to the visual cues provided. If the bread dough hasn't "come together in a ball," as described, you may need to add more flour—even if the recipe doesn't tell you to. You be the judge.

The recipes in this book were developed using standard U.S. measures following U.S. government guidelines. The charts below offer equivalents for U.S., metric, and imperial (U.K.) measures. All conversions are approximate and have been rounded up or down to the nearest whole number.

EXAMPLE:

| 1 teaspoon | = 4.9292 milliliters, rounded up to 5 milliliters |
| 1 ounce | = 28.3495 grams, rounded down to 28 grams |

VOLUME CONVERSIONS

U.S.	METRIC
1 teaspoon	5 milliliters
2 teaspoons	10 milliliters
1 tablespoon	15 milliliters
2 tablespoons	30 milliliters
¼ cup	59 milliliters
⅓ cup	79 milliliters
½ cup	118 milliliters
¾ cup	177 milliliters
1 cup	237 milliliters
1¼ cups	296 milliliters
1½ cups	355 milliliters
2 cups (1 pint)	473 milliliters
2½ cups	591 milliliters
3 cups	710 milliliters
4 cups (1 quart)	0.946 liter
1.06 quarts	1 liter
4 quarts (1 gallon)	3.8 liters

WEIGHT CONVERSIONS

OUNCES	GRAMS
½	14
¾	21
1	28
1½	43
2	57
2½	71
3	85
3½	99
4	113
4½	128
5	142
6	170
7	198
8	227
9	255
10	283
12	340
16 (1 pound)	454

CONVERSIONS FOR INGREDIENTS COMMONLY USED IN BAKING

Baking is an exacting science. Because measuring by weight is far more accurate than measuring by volume, and thus more likely to achieve reliable results, in our recipes we provide ounce measures in addition to cup measures for many ingredients. Refer to the chart below to convert these measures into grams.

INGREDIENT	OUNCES	GRAMS
1 cup all-purpose flour*	5	142
1 cup cake flour	4	113
1 cup whole-wheat flour	5½	156
1 cup granulated (white) sugar	7	198
1 cup packed brown sugar (light or dark)	7	198
1 cup confectioners' sugar	4	113
1 cup cocoa powder	3	85
4 tablespoons butter[†] (½ stick, or ¼ cup)	2	57
8 tablespoons butter[†] (1 stick, or ½ cup)	4	113
16 tablespoons butter[†] (2 sticks, or 1 cup)	8	227

* U.S. all-purpose flour, the most frequently used flour in this book, does not contain leaveners, as some European flours do. These leavened flours are called self-rising or self-raising. If you are using self-rising flour, take this into consideration before adding leavening to a recipe.

[†] In the United States, butter is sold both salted and unsalted. We generally recommend unsalted butter. If you are using salted butter, take this into consideration before adding salt to a recipe.

OVEN TEMPERATURES

FAHRENHEIT	CELSIUS	GAS MARK (IMPERIAL)
225	105	¼
250	120	½
275	135	1
300	150	2
325	165	3
350	180	4
375	190	5
400	200	6
425	220	7
450	230	8
475	245	9

CONVERTING TEMPERATURES FROM AN INSTANT-READ THERMOMETER

We include doneness temperatures in many of the recipes in this book. We recommend an instant-read thermometer for the job. Refer to the above table to convert Fahrenheit degrees to Celsius. Or, for temperatures not represented in the chart, use this simple formula:

Subtract 32 degrees from the Fahrenheit reading, then divide the result by 1.8 to find the Celsius reading.

EXAMPLE:
"Roast chicken until thighs register 175 degrees."
To convert:

175°F – 32 = 143°
143° ÷ 1.8 = 79.44°C, rounded down to 79°C

Index

A

All-Season Tomato Sauce, 199

Almond(s)

Spanish-Style Braised Green
Beans, 269

Spiced Pork Tenderloin with
Couscous, *132, 133*

and Tomato Pesto, Penne with,
176

American Chop Suey, 213

Anchovies

canned, taste tests on, 123

fillets vs. paste, 123

Appetizers

Asian Glazed Wings, *28, 29*

Barbecued Cocktail Franks, 31

Beef and Black Bean Taco Dip,
14, 15

Beer and Cheddar Fondue, 19

Chili con Queso, *20, 21*

Creamy Crab Dip, 12

Garlicky Shrimp, *24, 25*

Italian Sausage Cocktail
Meatballs, 26

Pepperoni Pizza Dip, 13

Refried Bean Dip, 18

Rosemary and Garlic White
Bean Dip, 16, *17*

Smoky Honey-Lime Glazed
Wings, 30

Spicy Mustard Cocktail Franks,
31

Spinach and Artichoke Dip,
10, 11

Tangy Mango Cocktail
Meatballs, 27

Warm Marinated Artichoke
Hearts with Feta and
Olives, 22, *23*

Apples and Kale, Harvest Pork
Chops with, 124

Applesauce Spice Cake, 292

Apricot-Ginger Glazed
Chicken, Easy, 89

Artichoke(s)

Braised, 264

and Capers, Lemony Chicken
with, 100

frozen, cooking with, 22

Hearts, Warm Marinated, with
Feta and Olives, 22, *23*

and Spinach Dip, *10,* 11

trimming, 264

Arugula

and Dried Cherries, Warm
Wheat Berry Salad with,
281

Salad with Balsamic-Mustard
Vinaigrette, 194

Asian Beef Noodle Soup, 42

Asian Chicken Lettuce Wraps,
114, 115

Asian Chicken Noodle Soup, 36

Asian Glazed Wings, *28,* 29

Asian-Style Braised Short Ribs,
254, *255*

Asparagus and Mushrooms,
Thai Chicken with, 101

Atlanta Brisket, 158, *159*

Avocados

Chunky Chipotle Guacamole,
142, 143

Monterey Chicken and Rice,
209

B

Bacon

Lemon, and Thyme, Brussels
Sprouts with, 271

taste tests on, 49

Baked Penne with Chicken
Sausage and Red Bell
Pepper Pesto, 215

Balsamic-Braised Chicken with
Swiss Chard, 250

Balsamic-Glazed Brussels
Sprouts with Pine Nuts,
270, 271

Balsamic vinegar, taste tests on,
109

Barbecued Cocktail Franks, 31

Barbecue sauce, taste tests on, 82

Basil

Cherry Tomatoes, and
Mozzarella, Orzo with,
282, 283

and Grapefruit Relish, Poached
Salmon with, 145

pesto, small-batch, preparing, 190

Bean(s)

Asian Beef Noodle Soup, 42

baked, taste tests on, 122

Black, and Beef Taco Dip, *14, 15*

Black, and Corn, Spicy, Stuffed
Bell Peppers with, 235

Black, Soup, 240

black, taste tests on, 240

Campfire, 285

Cheesy Chicken and Frito
Casserole, 204

chickpeas, taste tests on, 65

Cowboy Steak and, 122

dried, shopping for, 284

dried, sorting, 59